THE GEOMETRY OF PASTA

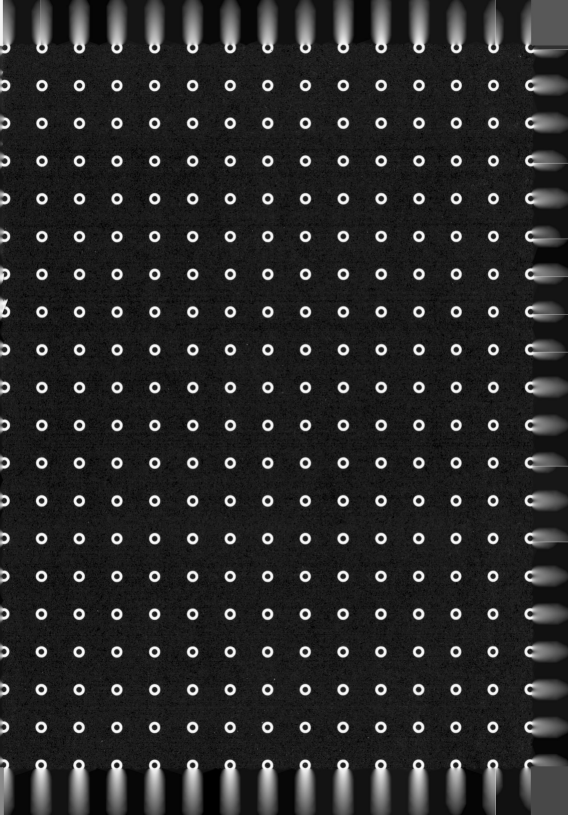

THE GEOMETRY
OF PASTA

CAZ HILDEBRAND & JACOB KENEDY

QUIRK BOOKS

PHILADELPHIA

For our mothers,
Haidee Becker and Judy Hildebrand

Library of Congress Cataloging in Publication Number: 2010927134

ISBN: 978-1-59474-495-2

Illustrations: Lisa Vandy
Design: Caz Hildebrand, Heredesign.co.uk

The publisher would like to thank Jane Morley for editorial support and
Martin Dominguez and Triet Tran for design assistance.

Printed by L.E.G.O. SpA, Italy

Distributed in North America by Chronicle Books
680 Second Street
San Francisco, CA 94107

10 9 8 7 6 5 4 3 2 1

Quirk Books
215 Church Street
Philadelphia, PA 19106
www.irreference.com
www.quirkbooks.com

First published 2010 by Boxtree
an imprint of Pan Macmillan, a division of Macmillan Publishers Limited
Pan Macmillan, 20 New Wharf Road, London N1 9RR
Basingstoke and Oxford
Associated companies throughout the world
www.panmacmillan.com

CONTENTS

INTRODUCTION

This book was not my idea, although I would be so very proud if it were. It was conceived by Caz, the graphic designer, in whose mind it grew over a period of more than five years before she first discussed it with me. Kudos is due.

The selection of pastas, writing, and recipes are all my own, but again I cannot take all the credit. Centuries of Italian invention, industry, agriculture, hunger, and politics have shaped pasta into its myriad forms and flavours. Few (if any) of the shapes described were designed by any one hand, and the same goes for the accompanying recipes. Instead, subtle differences have increased as methods to prepare modern Italy's staple food have passed from mother to daughter, neighbour to neighbour, and town to town. The startling diversity we wonder at in the natural world is mirrored in microcosm in pasta. Evolution is at work.

Pasta is different across Italy. In the poorer south, pastes of semolina and water are shaped by hand into chunky peasant forms. In south-central Italy, the same semolina dough is extruded by machine into simple long shapes and complex short ones, then dried, packaged, and sold. North and north-central Italy, wealthier by far, uses expensive egg yolks and refined flours to make fine golden-yellow marvels – silky ribbons and tiny stuffed shapes like fine jewellery. In the far north, cold and under the influence of Germany and Eastern Europe, white flour is often replaced by other starches – bread crumbs, chestnut, buckwheat, and rye. The properties of each type of dough, the mechanics of each shape, and the tastes and traditions of each region have determined also that an equal panoply of sauces exists, to match the requirements of the pasta and the people's palates.

This diversity is true at every level. From region to region, the same pasta is cooked with a different sauce. Oily sauces to coat, light ones to dress, rich ones to enhance and impress, fresh ones to lighten, and all to enjoy. From town to town, the same sauce with differing ingredients. From door to door, the same ingredients in differing proportions and to different effect, each cook convinced their method is the best, the only correct way. Whilst the majority of the recipes that follow are traditional in some respect, their precise formula is my own – just one of an infinite number of interpretations. It is this subtle influence I take ownership of – my contribution to the ongoing evolution of the taste and geometry of pasta.

Jacob Kenedy

The idea for this book began when I was thinking about the Italians' preoccupation with choosing the right pasta shape to go with the right sauce. As they will tell you, this makes the difference between pasta dishes that are merely ordinary and truly sublime.

Trying to understand the subject better led me to Pellegrino Artusi's wonderful book, *Science in the Kitchen and the Art of Eating Well*. Originally published in 1891, it was the first cookbook in Italian aimed primarily at the home cook. I was struck not only by the recipes and the entertaining text, but also the pure, graphic style of the illustrated instructions for making stuffed pasta. A chance encounter with a wall chart of plumbing grommets around the same time convinced me that using simple, geometric black-and-white drawings of the pasta shapes could demonstrate their differences and help to identify the individual characteristics that make them particularly suitable for certain sauces. With this concept in mind I approached Jacob, who contributed his totally delicious and definitive recipes. Together, we offer a guide to the geometry of pasta – pasta at its simplest and best, to be enjoyed as the Italians do.

Caz Hildebrand

IMPORTANT NOTES

SALT

Salt is one of those things that makes pasta delicious. To most chefs, the correct level of seasoning is as much salt as a dish can take without in any way being over-salty – this is, to my mind, the greatest difference between restaurant food and home cooking. In all the recipes, I have left the level of seasoning up to you (except in the dose of salt for pasta water on page 13, although this can be reduced to taste). It is probably best to consider, in deciding how much salt to use:

- Your enjoyment of the meal (the perfect amount of salt for the dish at hand).

- Your enjoyment of all your meals over a lifetime (and enjoyment of everything else, for that matter). Using less salt will help to prolong your life and improve its quality as time goes on.

Being a short-termist, I tend to favour the first argument in a live-fast, die-young mentality. I will likely regret this in later years.

FAT

Fat, just like salt, is key to the deliciousness of most pasta dishes. Unlike salt, in this book quantities of fat are specified – and are in the proportions you would be likely to find in a great Italian restaurant. Whilst these render the recipes to their perfect balance in my eyes, you may disagree. The quantities of butter, oil, or cream can be halved to produce a healthier, more domestic version of any of the dishes. The arguments for salt apply for fat as well.

QUANTITY

Except where otherwise specified, all recipes in this book serve two as a main course or light meal, or four as a starter (based on a 3½-ounce portion of dried pasta per person as a main course, or the rough equivalent for filled and fresh pastas). When recipes are easier to prepare in larger quantities, they produce a larger but sensible quantity. Whilst any recipe can be scaled up or down, it is worth making sure that you have enough room in your pan (and heat on your stove top) to cope.

COOKING PASTA

Boiling pasta requires a vessel capacious enough to let it move freely in the water, whilst sautéing sauces and pastas requires a pan large enough so they won't be crowded. Pasta should be cooked *al dente* ("to the tooth," or with a little bite) for the modern palate, but in ancient times it would have been cooked as it is today in English schools – almost to a mush. There is no rule regarding cooking times – each pasta is unique. Fresh pasta cooks much faster than dried, as it's already moist within.

It is important to drain pasta when slightly too *al dente* for your taste – it'll continue to cook in those precious moments between colander and plate, and even more so if, as in most of these recipes, it is cooked for a further minute in its sauce. This requires precision: Start tasting the pasta at 15–20 second intervals, from a minute or two before you think it might be ready.

You don't need any special equipment to cook pasta – just a pot, a pan, and a colander. If you want to invest in something of great utility, buy a pasta basket. It allows quick draining without losing the water – especially useful as this hot and slightly starchy water often finishes the pasta's sauce. If you drain your pasta through a colander instead, reserve a small jug of the water – in some parts of central and southern Italy, this jug would even be sent to the table, to allow guests to further moisten their pasta on the plate.

BASICS:
RECIPES FOR PASTA

SEMOLINA PASTA

The simplest sort of pasta to make, semolina pasta really is nothing more than flour and water.

On technique

It isn't worth making extruded pasta shapes yourself (*rigatoni, spaghetti,* and the like): Their thinner section actually benefits from drying beforehand, so the packaged products are ideal. These are also impossible to make at home without considerable investment in equipment.

The "peasant" pasta shapes – traditionally made by hand (*orecchiette, trofie, cavatelli,* anything that looks irregular) – are by their very nature thicker. These quite simply take too long to cook from dry – by the time the inside is beginning to cook, the outer surface will have turned to mush. Making these at home is laborious and time-consuming, but the returns are well worth the effort.

On ingredients

At least the dough is quick enough to make, once you've found the right flour: *semola di grano duro* – semolina, or a medium-ground flour made from strong wheat – or *semola di grano duro rimacinata,* more simply known as *semola rimacinata* (the same, but re-ground for a finer texture).

You can use store-bought semolina as a substitute for Italian *semola,* but since it isn't designed for pasta – or bread-making – the semolina you're likely to find outside Italy is lower in gluten. You will therefore need to use slightly less water, and the resultant pasta might have a little less bite. But when we blind-tasted the two, they were almost indistinguishable.

Semola di grano duro is kneaded with half its weight of water, then left to rest a few minutes before shaping (i.e., 3½ ounces, or ½ cup plus 1½ tablespoons *semola*, with 3 tablespoons water = pasta for 1 person). The texture of the dough should be soft enough to work (like a stress ball), but dry enough that it won't stick to itself too easily. A good way to test it is to press and smear the dough against a dry wooden surface – if it is easy to do, the pasta doesn't stick to the wood, and the top surface tears and roughens against your hand, the texture is right.

EGG PASTA

More commonly made at home, below are three recipes. Each has its own use, but all are interchangeable in practice.

On technique
Egg pasta is rolled in sheets before cutting or shaping. This is normally done with a machine nowadays (domestic ones are inexpensive). Roll the pasta on the thickest setting, then fold and turn 90°, repeating a few times to stretch the gluten in all directions before starting to roll progressively thinner. The traditional way, unsurprisingly, is to use a long (several-foot) rolling pin and a flat wooden table. The pasta sheet is rolled into a large disc and, when too large and thin to work effectively, is allowed to coil around the rolling pin like a sheet of wrapping paper. It is rolled until loose on the pin, then uncurled and re-rolled tight to the pin, the process repeated until the pasta is thin enough. As opposed to the mechanical method, this has the advantage of allowing (necessitating, in fact) the use of a softer, wetter dough, which in turn yields a more elastic, magical pasta when cooked. The disadvantage is the practice required to achieve any sort of results. Up to you . . .

The result
However you roll, you want to achieve an even, smooth sheet of pasta at the end. There should be no flour on the pasta, and if you work quickly it should be sticky enough to stick to itself, but not to anything else. You may therefore be able to close filled pastas without using egg or water as an adhesive, but will

have to let the pasta dry to a leathery state before cutting into unfilled pasta shapes (which would otherwise stick together).

On precision
Eggs vary in size, flour in humidity and gluten content, days in their weather, and locations in their climate – and you need to choose how stiff your dough is going to be (for machine- or hand-rolling). The measurements below are therefore imprecise. A little practice will tell you when to add a touch more flour or egg. As a general rule, your dough should have as much spring in it as a relaxed muscle in your forearm.

On ingredients
I mention only egg and flour below. Colours and flavours may be added, but these are a distraction and, to my mind, normally to be avoided. Your eggs and flour therefore are of the utmost importance. It may seem silly to state, but try to make sure the yolks are as dark a yellow as possible. Pale pasta looks, and somehow even tastes, insipid. I use Italian eggs whose hens were fed on God-knows-what (I believe a mixture of purest corn and carotene), but they make my pasta a glorious buttercup yellow.

The best flour is *"00" farina di grano tenero,* but plain all-purpose flour is fine. Up to a third may be substituted for *semola di grano duro,* which will give your pasta a little more bite at the expense of its velvety texture, and improve it for drying.

Egg equivalents
All eggs used in this book are extra large. You may substitute 1 large egg for 1 extra large one with impunity where few are used, or 10 large eggs for 9 extra large ones where many are used.

SIMPLE EGG PASTA

Good for any dish, especially typical of Umbria and Emilia-Romagna.

1 egg per 3½ ounces flour (½ cup plus 1½ tablespoons semolina, or 6 tablespoons plus 1 teaspoon semolina with 4½ tablespoons all-purpose flour if using a combination), kneaded well and allowed to rest for half an hour before rolling. 2 eggs and 7 ounces flour (1 cup plus 3 tablespoons semolina, or ¾ cup plus 2 teaspoons semolina with 8½ tablespoons all-purpose flour if using a combination) will make enough pasta for 3 as a main course (the same quantity as the following recipes).

ENRICHED EGG PASTA

A stronger colour makes this a little more dramatic, and it is a little richer. Good all-purpose pasta, for flat or filled shapes.

1 egg and 3 egg yolks per 7 ounces flour (1 cup plus 3 tablespoons semolina, or ¾ cup plus 2 teaspoons semolina with 8½ tablespoons all-purpose flour if using a combination).

PURE-YOLK PASTA

Very decadent, given the expense of eggs for much of modern history, pure-yolk pasta is used rarely. It is not so suitable for stuffing, as the dough lacks elasticity, and is especially typical of Piedmont, as in the famous *tajarin* (see page 254).

8 egg yolks per 7 ounces flour (1 cup plus 3 tablespoons semolina, or ¾ cup plus 2 teaspoons semolina with 8½ tablespoons all-purpose flour if using a combination).

PASTA WATER

All pasta should be cooked in an abundance of boiling water, with about 2 teaspoons salt per quart, and nothing else.

BASICS:
THREE TOMATO SAUCES

Tomato sauce is not only a sauce on its own, but a useful component of other dishes. Opposite are three sauces, subtly different in the making but quite different to eat.

The lightest sauce is best for the most delicate of pasta shapes (*spaghettini* in particular), or with subtly-flavoured filled pastas – *caramelle, ravioli, malfatti,* and the like. It is a fresh sauce, more water- than oil-based, tasting much like fresh tomato, and is used in quite a high proportion to the pasta. I always keep some in my fridge and use it as an additive to other sauces that need a touch of tomato.

The richest sauce is the opposite – reduced, concentrated, and oily; a small amount is enough to coat chunky long shapes such as *spaghetti* and *pici,* or tubular ridged ones: *penne rigate, tortiglioni,* and *rigatoni*. Its concentrated acidity also makes it great to keep in the fridge – whilst I use it less than a light sauce, it keeps for a long while.

The medium sauce is most like your garden-variety tomato sauce. It is, to my mind, neither one thing nor the other. It is a good all-around sauce, even if I prefer the other two for their character.

LIGHT TOMATO SAUCE

Yields about 2½– 2⅔ cups sauce, enough for 1 pound dried pasta
5 large ripe vine tomatoes (2¼ pounds)
3 garlic cloves, thinly sliced
6 tablespoons extra-virgin olive oil, divided
A small pinch of crushed red pepper flakes (optional)
Generous ¾ teaspoon fine sea salt

Cut the whole tomatoes into chunks, then puree (seeds and all). Fry the garlic in 4½ tablespoons of the olive oil for a few moments until cooked, but not yet coloured. Add the red pepper flakes followed by the pureed tomato and salt. Bring to a fairly brisk boil and cook until the sauce has a little body (you will see the bubbles get a bit bigger), but is by no measure thick. The tomatoes should taste fresh, but no longer raw. Season with black pepper and add the remaining 1½ tablespoons oil to finish.

MEDIUM TOMATO SAUCE

Yields 2¼ cups sauce, enough for 1¼ pounds dried pasta
3 garlic cloves, thinly sliced
½ cup plus 1 tablespoon extra-virgin olive oil
A small pinch of crushed red pepper flakes (optional)
3 ripe vine tomatoes (1 pound), chopped
1 pound canned tomatoes, chopped or crushed
Generous ¾ teaspoon fine sea salt

Fry the garlic in the oil until it just begins to colour, then add the red pepper flakes, then the tomatoes and salt, along with a few grinds of black pepper. Cook at a brisk simmer until thickened – about an hour. This sauce, of the 3, is closest to one you might buy at a shop. It is my least favourite, but is useful in a number of dishes, such as *malfatti al pomodoro*, *pasta alla Norma*, and others.

RICH TOMATO SAUCE

Yields 1¾–2 cups sauce, enough for 1½ pounds dried pasta
4 garlic cloves, thinly sliced
7½ tablespoons extra-virgin olive oil
A small pinch of crushed red pepper flakes (optional)
2¼ pounds canned tomatoes, chopped or crushed
Generous ¾ teaspoon fine sea salt

Fry the garlic in the oil until golden brown (it's ready when you start to become nervous of burning it, but before you actually do), then add the red pepper flakes, tomatoes, and salt. Bring to a boil, then simmer gently until the sauce is very thick, and the oil has all risen to the top. If your spoon (which you must use frequently – the thicker the sauce, the greater the risk of burning) is small and wooden, you may be able to stand it upright in the sauce when it's ready.

AGNOLOTTI

Dimensions
Length: 2 in
Width: 1 in

Synonyms
*agnellotti, agnulot,
angelotti, langaroli,
langheroli, piat d'angelot*

Also good with this pasta
butter and sage; *in brodo;*
stew juice; tomato sauce

Agnolotti are, in essence, *ravioli* (page 208), but instead of being made from two squares of pasta, they are made from one piece folded in half. The pasta sheet may be circular (for semicircular *agnolotti*, illustrated) or rectangular (for square or rectangular *agnolotti*). A speciality of Piedmont, they were named after their reputed inventor – a cook called Angiolino from Monferrato, known as "Angelot" (the ancient spelling, still sometimes found today, is *piat d'angelot or angelotti*).

In accordance with ancient custom, different fillings were made for feasting days (i.e., normal ones) and fasting days (at one time, no meat was eaten on 150 days in the year):

- *Agnolotti di magro* (for "lean" or fasting days) – filled with a mixture of greens, cheese, egg, and perhaps some bread crumbs. You can make these using the fillings from *pansotti di preboggion* (page 182), or spinach and ricotta *ravioli* (page 210).

- *Agnolotti di grasso* (for "fat" or feasting days) could be filled with boiled breast of veal, the stock used first for cooking the meat, then cooking the *agnolotti*, and finally eaten with them bobbing in it. Alternatively, they could be filled with pot-roasted meats, as in the recipe on page 22, and dressed with the pan juices before serving.

As with all Piedmontese pastas, these are dressed with butter and cheese – a sign of the wealth of the area, and a symptom of its poor climate for olives.

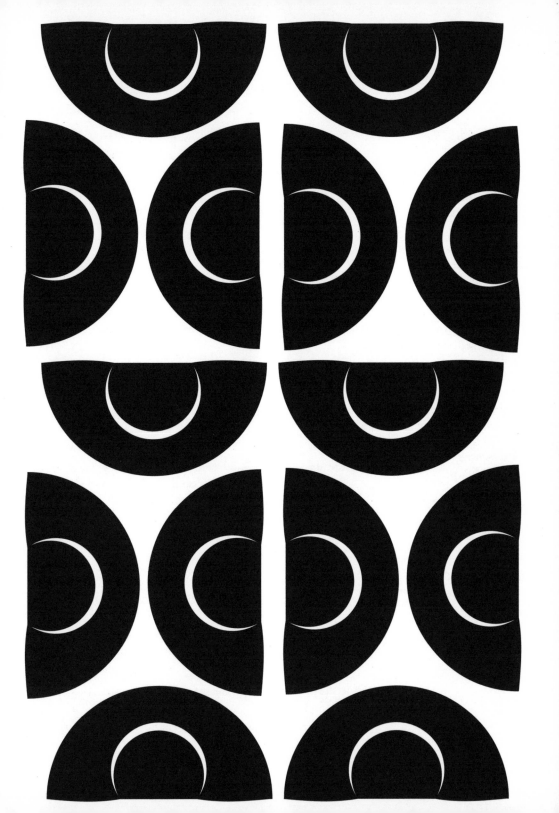

MAKING AGNOLOTTI

Serves 16 as a main

3 pounds enriched egg
  pasta dough (page 13)
½ pound calves' or
  lambs' brains
½ head escarole (about 8
  ounces), chopped roughly
7 tablespoons butter
½ pound lean veal (loin,
  fillet, or scallop meat), cut
  in ¾-inch cubes
½ pound lean pork (loin or
  leg meat), cut in ¾-inch
  cubes
1 medium onion, chopped
1 garlic clove, chopped
3 rosemary sprigs,
  leaves only
15–20 sage leaves
3½ ounces sliced
  prosciutto
2 eggs
1¾ cups grated Parmesan
⅓ cup heavy cream

This filling is similar to that for *agnolotti dal plin* (page 22) and is in some ways easier to make (you don't have to make a pot-roast first), in some ways more challenging (everything is cooked from raw, and you need to source some offal). Choose whichever recipe seems more convenient to you — both are delicious.

Poach the brains in salted water for 10–12 minutes at a gentle simmer, leave them to cool in the water, and pick off any nasty-looking bits of membrane. Boil the escarole in well-salted water until tender (2 minutes), drain, refresh with cold water, and squeeze as dry as possible.

Heat the butter and brown the veal and pork over a medium-high heat for 10 minutes, until caramelised all over. Add the onion, garlic, rosemary, and sage, and fry for a further 10 minutes on a slightly lowered flame until softened. Leave to cool in the pan.

Add the rest of the ingredients, transfer to the bowl of a food processor (make sure all the buttery meat juices go in too), and work until you have a finely textured pâté. This will yield more than 2 pounds of filling, enough for about 3 pounds of pasta dough, or a lot of *agnolotti*. Less can be made, and the filling frozen for future use, either in *agnolotti*, or other shapes like *tortellini* (page 262), *ravioli* (page 208), *cannelloni* (page 50), et al. In this case, use 5 parts of filling to 6 parts of pasta by weight, allowing a generous 2½ ounces filling per main course per person — 5¼ ounces *agnolotti*, allowing for wastage of the dough. Or be prepared to spend a long time forming these little pastas and freezing the ones you don't need today.

Roll a reasonably sized piece of dough to just under 1 millimeter thick, the second-thinnest setting on most machines. Cut into 2-inch rounds with a pastry cutter and dab a piece of filling the size of a chickpea in the center of each. Working quickly, pick up each disc and fold into a semicircle to enclose the filling, pinching the edges to close and exclude air. If too dry to stick to itself, or if you've got flour on the dough (you shouldn't need any flour at all to roll the pasta), mist with a little water before you start picking up the discs. Keep the *agnolotti* on a tray dusted with semolina until ready to cook.

AGNOLOTTI ALLE NOCI
Walnut sauce

Serves 4

1¼ pounds (¼ recipe) agnolotti

WALNUT SAUCE
¾–1 cup shelled walnuts
2 hefty slices bread (about 2 ounces)
6 tablespoons milk
1½ tablespoons fresh oregano leaves, or 5 sage leaves
1 cup grated Parmesan, plus more to serve
½ cup plus 1 tablespoon extra-virgin olive oil

Also good with this sauce
fettuccine, pappardelle, ravioli, tagliatelle, tortellini

This sauce is almost identical to that for *corzetti* (page 82), but for the omission of garlic and the extra water. The lack of garlic is my preference, but if you do make too much of the raw sauce used for *corzetti*, you can always dilute it for use here.

Only if they look dark and slightly bitter, soak the walnuts in boiling water for 15 minutes, then drain and pick off any extraneous bits of dark skin. Soak the bread in the milk, then combine with the nuts, oregano or sage, and Parmesan in a food processor. Here you can choose to leave a little texture or to grind the mixture finely. Both options have their advantages; I lean towards a finely textured, creamy sauce.

Add the oil and then, gradually, 1 cup plus 2 tablespoons water. Season with salt and pepper.

When you put your pasta on, heat the sauce in a wide pan. It will do an amazing thing: The greenish hue from the herb will turn purple, from the walnut skins. Drain the pasta *al dente*, and toss into the sauce. Cook until well coated, and serve with more grated Parmesan.

AGNOLOTTI DAL PLIN

Dimensions
Length: 1.64 in
Width: 0.92 in

Also good with this pasta
cream; *in brodo;* stew juice;
tartufo d'Alba; walnut sauce

Agnolotti dal plin are pinched or pleated tiny *agnolotti* (see page 16), *plin* being a pinch in Piedmontese dialect. They are almost always stuffed with a meat filling and may be served *in brodo* (in a broth) where the pleat improves the mouthfeel, or in a sauce, which the pleat helps to catch on the pasta. As with *tortellini* (the Bolognese equivalent, page 262), they may be further condimented with white truffles, especially when served in broth, for particularly festive occasions. The small size and dainty work required means these have never been an everyday pasta, rather for times when there is something to celebrate, or when housewives had to fill long winter evenings with some sort of activity.

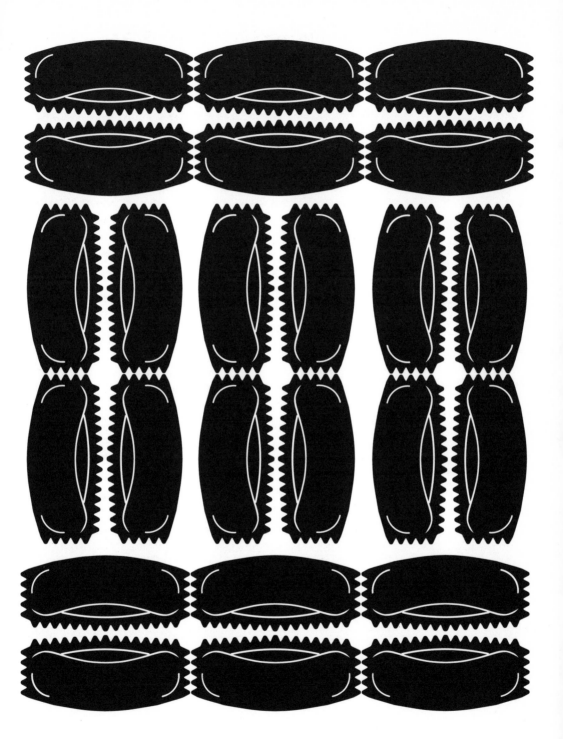

MAKING AGNOLOTTI DAL PLIN

Serves 4

1 recipe enriched egg pasta
  dough (page 13)
⅓ pound cabbage or
  escarole
2 tablespoons butter
¾–1 pound leftover braised
  or pot-roasted veal or
  pork*
4 sage leaves
1 cup grated Parmesan
1 egg
Grated nutmeg to taste

*Substituting 3½ ounces
boiled veal brains for a
quarter of the meat makes for
a smoother, richer filling. If
you need to braise your meat
specifically for this dish, start
with 1–1½ pounds of raw
meat, brown it in butter, add
some herbs, and white wine
and simmer with a lid on for an
hour or 2.

This filling is a simplified version of that for *agnolotti* (page 18) – the two can be used interchangeably. This recipe makes more filling than you'll need; freeze what you don't use.

For the filling, boil the greens in salted water until tender. Drain well, and leave to steam-dry spread out on a cloth. Chop finely, squeezing any extra water out in your hands, then fry gently in the butter for a few minutes. Leave to cool, then combine with the other ingredients in a food processor until quite smooth.

To make the *agnolotti dal plin* roll the pasta just under 1 millimeter thick (the thinnest setting on most machines), and cut into long, 2-inch-wide strips. Along the center, dot even, hazelnut-sized pieces of filling ½ inch apart. Barely moisten the flap of dough with egg or water only if it is too dry to stick to itself. Fold the strip over along its length, towards you (with the fold away from you and the 2 edges facing you) to loosely enclose the filling. For "normal" filled pasta, you would press down to seal between the little dumplings – not so here! Pinch to either side of each lump of filling, to make a vertical pleat in the top layer of pasta and exclude any air. Now press down – both to flatten the pleat towards you and to close the long open edge of the folded pasta. Use a rotary dough cutter (anything really) to cut the dumplings apart – one which cuts frilly edges is often preferred. Spread out in a single layer until ready to use, or freeze for future use.

AGNOLOTTI DAL PLIN CON BURRO E SALVIA
Butter and sage

½ pound *agnolotti dal plin*
½ cup butter
16 sage leaves
Grated Parmesan, to serve

Also good with this sauce
agnolotti, cappelletti, ravioli, tortelli, tortellini, tortelloni

Burro e salvia, or "butter and sage," is one of the simplest sauces for stuffed pasta, and one of the best. Sage is one of my favourite herbs, reminding me of a kindly older lady in flavour — elegant, feminine, complex, and slightly dusty. It marries beautifully with butter, especially when lightly caramelised, and together they act as an excellent foil to even the simplest of fillings.

As usual, cook the pasta in boiling, salted water (in this case, for 2–3 minutes). Whilst they boil, you have a short window of time in which to make your sauce. Fry the butter and sage until the butter caramelises (the solids turn hazelnut-brown), then add a ladleful (about ⅓ cup) of the pasta water, and shake the pan. It will foam up and start to emulsify and thicken as you shake. It should still be a little runny when you add your drained *agnolotti* (leave the pasta slightly under-done; it will cook for 20 seconds more in the sauce), as it will thicken more as the sauce bubbles away on a medium heat. The sauce is done when it coats the pasta like cream. Taste for seasoning (your pasta water may have already provided enough salt), and serve with a liberal grating of Parmesan.

ALFABETO

Dimensions
Length: 4.5 mm
Width: 3.5 mm

Also good with this pasta
acquacotta; chicken or
capon broth

Aka "alphabetti spaghetti," *alfabeto* is a *pastina* (tiny pasta for soups) made in the shape of the letters of the alphabet. Almost certainly invented to appeal to children, it might also appeal to parents as an educational tool and a source of nostalgic pleasure.

MINESTRA DI ALFABETO
Alphabet soup

2¾ ounces *alfabeto*
1 small bunch asparagus
1 zucchini, diced ½ inch
1⅓ cups chicken broth,
   preferably clarified (see
   page 242), or vegetable
   stock
10 basil leaves
1½ tablespoons extra-
   virgin olive oil to serve

Also good in this soup
*canestrini, quadrettini,
stelline*

Using an A to Z of vegetables (only two — asparagus and zucchini), this broth is appealing to children and tasty enough for grown-ups willing to forgive the gimmick.

Trim the tough parts of the stem from the asparagus and cut the tender remainder into ½-inch lengths, leaving the tips intact.

Heat the broth or stock until boiling, check for seasoning, and add the pasta. About a minute before it is done, add the vegetables. Serve with the basil stirred in and the oil drizzled over.

ALFABETO WITH KETCHUP

*Serves 1 adult, or more
likely 2 children*

3½ ounces *alfabeto*
3 tablespoons ketchup,
   plus a little more for
   decoration
3 tablespoons butter,
   divided

Boil the *alfabeto*. Meanwhile, warm the ketchup with half the butter and a dash of pasta water to make a sauce. Drain the *alfabeto*, and mix with the remaining butter. Spread the sauce out on a warm plate, and make a mound of pasta in the middle. Decorate the top with a bit more ketchup — polka dots, or the eater's initials if you have a squeezy bottle of ketchup and great dexterity.

ANELLETTI

Dimensions
Diameter: 0.32 in
Length: 2.5 mm
Wall thickness: 1.5 mm

Synonyms
cerchionetti; taradduzzi;
in Sicily anidduzzi,
anelloni d'Africa, or anelli

Similar forms
anelli, anellini

Also good with this pasta
in brodo

Anelloni d'Africa, which can still be found in southern Italy, are great hoops of pasta. They originated in the 1930s, probably inspired by the huge earrings worn by some African women, who became known to the Italian military during campaigns in the First World War. *Anelletti* are their little brother, meaning "little rings." They are now widespread, although they are best known in a Sicilian baked pasta that is itself made in the shape of a ring. Best eaten cold, this is traditionally the dish taken to the beach for *Ferragosto* (the mid-August bank holiday). The recipe is opposite.

Anelletti have other uses within Italy – primarily in soups. But it is likely that by far the majority of their consumption is outside her borders – open a can of pasta hoops (perhaps the most popular remaining canned pasta), and *anelletti* is what you get.

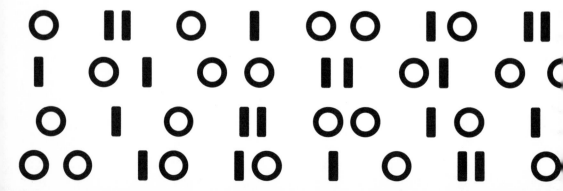

ANELLETTI AL FORNO
Baked in a ring

Serves 6–8 as a picnic dish

2/3 pound *anelletti*
1 medium onion, diced
1 celery stalk, diced
1 garlic clove, chopped
3 tablespoons extra-virgin
 olive oil
2–3 tablespoons butter, plus
 extra for greasing the pan
1 ounce minced pork or veal
3/4 teaspoon crushed red
 pepper flakes
3/4 cup wine (red for pork,
 white for veal)
2 cups tomato *passata*
1 2/3 cups frozen peas, or
 blanched fresh ones
4 1/2 tablespoons chopped
 flat-leaf parsley
4 1/2 tablespoons chopped
 basil
3 1/2 ounces *caciocavallo* or
 provolone cheese, diced
1/2 cup grated pecorino
1–2 eggs (optional)
1/3 cup fresh bread crumbs

Also good in this dish
ditali

Anelletti al forno, baked rings of pasta, the whole dish often formed as a great ring itself, is a classic Sicilian dish. A favourite for Easter time, and picnicking in general, it is best served at room temperature — perfect for those who like to cook in advance or aren't sure what time their guests will arrive for dinner. A vegetarian version can be made by omitting the meat and stirring in 3/4 pound diced buffalo mozzarella just before the pasta goes into the baking dish.

Preheat the oven to 425°F (or 390°F for convection ovens).

Fry the onion, celery, and garlic in the butter and oil over a medium heat with a hefty pinch of salt until softened — about 10 minutes. Add the meat and red pepper flakes, increase the heat to high, and fry for a quarter of an hour until the meat is partly browned. You'll want to break it up with a spoon for the first 5 minutes, until the meat is grey and particulated, then stir only occasionally to give it a chance to caramelise properly. Add the wine and let it reduce by half, then add the *passata* and peas, reduce the heat to low, and simmer for 45 minutes until well thickened. Taste for seasoning.

Cook the pasta until *al dente*, drain, and mix with the sauce. Stir in the herbs and most of both cheeses. You can add an egg or 2 if you want a more robust texture; I prefer mine a little crumbly, so I follow tradition and leave the eggs out. Butter a suitable baking dish (a 9-inch round cake pan or 11-inch ring mold is best), line the bottom with buttered parchment paper if practical, and thoroughly coat with the bread crumbs, keeping any excess crumbs to one side. Pour in the pasta mixture, pressing down with the back of a spoon, and top with the remaining cheeses and leftover bread crumbs. Bake for 45 minutes until browned on all sides. Leave to cool for at least 2 hours before turning out onto a plate — this dish should be served at room temperature and won't hold together when still hot.

BIGOLI

Dimensions
Length: 6.2 in
Diameter: 2.5 mm

Similar forms
fusarioli, passatelli, pici

Also good with this pasta
*arrabiata; pesto Genovese;
puttanesca; sausage sauce;
scallops and thyme; tartufo
dei poveri; tocco*

Until recently, there was scarcely a home in the Veneto that didn't have its own *bigolario* – a rugged hand-cranked press bolted onto the kitchen table or a work-horse – that would force a stiff dough of whole wheat flour, water, and perhaps a duck egg through a brass die. The resulting strands, like thick *spaghetti* with a rough-textured surface, are *bigoli*, the signature pasta of the region. They are supposed to be as thick as knitting needles used to knit tights, but nowadays as few homes have knitting needles as they do *bigoli* presses. The haberdashery parallel doesn't stop, however: There is a lesser-known variant, *fusarioi*, with a name that comes from *fuso da filare* – a knitting spool.

There are three key features of this pasta that render it unique. Firstly, the whole wheat flour – whole wheat doughs are unusual, in this case lending an earthy flavour and pleasant texture, and also being rather healthy, incidentally. Secondly, the freshness – this is the only cylindrical pasta traditionally cooked from fresh (rather than dried), apart from *pici* (page 198). This allows its thick shape to cook quickly, the interior already being moist, leading to a finished product that is springy and chewy, rather than faintly crunchy, when *al dente*. Thirdly, the roughness, produced by a coarse dough rubbing against a bronze die, which allows the pasta to take up more sauce than its counterparts.

MAKING BIGOLI

2¾ cups plus 2 generous tablespoons whole wheat flour (finely ground, if possible)

¼ cup plus 2 generous teaspoons *semola* (this is not traditional but pleasing; you could use an extra 6 tablespoons plus 2 teaspoons whole wheat flour if you are a staunch traditionalist)

3 eggs

This recipe is nearly impossible to follow exactly, as it relies on the use of a *bigolario* — something resembling a gymnastics horse which you sit astride, with a brass hand-cranked press attached to one end. Given that probably only a very small minority of families in the Veneto (where *bigoli* come from) have such a device, it seems a fair assumption that even fewer of my readership will.

There are ways to cheat:

1) Buy dried *bigoli*.
2) Buy dried whole wheat *spaghetti*.
3) Buy fresh *spaghetti*.
4) Roll the dough 1.5 millimeters thick, and cut (with a knife or the *tagliolini* cutter of a pasta machine) into very thin square noodles — not the right shape, but still nice.
5) Not my idea, but a workable one: Remove the blade from a meat mincer, and pass the dough through the finest plate.

Here is a recipe for those who happen to have a *bigoli* press, or who wish to attempt one of the latter options above.

Combine all ingredients with 3 tablespoons of water and knead thoroughly (15 minutes of hard labour), then let rest for an hour before passing through your press. Allow the *bigoli* to fall directly on a board dusted liberally with *semola* and dust themselves, lest they stick. Use fresh.

BIGOLI IN SALSA
Anchovy sauce

½ recipe fresh *bigoli* (or ½ pound dried)
8–11 salted anchovy or sardine fillets
1 medium onion
6 tablespoons extra-virgin olive oil
⅓ cup white wine
2 tablespoons chopped flat-leaf parsley

Also good with this sauce
bucatini, maccheroni alla chitarra, pici, spaghetti

Clearly, there is only one sauce to go with *bigoli*. If you like anchovies, it's the bomb . . .

Like *tartufo dei poveri* (page 158), this is a somewhat dry sauce that goes excellently with fresh noodles – fresh spaghetti are the most readily available substitute if you can't get or won't make *bigoli*.

Chop the anchovy or sardine fillets, but no need to do so very finely.

Halve the onion and slice very thinly across the grain. Put into a cold frying pan large enough to hold the pasta along with the fish and the oil. Fry over a medium heat for about 10 minutes, stirring away until the anchovy or sardine has disintegrated and the onion is soft and just starting to colour. Add the wine and 1 cup water, and simmer gently for 45 minutes or so, until the sauce attains a thick, dry texture.

Cook the pasta and add to the sauce marginally undercooked, along with a few tablespoons of the pasta water and 1½ tablespoons of the parsley. Cook together until the pasta is well coated in the sauce – it should look a little dry but not taste so (if it does, add a splash of water).

Serve with the remaining parsley on top. I am not, in general, one for over-refining presentation – nor am I averse to ubiquitous brown food, which often tastes so nice. The particular hue of this sauce is so unappetising, however, that it may be worth going the extra mile and serving it as *nidi* (nests), by winding large forkfuls against a spoon and carefully depositing a few of these neat, domed mounds on each plate before adding the final parsley.

BIGOLI ALL'ANATRA
Duck sauce

½ recipe fresh *bigoli* or ½ pound dried

DUCK *RAGÙ*
1 whole duck (4–5½ pounds)
2 onions
2 carrots
3 celery stalks
4 garlic cloves
4 bay leaves
3½ tablespoons butter
1½ cups red wine
About 1 cup canned chopped tomatoes or pureed fresh tomatoes (½ pound)
Grated *grana* cheese (such as Parmesan), to serve

Also good with this sauce
maccheroni alla chitarra, maltagliati, pappardelle, pici, spaccatelle

On second thought, there may actually be more than one sauce for *bigoli*. The following method of cooking the pasta in the broth from a boiled duck, and using the meat to make the sauce, is as ancient as it is worthwhile.

Remove the giblets from the duck. Finely chop the gizzard, heart, and liver, and set aside. You are going to boil the duck and use the leg meat to make the *ragù*. You can leave the breasts on (and serve them with boiled potatoes and *mostarda* as a second course), or cut them off raw and use in a grander dish.

Take 1 onion, 1 carrot, 1½ celery stalks, 2 garlic cloves, and 2 bay leaves and put with the duck in a large pot. Just cover with water, season with some salt (not too much), and simmer gently for 1½ hours. Drain the duck, then set aside until cool enough to handle. Strain and skim the stock, and return to the pan for later use.

If you've boiled the bird with the breasts on, cut them away and set aside for later. Pick all the other meat off the legs, wings, and body (don't forget the neck), and chop roughly. I like to leave on most of the skin to enrich the *ragù*, but you can discard it if you prefer.

Finely dice the remaining vegetables and chop the remaining garlic. Heat the butter (you could use the fat skimmed from your stock if you had a mind to) in a medium pan, and fry the vegetables, bay, and chopped giblets in it for 10 minutes, until soft.

Add the wine and reduce by half, then add the tomatoes, chopped duck meat, and 1 scant cup of the stock. Simmer the sauce until very thick and reduced, about 45 minutes.

When ready to eat, bring the duck stock back to the boil, check it is well seasoned with salt, and cook the pasta in it.

Drain when just on the uncooked side of *al dente,* toss in the heated sauce and cook together for a minute before serving with grated *grana* cheese at the table.

BUCATINI

Dimensions
Diameter: 3 mm
Length: 10.4 in
Wall thickness: 1 mm

Synonyms
boccolotti (from *boccolo*,
"ringlet" or "roll"), *fidelini
bucati, perciatelli* (from the
French *percer*, "to pierce");
in Sicily *agoni bucati, spilloni
bucati* ("hat pin with a hole")

Also good with this pasta
aglione; amatriciana;
anchovy sauce; *arrabbiata;*
cacio e pepe; cream
and prosciutto; *gricia;*
Norma; pork and pigskin;
puttanesca; ricotta and
tomato; *sugo di coda;* tuna
belly and tomato

Their name stems from *buco* ("hole"), or *bucato* ("pierced"),
and the hole has a specific function. A pasta with a large cross-
section takes a long time to cook. Above a certain diameter
(see *bigoli*, page 28, and *pici*, page 198), the form would take so
long to cook from dry that the outside would be overcooked
before the middle was *al dente*. These forms are therefore
always made fresh, so that the inside, already hydrated by the
water the pasta was made with, takes less time to cook. *Bucatini*
on the other hand are an industrial, die-extruded pasta (the
modern equivalent of *maccheroni inferrati*, page 160), and
the manufacture and distribution processes require that the
product be dried before packaging. The ingenious solution is
the fine hole that gives this pasta its name. Water enters as the
pasta boils, reducing the cooking time to no longer than that
of *spaghetti*. Long before the advent of the microwave, people
were finding ways to cook their food from the inside out.

By far the most famous dish they star in is the Roman *bucatini
all'Amatriciana*. In Amatrice, this is made *in bianco* (without
tomato, like *gricia* on page 220); in Rome *Amatriciana* is red
with tomato. Not out of any desire to be obtuse, a recipe for
Roman *pasta all'Amatriciana* can be found under *rigatoni* (page
221). I lived for some time in Rome and remember fondly
rigatoni served in this sauce at my favourite *trattorie*, notably
Trattoria da Marcello in San Lorenzo.

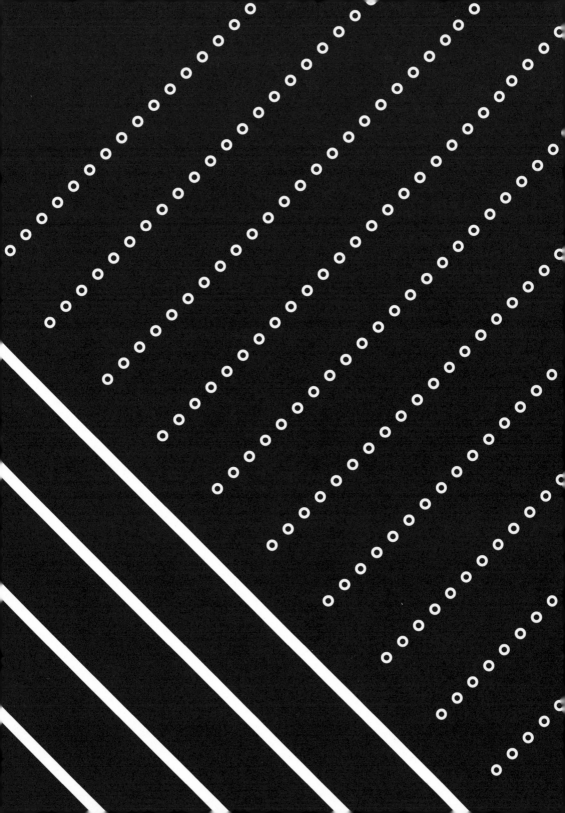

BUCATINI CARBONARA

½ pound *bucatini*
3½ ounces *guanciale*, sliced
    thickly, then across into
    ¾-inch-wide lardons
2 teaspoons olive oil
2 eggs
¾–1 cup grated pecorino
    Romano (or Parmesan,
    or mixture of the 2), plus
    extra to serve

Also good with this sauce
*fettuccine, maccheroni
inferrati, spaghetti,
tagliatelle*

This famous pasta is unrecorded before the Second World War. There are any number of unsubstantiated tales of its origin, including that it was traditional sustenance for charcoal workers (*carbone* meaning "charcoal"), or that it was named after the *Carbonari* ("charcoalmen" – a secret society prominent in Italy's unification). Whatever the origins, they were likely in Rome, which remains the spiritual home of this pasta today. A good *carbonara* is luscious, unctuous, piggy, and almost a heart attack on a plate. It is surely a good way to go . . .

Guanciale is pig's cheek cured like pancetta or bacon. The result is a fatty, porcine treat, hard to find but worth seeking out.

Put the pasta on to boil. Fry the *guanciale* in the oil over a high heat until the fat has blistered and browned a little on the outside, but is still soft within. It will smoke profusely. Take the pan off the heat. Beat the eggs with the cheese in a large bowl, seasoning generously with plenty of freshly crushed black pepper. It is a good idea to warm this over the boiling water – not to cook, but just to take the chill off. When cooked (but of course *al dente*), drain the pasta, and toss in the pan of *guanciale* until well coated in the fat. Transfer immediately to your bowl, and stir well for about a minute until the eggs have partially thickened. Check for seasoning, and serve with extra cheese on top.

BUCATINI AL CONIGLIO ALL'ISCHITANA
Rabbit and spicy tomato

Serves 4

2/3–3/4 pound *bucatini*
1 farmed rabbit
1/2 cup olive oil
6 garlic cloves, peeled and broken but whole
1 or 2 whole dried chilis
3/4–1 cup white wine
5 medium ripe tomatoes (1 pound 10 ounces), cut into chunks (probably eighths)
3/4 cup chopped flat-leaf parsley (1 ounce)
Grated pecorino Romano, to serve (optional)

Also good with this sauce
maccheroni inferrati, reginette, spaghetti

This is a punchy dish with concentrated flavours that work just as well at any time of year. Hailing from beautiful Ischia, it serves four as two courses of a meal.

Cut the rabbit into joints (cut the legs and shoulders off the spine; cut off tail, neck, and ribs; cut the torso into 4 sections, leaving belly flaps, liver, and kidneys attached).

Heat the oil in a very wide pan (16 inches – you need space to brown the rabbit, although this can be done in 2 batches in a smaller pan). Fry the garlic with the chili(s) until the garlic begins to brown; remove with a slotted spoon and set aside. Add the rabbit, seasoned with salt and pepper, and brown very well over a medium heat – this will take a good 15 minutes if the heat isn't too high. Return the garlic and chili(s) to the pan, and add the wine. Allow to bubble slowly, uncovered, turning the rabbit every 5 minutes or so. After half an hour, when almost all the wine has evaporated, add the tomato and parsley, and season to taste. Continue to cook over the same heat, still turning the rabbit every few minutes, for longer than you might think.

This sauce is cooked until it is incredibly reduced and the rabbit is coated in a concentrated paste of tomato in which it again starts to fry. This should take about 40 minutes from when you add the tomatoes, but keep on going until you are afraid the tomato might burn. Put the pasta on at this point.

There will appear to be almost no sauce for your pasta, but adding 3/4 cup of water will rejuvenate and extend the meager scrapings that stick to pan and rabbit. Remove the meat (keep it somewhere warm for your second course), and add the pasta (drained and *al dente*) to the pan and cook for a minute in the sauce. Serve as is, or with a little pecorino if you like.

PASTA CU LI SARDI
Sardines and fennel

½ pound *bucatini*
⅔ pound fresh sardines (or
⅓ pound fresh sardine
fillets)
1 whole salted anchovy, or
2 fillets
1 slice bread, crustless, torn
up (about 1 ounce)
6 tablespoons extra-virgin
olive oil, divided
1 small fennel bulb (with as
many leaves as possible,
or a small bunch of wild
fennel if you can get it)
1 medium onion, diced
3 tablespoons pine nuts
2 tablespoons raisins
About ¹⁄₁₆ teaspoon or ½
pinch fennel pollen (or
fennel seed, crushed)
1 pinch saffron strands, in
1½ tablespoons boiling
water

Also good with this sauce
*maccheroni inferrati, penne,
rigatoni, sedanini, spaghetti*

This dish seems to summarise Sicily on a plate, with earthy tones of pine nuts, fennel, and saffron representing the wild and beautiful hills, combined with sardines, just one of the oily fish so loved on the island.

First clean and fillet the sardines and anchovy, if using whole fish.

For the sardines, rub them under running water with your thumb to scale them. Then grasp a fish in your left hand (assuming you're right-handed) with the dorsal fin against your palm, belly facing out. With your right hand, pinch the nape of the neck to break the flesh above the spine. Now gently pull the head forwards towards the belly – it should, if you're lucky, draw out the spine and guts together, leaving 2 clean fillets in your left hand.

For the anchovy, rinse off the salt. Under running water, use your thumb to open up the 2 fillets, then pull out the spine. Blot the fillets dry.

Toss the bread with 3 tablespoons of the oil, salt, and pepper, and toast in a moderate oven until golden, then crush to crumbs.

Bring a pot of salted water to the boil. Halve the bulb of fennel (green stalks and all) and boil until tender, about 10 minutes.

In another, wide pan, fry the onion on a medium-low heat in the remaining oil until translucent – about 10 minutes. Then add the pine nuts, raisins, and fennel pollen, and fry for a further 10 minutes, until the onion is completely soft. Meanwhile, remove the fennel from the water (leave it boiling) and chop.

Remove any fins from the sardines, and chop up the sardines and anchovy. Season with salt, add to the pan and cook for a minute, then add the fennel and cook for a final 5–10 minutes.

At about the same time that you add the sardines, put the pasta into your still-boiling fennely water. Cook until firmly *al dente*, then add a spoonful of the water to your sauce. To finish the sauce, add the saffron and its water, and taste for seasoning. Drain the pasta and add to the sauce. Cook for a minute or 2 before serving with the bread crumbs on top.

BUSIATI

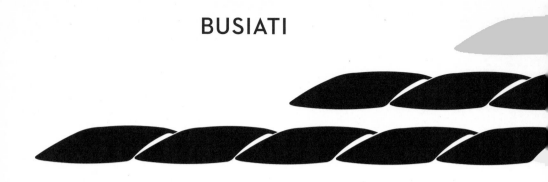

Dimensions
Length: 3.2 in
Width: 0.4 in

Synonyms
subioti, fusarioi, maccheroni bobbesi, busa, ciufolitti (Abruzzese term from *zuffolo*, "panpipes"), *gnocchi col ferro*

Also good with this pasta
garlic sauce; green beans; *pesto Genovese; tocco;* tuna belly and tomato

There are two forms of *busiati*, made in almost identical manners but looking quite distinct. The other is listed under *maccheroni inferrati* (page 160) and is more similar to handmade *bucatini* (page 34) or hollow *pici* (page 198) – the version described and illustrated here looks and behaves like a coiled telephone wire. From Sicily (and Trapani in particular) this, along with *spaccatelle* (page 228) and *cuscussù* (page 84), makes up the triumvirate of Sicilian pastas. Notwithstanding that all pasta came to Europe via the Arabs, the link between the Latins and the Moors is particularly strong in Sicily. *Cuscussù* is an obvious result – but this marriage of races is also evident in *busiati*, which take their name from *busa* (a type of reed), itself stemming from the Arabic *bus*. Early recipes for *busiati* replace water with egg whites and rosewater in the dough (in 1456 in *Libro de Arte Coquinaria*, Maestro Martino referred to this as *maccheroni Siciliani*). This may have helped the pasta to store when dried for sailors about to embark on long voyages, but must have been especially wonderful with *pesto Trapanese*, the recipe given opposite.

MAKING BUSIATI

To make spiralled *busiati* for 2, make a semolina pasta dough (page 10) using 7 ounces of *semola*. Take a piece the size of a lime and roll it out into a strand about ¼ inch across, then

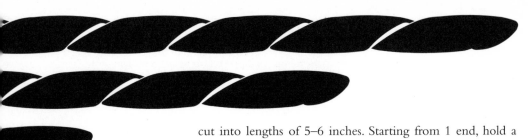

cut into lengths of 5–6 inches. Starting from 1 end, hold a wooden skewer or thin dowel, or a thin iron rod like an old knitting needle, at a 45° angle to your worm of pasta. Wind and stretch the pasta around the rod with a rolling motion, applying some pressure to help the stretching process. Roll back and forth a couple of times to loosen them from the rod, and pull it out from the pasta. The finished *busiati* should look somewhat like telephone wires – fairly tightly coiled, flattened strands of pasta. This is the real deal – the inspiration behind *fusilli bucati* (page 108).

BUSIATI CON PESTO TRAPANESE
Almond pesto

1 recipe *busiati*
2/3–3/4 cup blanched
   almonds
2 garlic cloves, crushed
1 (3/4–1 ounce) bunch basil
10 1/2 ounces ripe cherry
   tomatoes
1/3 cup extra-virgin olive oil
Grated pecorino Romano, to
   serve (optional)

Also good with this sauce
*casarecce, cavatappi,
fusilli bucati/fatti a mano,
gemelli, maccheroni inferrati,
spaghetti, trenette*

Few sauces going by the name of "pesto" are worth eating, other than the famous *pesto Genovese* (page 276). This is one of those rare exceptions.

Cook the pasta in plenty of boiling, salted water until *al dente*.

Meanwhile, grind the nuts and garlic in a food processor until fine, then add the basil leaves followed by the tomatoes. When you have a fine, but still textured paste, stir in the oil by hand. Season with salt and pepper to taste.

This sauce may be served on top of pasta or stirred through it, but never cooked with it in a pan. Great with grated pecorino, or without.

CAMPANELLE/GIGLI

Dimensions
Length: 1 in
Width: 0.52 in

Synonyms
lilies or, with a turn-of-the-screw shape, *amorosi, cornetti,* or *jolly*

Also good with this pasta
artichokes, peas, and broad beans; green beans; green olives and tomatoes; Hungarian fish soup; lamb sauce; lentils; *norcina;* pureed broad beans; *puttanesca; ragù Bolognese;* tomato sauce; Treviso, speck, and fontina

Unmistakably floral, even in name (*gigli* means "lilies," *campanelle* "bells" or "bellflowers"), these pastas are made from a single sheet of pasta with a frilly edge, twisted into a tapering helix – just as a baker might make flowers from sugar paste. They are a fantasy pasta shape – designed to meet consumer desire for something new – but the designers bore in mind the need for a shape that looked good, cooked evenly without breaking, and was a good vehicle for sauce, and so *campanelle* have become a well-used and respected form. As with a number of fantastical shapes, these may be made with semolina dough (in general, from larger and more industrial producers) or with a richer egg pasta from more artisanal production, but they are always sold dried.

CAMPANELLE CON SGOMBRO E ROSMARINO
Mackerel, tomato, and rosemary

½ pound *campanelle/gigli*
1 medium mackerel (about ⅔ pound)
½ cup extra-virgin olive oil
1 garlic clove, finely chopped
1½ tablespoons finely chopped fresh rosemary
⅜ teaspoon crushed red pepper flakes
2 ripe tomatoes, chopped in ½-inch pieces
3 tablespoons chopped flat-leaf parsley

Also good with this sauce
canestri, torchio

Fillet the mackerel, leaving the skin on. To avoid onerous pin-boning, cut each fillet in 2 by slicing down either side of the red central line, which you can discard along with the pin bones. Cut these 4 quarter-fillets across to make rough ¾-inch dice.

Put the pasta on to boil. Heat the oil until fragrant, but a long way from smoking. Add the garlic, rosemary, and red pepper flakes, and fry for a few seconds to release the flavours, then add the mackerel and tomatoes. Season with salt and pepper, and cook over a medium heat for 3–4 minutes, until the fish is cooked and the tomatoes break up. Drain the pasta while it is still *al dente*, and add it, allowing it to cook for a minute in the sauce. Add the parsley, and a splash of the cooking water only if it all looks a bit dry.

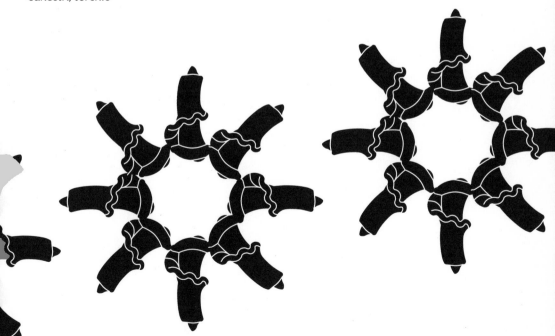

CANEDERLI

Dimensions
Diameter: 1.68 in
Synonyms
*gnocchi di Pane,
canedeli, knödel*

Canederli hail from the Alpine regions of Italy, Trentino–Alto Adige in particular, where the buildings, culture, customs, and food seem altogether more Germanic than Italian. Indeed this pasta is German in origin, its name still similar to the original *knödel*. Plain ball-like dumplings, the simplest are made from seasoned bread crumbs, but any number of variations combine ingredients readily available to mountain farmers. Wild herbs, cheeses, cured meats, or pike might make an appearance, while sweet versions use a dough made from potato and are stuffed with plums or apricots.

The savoury versions tend to be firm and substantial. Most commonly served in broth, they might instead be eaten with cabbage, greens, dandelion, or sauerkraut cooked au gratin (with cheese); or served as a starch with a *spezzatino* (scarce stew).

CANEDERLI IN BRODO
Bread dumplings in broth

1/2 medium onion, very finely
   chopped
3 1/2 tablespoons butter
3–4 slices good day-old
   bread (about 5 1/4 ounces,
   weighed without crust),
   finely diced
1/3 cup all-purpose flour, plus
   plenty extra for rolling
2 eggs
Scant 1/2 cup milk
1 1/2 ounces pancetta or
   lardo, finely chopped,
   or 2 2/3 ounces Italian
   sausage, skin removed,
   broken up
2/3 cup grated Parmesan,
   plus extra to serve
3 tablespoons finely
   chopped parsley
A grating of nutmeg
Some finely chopped chives
   (optional)
4 1/4 cups good broth (page
   242)

These light bread dumplings are delicious in broth, but can also be cooked (after boiling) au gratin with butter, herbs (sage, rosemary, or thyme), and Parmesan. They can be made vegetarian by the omission of the pancetta, with no real loss of flavour. The only challenge is to make a good enough broth without meat, but dried wild mushrooms would do the trick.

Gently fry the onion in the butter until soft, then leave to cool. Mix together well with all the ingredients (except the broth) to make a soft, sticky dough (which won't be entirely smooth). Season with salt and pepper.

Take a small lump of dough, roll in flour, and test to see if it holds together when dropped in boiling water. If it fails, add a bit more flour to the mixture and try again. When satisfied that you are on safe ground, roll golfball-sized spheres of dough with generously floured hands. Refrigerate for at least an hour before cooking. Cook in the broth at a gentle simmer, seasoned with salt to taste. They will take about 20 minutes. Serve in their broth, with a scattering of Parmesan atop.

CANEDERLI GRATINATI
Bread dumplings au gratin

1 recipe *canederli*, cooked
   as above
4 1/2 tablespoons fresh bread
   crumbs
4 1/2 tablespoons grated
   Parmesan
1 tablespoon finely chopped
   fresh sage or thyme

While the *canederli* cook, preheat the broiler. Drain the *canederli*, reserving the flavoursome broth. Put them in a buttered baking dish, dot each dumpling with butter, and sprinkle over a mixture of fresh bread crumbs, grated Parmesan, and herbs. Cook under the broiler until browned on top, and serve moistened with just a few tablespoons of the cooking liquid – keep the rest of the broth for some other use.

CANEDERLI DOLCI
Fruit dumplings

Serves 6

3–4 floury potatoes (17½ ounces), such as Russet or Idaho
1 egg
1 egg yolk
1²/₃ cups flour, plus plenty extra for rolling

FILLING
12 apricot kernels or bitter almonds (if you can get them; otherwise 1½ teaspoons almond extract)
7 tablespoons superfine sugar
4½ tablespoons rum
¾ teaspoon ground cinnamon
Grated zest of 1 small lemon
3½ ounces marzipan
6 ripe apricots/small plums, 12 soft dried prunes or apricots, or 12 dates

THE DISH
3½ tablespoons butter
¼ cup fresh bread crumbs
3½ tablespoons superfine sugar
Scant ¾ teaspoon ground cinnamon

If the idea of a potato dessert seems bizarre, it is suggested you try the recipe below. Delicate and aromatic, and a substantial winter treat, these are a winner …

For the dough, boil the potatoes whole, skins on, until cooked through. Drain, peel with your fingers while still hot, and pass through a food mill or potato ricer. When cool enough to handle, mix in the remaining ingredients. Knead just enough to make an even dough, like that for *gnocchi* (page 116), only stiffer. Do not mix too much or the texture will be unpleasant.

For the filling, pound the apricot kernels (if using) to a fine paste. Stir in the sugar, rum, cinnamon, and zest, then work into a paste with the marzipan (with almond extract, if not using kernels). Remove the pits from the fruit, replace with as much filling as you can cram in, and close the fruit around. (If using dried fruits, open them up like butterflies, and enclose the filling in 2 butterflied wrappers.)

To assemble the dish, divide the dough into 6 balls. Take 1 in your hand, flatten, and carefully wrap around 1 fruit. Be sure to get an even coating, with no little holes for water to enter. Roll each in abundant flour. They have a tendency to stick to the bottom of the pot as they boil; to prevent this, cut 6 rough 6-inch squares of waxed paper, loosely wrap each ball, and lower it into a gently boiling pot of salted water, so the paper comes between pot and dumpling. Simmer for 45 minutes.

Meanwhile, fry the bread crumbs in the butter in a wide pan until golden. When the dumplings are ready (they should have bobbed on the surface halfway through the cooking time), lift them gently from the water on a slotted spoon, and turn in the buttery bread crumbs to coat. Mix the cinnamon and sugar together – either roll the dumplings in this, or sprinkle on top. Serve hot, with a scoop of vanilla, almond, or cinnamon ice cream if you like.

CANESTRINI AND CANESTRI

Canestrini are "little baskets," shaped like old-fashioned wicker baskets that might be taken to market, into the woods for foraging, or into the fields to gather flowers. They are an intermediate size, between the identically shaped but smaller *fiocchi di avena* ("rolled oats"), and the larger *canestri*, which may be used interchangeably with *farfalle* and *farfalle tonde* (page 92). The shape is, in fact, a derivation of *farfalle,* and whilst it can be easily made at home, it can be purchased with even less effort. With its double-cupped shape, it provides an excellent scoop for sauces, especially types of fish and meat *ragù* in larger sizes; the texture of smaller ones is delightful in soups and broths. Both semolina and egg versions can be found – and chosen to your personal preference.

CANESTRINI IN ACQUACOTTA
Vegetable soup with poached egg

Serves 2 as a substantial starter or light main

1¾ ounces canestrini
⅛–¼ ounce dried porcini
1 garlic clove, thinly sliced
1 medium onion, chopped
1 or 2 celery stalks, sliced across into crescents
1 bay leaf
½ cup extra-virgin olive oil, divided
5 cherry tomatoes, cut into eighths
About 1/2 cup spinach or baby chard (1¾ ounces)
2 eggs
10 basil leaves
Grated Parmesan, to serve

Also good with this soup
alfabeto, cavatelli, orzo, quadretti, stelline

Acquacotta is a simple peasant soup, normally made with bread. It is not dissimilar to *pancotto* (only thinner) or *ribollita* (only less beany). Here pasta replaces bread as the starch. The remaining ingredients are similarly open to interpretation — in spring, one might add peas, broad beans, or artichokes; in summer, all sorts of greens; in autumn, fresh mushrooms; and pulses in winter.

Soak the porcini in ⅓ cup boiling water, drain (reserving the liquid), chop, and return to their liquid. Fry the garlic, onion, celery, and bay in half the oil until barely tender, about 5 minutes. Add the porcini, their liquid, and 2 cups of water. Bring to a very gentle simmer, season to taste, and cook for 5–10 minutes until the vegetables have lost their bite, then add the pasta and the tomatoes. Continue to simmer until the pasta is 2–3 minutes from being done, then stir in the spinach and gently crack the eggs into the broth to poach. When the pasta and eggs are done (the yolks should still be soft), stir in the basil (shredded or torn) and drizzle with the remaining oil. Serve straightaway in wide bowls with a fair bit of Parmesan on top.

CANNELLONI

Dimensions
Length: 4 in
Width: 1.2 in

Synonyms
cannaciotti, canneroncini,
canneroni, manfriguli, or
manfrigoli in Valtellina;
cannerone or cannarone in
Naples; cannarune in Puglia;
cannoli or crusetti in Sicily

Cannelloni are sheets of pasta wrapped around a sausage of filling and baked. It is possible to buy dried tubes of pasta to blanch and stuff, but to my mind these should really be called *manicotti* (page 168). Their name derives from *canna* ("cane"); thus *cannelloni* means "large reeds" – the same stem as *cannella* (cinnamon – "little reed"). The idea of stuffing a soft pastry with a savoury filling isn't new in Europe – *crêpes* have been around forever, and references to *macheroni ripieni* date back to around 1770 – but *cannelloni* were first mentioned in print at the beginning of the twentieth century, likely the time they were invented. Their popularity took off and went global after the Second World War, for the dual reasons of their ease of advance preparation (they can be made ready to go in the oven even the day before) and of being the symbol of domestic bliss – the housewife at her gleaming white enamel oven. The pasta can be replaced with a *crêpe* in all recipes, if that seems easier or better to you; in both forms, *cannelloni* are equally popular in Italy, the UK, the USA, and Spain (Catalonia in particular).

VEAL AND SPINACH CANNELLONI

Serves 5 as a main course

FILLING
2 garlic cloves
6 tablespoons extra-virgin
  olive oil
1 smallish onion, diced
1 celery stalk, finely diced
2/3 pound minced veal
1½ teaspoons finely
  chopped fresh rosemary
1½ tablespoons finely
  chopped fresh sage or
  oregano
¾ cup white wine
2–2¼ cups fresh spinach
  (½ pound)
Generous ½ cup fresh
  ricotta
1 cup grated Parmesan
1 egg
A good grating of nutmeg
⅓ cup fresh bread crumbs
  (if required)

BÉCHAMEL
½ cup butter
1 bay leaf
¾ cup plus 2 tablespoons
  flour
4¼ cups milk
Nutmeg to taste

The following recipe is an Americanised one; it has everything inside (meat, cheese, vegetable), where an Italian recipe might be simpler – you could use the spinach and ricotta filling (page 210) from *ravioli* to great effect. Both are delicious.

To make the filling, break the garlic cloves to release the flavour and fry in a wide pan in the oil until starting to brown. Remove and discard the garlic, adding the onion and celery along with a good pinch of salt. Fry together until tender (5–10 minutes), then add the meat. Fry over a high heat, stirring and breaking up with a spoon for the first 5 minutes, then as little as possible to give the meat a chance to brown. Add the herbs, closely followed by the wine, which you should allow to bubble away to almost nothing (you really want it quite dry) before taking the pan from the heat to cool.

Blanch the spinach in boiling salted water until just tender, drain, refresh under cold water, drain again, and squeeze dry with all your might. Chop as finely as you can by hand, then stir vigorously with the ricotta, Parmesan, and egg to make a smooth paste. Mix this paste with the cooked veal, and season with a good grating of nutmeg, salt, and pepper. Add some bread crumbs if the mixture looks a little damp. Refrigerate until ready to use.

To make the béchamel, melt the butter over a medium heat, add the bay leaf and flour, and stir until incorporated and bubbling. Add the milk – the daring add it all at once and whisk, the cautious bit by bit, beating with a wooden spoon with each addition of milk until the mixture is smooth and returns to the boil. Season with salt, pepper, and nutmeg, and make sure the sauce comes to a boil when all the milk is added, at which point it can be taken from the heat.

THE DISH

2/3 pound simple or enriched egg pasta dough (page 13)

1/3 cup light tomato sauce (page 15), optional

1 cup grated Parmesan

Also good with these fillings
veal and pork (page 18); chicken and ricotta (page 60); spinach and ricotta (page 210)

Preheat the oven to 465°F (or 425°F for convection ovens).

To make the dish, roll the pasta just under 1 millimeter thick and cut into rough 6-inch squares — you'll get about 15 of them. Blanch these for 30 seconds in boiling, salted water, and refresh in cold water.

Take 1 square at a time and lay a sausage of filling (about ¾ inch wide — as wide as a sausage) along 1 edge. Roll up like a carpet, and repeat for the remaining squares. Spread one-third of the béchamel on the base of a baking pan large enough to accommodate the *cannelloni* without crowding them. Lay the *cannelloni* on top, cover evenly with the remaining béchamel, drizzle with the tomato sauce (if using), and sprinkle with the Parmesan. Bake for 45 minutes, until browned on top. They will be lethally hot fresh from the oven — best to wait 10 minutes before serving.

CAPELLI D'ANGELO

Dimensions
Length: 10.4 in
Diameter: 1 mm

Synonyms
capelvenere, ramicia, or in
Calabria *capiddi d'angilu,
vrimiciddi*

Similar forms
capellini (slightly thicker),
vermicelli (slightly thicker
still)

Also good with this pasta
fideuà; frittata; lokshen
pudding

These thin, thin strands of pasta ("angel's hair" or "little worms") can be a challenge in the modern kitchen: They cook very fast, they overcook easily, and their fine texture can become porridgy if served in a thick sauce – they have no backbone to hold it up. It was a different challenge that led them to be so highly esteemed during the Renaissance. So difficult to make by hand as to be nigh-on impossible, they were the height of refinement. Specialist nuns would make them in their convents, particularly to feed to new mothers, as the pasta was believed to help their milk to "drop." Their exceeding fragility means they are always dried in *nidi* ("nests"), as they are too delicate to hang up to dry or to transport otherwise.

CAPELLI D'ANGELO AL BURRO E LIMONE
Butter and lemon

½ pound *capelli d'angelo*
⅓ cup butter
Grated zest of 1 lemon
A grating of nutmeg
A few drops of lemon juice
A little grated Parmesan, to
  serve
A few basil leaves (optional)

Also good in this dish
tagliatelle, tagliolini

This dish, fine-textured and subtle, is somewhat ethereal. You might call it bland, but not in a pejorative sense.

While the *capelli d'angelo* are cooking, pour about ⅓ cup of their water into a pan and boil, swirling in the butter to make a *beurre fondu*. Add the lemon zest, nutmeg, and a little pepper and salt if needed. Allow to reduce to the consistency of light cream (add water if it goes too far), then add the pasta (drained and, as ever, slightly on the undercooked side). Stir in and add a very few drops of lemon juice to taste.

Serve with a little Parmesan. A few basil leaves, stirred in at the same time as the lemon juice, are a pleasant addition.

PASTA FRITTA ALLA SIRACUSANA
Fried in nests

⅓ pound *capelli d'angelo*
  (or ½ pound *spaghetti* or
  spaghettini)
1½ tablespoons butter
½ cup grated pecorino or
  caciocavallo cheese
2 eggs
3 tablespoons fresh bread
  crumbs
6 tablespoons olive oil

Also good in this dish
*spaghetti, spaghettini,
tagliolini*

This dish of fried nests of pasta is just like a free-form *frittata* and originates from Syracuse.

Cook the pasta until *al dente*, drain, and toss in the butter. Beat the cheese into the eggs along with the bread crumbs, then stir into the hot pasta. Heat the oil over a medium heat in a wide pan. Use a fork and twisting action to make individual pasta nests (as you would when eating the pasta, only make the nests as big as you can), dropping them into the oil as you go. Flatten each nest slightly and fry for 2–3 minutes on each side until golden. Serve piping hot.

PASTA SOUFFLÉ

Serves 4

2¾ ounces *capelli d'angelo*
½ cup finely grated
    Parmesan
3 tablespoons butter, plus
    more for ramekin(s)
4½ tablespoons all-purpose
    flour
A little nutmeg
A bay leaf, if you like
¾ cup milk
4 eggs, separated

Also good in this dish
tagliolini, vermicellini

This recipe comes from my grandmother, who remembers the dish from Rome in the 1950s. We have had some interesting times cooking it together, since the original recipe went missing a few years ago. Here at last is a new working version, to avoid the dramas of impossibly thick béchamel and collapsed dreams.

Preheat the oven to 425°F (or 390°F for convection ovens).

You will need 4 (1½-cup) soufflé ramekins, or 1 larger ramekin. Butter the dish(es) generously. Add a handful of Parmesan to 1 ramekin, and coat the sides by turning the ramekin in a rolling motion. Tip the remaining cheese into the next, and continue until you return the excess to your heap of grated cheese.

Crush the nests of pasta into boiling, salted water, and cook for half the stated time – it should be very *al dente*. Drain and cool under cold running water.

Melt the butter over a medium heat, then add the flour, quite a few gratings of nutmeg, the bay leaf, and plenty of pepper. Fry for a minute, then gradually add the milk, beating ferociously with a wooden spoon. Patience with the milk will yield a smooth sauce. Season well with salt.

Combine the pasta with the béchamel, egg yolks, and remaining cheese in a large bowl. Beat the egg whites with a small pinch of salt until stiff, but not dry. Mix one-third of the whites into the pasta mixture to slacken it a little, then very gently fold in the rest with a metal spoon. Divide between the ramekins (it should come about ½ inch below the rim), and bake for 20 minutes or until risen, browned and firm. (A single, larger soufflé will need up to twice as long at a slightly cooler temperature.) Serve immediately.

CAPPELLETTI

Dimensions
Length: 1.68 in
Width: 1.2 in

Synonyms
cappelli, cappelli del prete
("priest's hats" – tricorn or
three-cornered hats), *nicci*
in Tuscany

Similar forms
agnolotti, tortelli, tortelloni,
turtei con la cua

Also good with this pasta
asparagus and cream;
butter and sage; cream; *in
brodo;* morels

Fashioned after an Alpine trooper's or cardinal's hat, *cappelletti* ("little hats") are closely related to *tortelli* (page 260) and *tortelloni* (page 266), but with a subtle difference in the way they are formed, leading to a more elongated shape (like an eye when viewed from on top). Whilst all in this family of stuffed and twisted pasta can be made from squares or circles of dough, most are more elegant when made from squares, and this is especially true of *cappelletti*. In Emilia-Romagna, and Modena in particular, these are a permanent feature of Christmas lunch, where they appear as a first course stuffed with ricotta, lemon zest, and nutmeg and served in a limpid pool of capon broth. As with many older dishes, there are also vegetarian varieties (*cappelletti di magro*) for lean or fasting days.

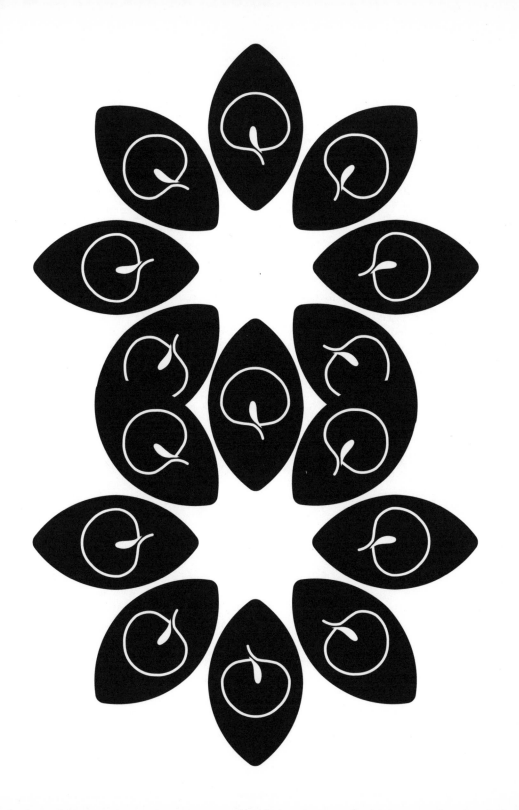

CHICKEN AND RICOTTA CAPPELLETTI

Serves 6 as a main

1 pound enriched egg
    pasta dough (page 13) –
    equivalent to about 1¼
    cups semolina
⅓ pound chicken or capon
    breast, diced about ¾
    inch
3 tablespoons butter
1 egg
¾ cup grated Parmesan
Generous ¾ cup ricotta
Grated zest of 1 small
    lemon (optional)
Grated nutmeg to taste

Also good with these fillings
ricotta (page 267); spinach
and ricotta (page 210);
tortellini filling (page 264)

If one were to serve the *cappelletti in brodo* ("in broth"), it would be advisable to take a small chicken or, better still, a capon and poach it for an hour or two to give a flavoursome broth in which to cook and serve the pasta. The cooked breast meat could then be picked off the carcass and added directly with the other ingredients to the food processor or mincer, the butter having been softened beforehand.

It is worth noting that this filling has a relatively high proportion of moisture inside, and freezing the stuffed pastas runs a risk that the filling expands, cracking the surrounding dough. If you want to serve fewer than 6 people, you would do well to freeze some of the filling in a lump, for future use in *cappelletti, tortelloni* (page 266), or *cannelloni* (page 50). It hardly seems worth making less of the filling, but if you wish to, 1 large egg would bind 3½ ounces chicken breast, ½ cup Parmesan, and a generous ½ cup ricotta for 4; half those quantities, with a medium egg, would serve 2.

Fry the chicken in the butter over a medium heat until just cooked and lightly browned. Allow to cool in the pan, then combine the meat and juices in a food processor with the egg and Parmesan, and process until smooth. Stir in the ricotta by hand, seasoning with salt, pepper, lemon zest, and nutmeg.

Roll the pasta just under 1 millimeter thick, the second-thinnest setting on most machines, or about as thin as any but the most experienced of hands can go with a rolling pin. Cut into squares about 2½ inches large, and dollop a generous 1½ teaspoons (roughly ¼ ounce) of filling in the center of each. Make sure the pasta dough is wet enough to stick to itself (a good one will be); if not, mist lightly with water. Fold in half diagonally, and press to seal the edges and exclude any air.

Take 1 of these triangular parcels. Holding it in the horizontal plane, bring the 2 longer arms together (always in the same plane), as though bringing your own arms from an outstretched position together, pointing in front of you. Press these praying hands of pasta together to seal – the shape should have become somewhat like a naval hat.

CAPPELLETTI CON PORCINI E PANNA
Porcini and cream

½–⅔ pound *cappelletti*
½ pound firm, small, fresh porcini
3 tablespoons butter
⅓ cup heavy cream
Grated Parmesan, to serve

Also good with this sauce
canestri, caramelle, farfalle, farfalle tonde, maltagliati, tortelli, tortellini; tortelloni

This recipe calls for generous quantities of expensive or rich ingredients — such as might grace the table of the cardinal whose hat inspired the shape of the pasta. If your pocket or diet doesn't allow such excess, the quantities of any or all of the mushroom, butter, and cream can be halved. But here is the real deal.

Use a sharp knife to pare the dark skin from the mushroom stalks, leaving them pearly white, and a damp cloth to clean the caps if soiled. Slice the mushrooms ¼ inch thick.

Neither the fresh pasta nor the sauce will take very long – put the pasta into the water at the same time as the mushrooms go into the butter, which has just started to foam over a medium-high heat. Cook the mushrooms, stirring only once or twice, for about 2 minutes or until partly browned and just tender. Add the cream and let bubble until as thick as it was in the fridge, then drain the pasta and add to the sauce. Add a touch of the pasta water if needed, and serve with grated Parmesan on top.

CARAMELLE

Dimensions
Length: 3.2 in
Width: 0.84 in

Similar forms
turtei con la cua

Also good with this pasta
marjoram and pine nuts;
morels; porcini and cream;
tomato sauce

To read a book in translation is like sucking a sweet in its wrapper.
—Proverb

Caramelle – "bonbons" or "candies" – are stuffed pastas shaped like sweets whose plastic wrappers are twisted at both ends, and they are the one candy better in its wrapping. They are made like miniature, half-filled *cannelloni* (page 50), the ends twisted to seal them. This at once encloses the filling so it can be boiled, provides a texture that is capable of holding some sauce, and makes a shape that is reminiscent of happy childhood days. Perhaps for this last reason *caramelle* are generally served on festive days or Sunday lunch, particularly in Parma and Piacenza. They are invariably made from an egg pasta dough (or should be – avoid like the plague any that are pale) and may be stuffed with any manner of filling, but are best with one that is subtle and delicate.

POTATO CARAMELLE

¾ pound simple or
enriched egg pasta dough
(page 13) – equivalent to
1 cup plus 3 tablespoons
semolina
1 medium floury potato (½
pound), such as Russet or
Idaho
1½ tablespoons very finely
chopped fresh rosemary
3 tablespoons butter
¾–1 cup grated Parmesan
1 egg yolk

Also good with these fillings
chicken and ricotta (page
60); veal and spinach (52);
spinach and ricotta (page
210)

This filling also works well for *ravioli* (page 208). Potato, for such a humble foodstuff, makes a tasty, subtle filling. It is delicious either with rich, flavoursome sauces (as a starchy foil to the real business of the sauce) or delicate, similarly plain ones in harmony, such as the simplest of butter sauces.

Boil the potato in salted water in its skin until cooked, then peel and put through a ricer while still hot.

Fry the rosemary in the butter until the butter foams, but before it browns.

When the potato and butter are cool enough to handle, knead together with the Parmesan and egg yolk. Season with salt and pepper. Shape into a block and chill in the fridge before trying to make the pasta, or you won't have much luck.

Roll the pasta 0.7 millimeter thick (this is quite thin), in long strips (as long as your work surface) 2 inches wide. Make sure there is no flour on the surface or pasta.

Cut the filling into little bricks, 1-by-1-by-1½-inches, and lay these along the pasta leaving 2 inches between blocks of potato. Mist the pasta with a little water if too dry to stick to itself, then carefully roll the whole length up, like a giant sushi roll. Make sure the pasta is closed up around the filling. Cut halfway between pieces of filling, pinch to flatten the loose ends and exclude any air, and twist both ends like a sweet wrapper.

Keep on a tray lightly dusted with *semola*, making sure the *caramelle* aren't touching each other until ready to cook and serve.

CARAMELLE AL RAGÙ BOLOGNESE
Bolognese sauce

Serves 4

1 recipe *caramelle*
3 cups *ragù Bolognese*
   (page 250)
3 tablespoons butter
Grated Parmesan, to serve

While the *caramelle* are cooking, heat the *ragù* with a small ladleful of the pasta water. Enrich it (as if it needs enriching) with the butter, and toss in the *caramelle*. Serve with grated Parmesan.

CASARECCE

Dimensions
Length: 1.48 in
Width: 4 mm

Also good with this pasta
braised bacon and peas;
broccoli rabe; broccoli rabe
and sausage; chicken and
prunes; garlic sauce; *pesto
Genovese; pesto Trapanese;*
rabbit and asparagus;
Romanesco broccoli;
sausages and cream;
sausage sauce; *sugo di
coda;* tuna belly and tomato;
salad of zucchini, lemon
zest, and pine nuts

Casarecce means "homemade," so it is somewhat ironic that this semolina pasta is industrially produced by extrusion to create an s-shaped section in short lengths of pasta. The form surely has its roots in the home, as it would be relatively easy to make from short lengths of flat pasta, cut between the widths of *tagliatelle* and *pappardelle*. Unlike most shapes of semolina pasta that were once made by hand (see page 10 and *orecchiette, cavatelli, trofie,* etc.), this one has mechanised well and is an excellent pasta to use, particularly for fresh, chunky sauces.

CASARECCE CON RUCOLA E CIPOLLA DI TROPEA
Arugula, tomato, and onion

½ pound *casarecce*
1 medium red onion
6 tablespoons extra-virgin olive oil
1 garlic clove, thinly sliced
7 ounces cherry or baby plum tomatoes, halved
1¼ cups arugula (3½ ounces), chopped
Grated *caciocavallo* cheese to serve (or Parmesan, *provolone piccante*, *ricotta salata*, or pecorino, in a pinch)

Also good with this sauce
cavatelli, garganelli, passatelli, radiatori, spaccatelle, trofie

The combination of tomatoes and arugula is a classic — not only as a salad, but as a pasta sauce. There are many ways to accomplish this — adding arugula along with the pasta to a rich tomato sauce (page 15), chopping it into a raw tomato sauce (page 238), or sautéing with cherry tomatoes, or with tomatoes and onion as below.

The sauce will take about as long to cook as your pasta.

Have a frying pan heating up — you want it smoking hot. Top, tail, halve, and peel the onion, then slice thinly lengthways. Put it in the pan (the oil would burn if it went in first), closely followed by the oil. Allow the onions to colour before turning gently with a spoon. When they are partly softened and well browned in places, add the garlic and tomatoes. Toss together, season with salt and pepper, and cook for a couple of minutes until the tomatoes are hot and a few starting to break down, but mostly still whole. Add the arugula, sauté for a minute more, then toss in the drained pasta and a touch of its water.

Serve with a grating of *caciocavallo*.

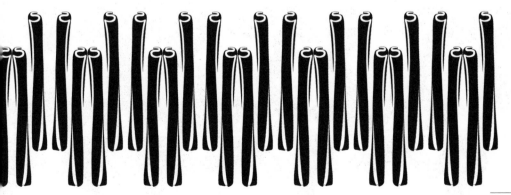

CAVATAPPI

Dimensions
Length: 1.2 in
Diameter: 5 mm
Wall thickness: 1 mm

Synonyms
cellentani ("whirls")

Also good with this pasta
al forno; braised bacon and
peas; chicken and prunes;
green beans; macaroni and
cheese; *norcina; Norma;
pesto Trapanese; ragù
Napoletano;* ricotta and
tomato

A modern form, in the shape of a hollow corkscrew (from which the pasta takes its name) or pig's tail. *Cavatappi* are not just a gimmick, but are delicious with most sauces designed for smaller tubular pastas, particularly *maccheroncini* (page 152) and *sedanini* (page 224).

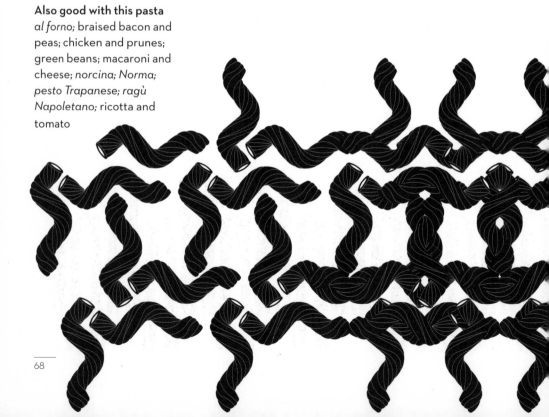

MACARONI SALAD

Serves 3–4 as a side dish

½ pound *cavatappi*
⅓ cup mayonnaise (store-bought)
½ carrot, coarsely grated

Also good in this salad
chifferi rigati, ditali, maccheroncini, sedanini

This is one of the classic components of a Hawaiian plate lunch – the others being rice, iceberg salad, and some sort of meat (teriyaki, sweet and sour, or similar). It should be made with "macaroni" (such as *maccheroncini*), but I like it at least as well with *cavatappi*. The macaroni component is in some ways like coleslaw, except that almost all the healthy part of slaw (already in a minority) has been removed and replaced with processed starch. Small wonder Hawaii performs so well in Sumo championships . . .

Cook the pasta more than usual (not overcooked, but no longer really *al dente*), drain, and refresh under cold running water, then drain again. Toss with the mayonnaise (the quantity here is the minimum – you can use even more if you dare) and carrot, taste for seasoning, and serve.

CAVATELLI

Dimensions
Length: 0.8 in
Width: 0.28 in

Synonyms
gnocchetti, manatelle,
orecchi di prete ("priest's
ears"), strascinari, truoccoli;
in Basilicata capunti, cingule,
minuich, rascatelli (3-finger),
zinnezinne; in Calabria
cavateddri, rascatielli; in
Campania and Puglia
cantaroggni, cavatieddi,
cecatelli/cicatelli (1-finger),
cecatidde, mignuicchi,
strascenate, tagghjunghele;
in Le Marche pincinelle; in
Molise cavatielle 'ncatenate
("chained" – 2-finger),
cazzarille, ciufele; in Sicily
cavasuneddi, cavatuneddi,
gnucchitti, gnocculi

Also good with this pasta
acquacotta; broccoli rabe;
green beans; pasta e ceci;
pork and pigskin

These little pastas are so simple to make, so delicious fresh and
so disappointing dry. Essentially short sections (as long as the
breadth of one, two, or three fingers) of thick cylindrical pasta
dough, they are made hollow (like a comma in cross-section,
almost curled around to make a tube) with a simple and quick
action of the fingers.

Cavatelli are mostly associated with Puglia, but they are also
one of the pastas of choice in Molise, Basilicata, and Calabria
– the deep south of mainland Italy. Here, where vegetables are
exalted and use of meats scarce, *cavatelli* of appropriate sizes
are paired with almost any single vegetable that grows locally.
With potato, or broccoli rabe and chili, or cooked arugula, or
wild turnips (*lassini*), or cannellini beans, or perhaps simply
dressed with cheese (*ricotta salata* or *cacioricotta*), or in a soup.
In hard times they would have used a poorer flour – notably
made from acorns or perhaps chestnuts – but today they are
made only with semolina. This flour, however, may be in its
usual form or *di grano arso* – made from charred wheat, with a
near-black colour and smoky flavour – which is impossible to
find outside of Puglia, but worth trying if you visit.

MAKING CAVATELLI

To serve 2, make 10½ ounces semolina pasta dough (page 10), using 1 cup plus 3 tablespoons *semola* and ⅓ cup water. Let it rest for a while, then roll walnut-sized pieces into long, thick noodles 4–5 millimeters across, working on a dry wooden or marble surface. Cut these into lengths:

For "1-finger" *cavatelli*, ¾ inch long
For "2-finger" *cavatelli*, 1¼–1½ inches long
For "3-finger" *cavatelli*, 1¾ inches long

Press the appropriate number of fingertips into one of these lengths, and make a flicking motion towards you. The finger should stretch the pasta out, the *cavatello* wrapping itself upwards towards your fingernail. Flick it out of the way, then do the next one. Leave these to dry slightly (they should get leathery outside but stay soft in the middle) before cooking.

CAVATELLI AI FAGIOLI CANNELLINI
Cannellini beans

1 recipe "1-finger" *cavatelli*, or ½ pound dried *cavatelli* (distinctly inferior)
6 tablespoons extra-virgin olive oil, plus more to serve
2 garlic cloves, thinly sliced
6 ounces cherry or baby plum tomatoes, halved

Time the pasta so it's cooked a couple of minutes after the beans go into the pan. Heat the oil in a wide pan, then add the garlic, tomatoes, and red pepper flakes all at once. Fry over a high heat for just a minute or 2, shaking the pan every few seconds. Add the beans, along with their cooking liquid, and the chopped arugula. Season with salt and pepper.

A good pinch of crushed red
pepper flakes
1¼ cups cooked, drained
cannellini beans (10½
ounces)
⅓ cup bean cooking liquid
(or water, if using canned
beans)
⅔ cup arugula (1¾ ounces)
or ½ ounce parsley, or 10
basil leaves, chopped

Also good with this sauce
chifferi rigati, strozzapreti

Drain the pasta and add to the pan when the beans have
bubbled for a couple of minutes. Cook for a minute more,
and serve with a final drizzle of oil.

CAVATELLI CON SALSICCIA E BROCCOLETTI
Broccoli rabe and sausage

1 recipe "2-finger" *cavatelli*
or ½ pound dried (less
good)
1 small bunch (¾–1 pound)
broccoli rabe, less if
tender, more if mature
½ pound Italian sausage,
skin removed, crumbled
2 garlic cloves, thinly sliced
6 tablespoons extra-virgin
olive oil
⅜ teaspoon crushed red
pepper flakes
Grated pecorino, to serve
(optional)

Also good with this sauce
*casarecce, fusilli a mano,
gramigne, orecchiette,
reginette, spaccatelle,
strozzapreti*

Having gone into far too much depth on broccoli rabe in
another recipe (see *orecchiette*, page 173), I suggest you
look there if you need advice on its preparation. This recipe
is best made with longer (2- or 3-finger) *cavatelli*.

Put the pasta on to boil. Time the cooking of the broccoli
rabe as described on page 173. Put the crumbled sausage,
garlic, and oil in a pan, and fry over a medium heat until
starting to colour – break the meat up with a spoon as much
as you can. Add the red pepper flakes, then a few seconds later
the drained broccoli rabe. Sauté briefly, seasoning with salt
and pepper, adding a little pasta water and allowing to bubble
down until pretty much dry again. Now add the drained pasta
with a few more tablespoons of its water. Cook together for a
minute, and serve either with grated pecorino or without.

CHIFFERI RIGATI

Dimensions
Length: 0.92 in
Width: 0.56 in
Diameter: 0.32 in

Also good with this pasta
braised bacon and peas;
chicken and prunes;
chickpeas and clams;
Gorgonzola; Hungarian fish
soup; lentils; macaroni and
cheese; macaroni salad;
mussels and beans; *pasta e
ceci; pasta e fagioli;* ricotta
and broad beans; warming
red pepper and whiskey
sauce

Chifferi (smooth) and *chifferi rigati* (ridged, as illustrated) are industrially made pasta in the shape of *kipferl*, the Austrian cookies. As fresh pasta used to be made by bakers (there are still some shops that perform both functions), it is likely that this form drew inspiration from Italian *mezzelune* (half-moon cookies), themselves an adaptation of *kipferl*.

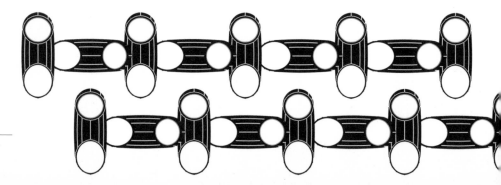

CHIFFERI ALLE OLIVE VERDI
Green olives and tomatoes

½ pound *chifferi rigati*
½ pound bitter green olives (cracked ones or Lucques)
½ cup extra-virgin olive oil
2 garlic cloves, thinly sliced
¾ teaspoon crushed red pepper flakes (optional)
1–2 fresh tomatoes cut into chunks, or ½ pound halved cherry tomatoes
3 tablespoons chopped flat-leaf parsley
⅓ cup light tomato sauce (page 15) or tomato *passata*

Also good with this sauce
campanelle/gigli, fusilli, fusilli fatti a mano, spaccatelle

This recipe is based on one from the province of Bari, where raw (and incredibly bitter) ripe black olives are cooked in a manner between a sauté and a stew with fresh tomato, garlic, and oil until soft, when their flavour tempers to produce a pleasingly bitter and astringent dish, often eaten simply with bread. Given the short season, and difficulty in procuring uncured eating olives far from the Mediterranean, the present recipe is an approximation in flavour – green cured olives providing a more restrained bitterness.

Pit the olives and cut them in half – easiest achieved by pressing each firmly with the flat of a knife, which will at once split the flesh in 2 and loosen the pit. Heat a wide frying pan over a medium heat, add the oil and garlic, and fry until it barely starts to colour. Add the red pepper flakes (if using), closely followed by the tomatoes. If the olives were fresh, they would be added (whole, pit-in) at the same time, but cured olives don't need quite so long to cook. Let the tomatoes fry for about 5 minutes, until some skins start to colour and other tomatoes start to turn to mush. Add the olives now, and continue to cook for a further 4–5 minutes, until the sauce starts to look more like a sauce and less like a stir-fry. Reduce the heat to low, add the parsley and tomato sauce, and simmer for 5 minutes until thickened.

This sauce can be used immediately, or made in advance to be reheated as the pasta is cooking.

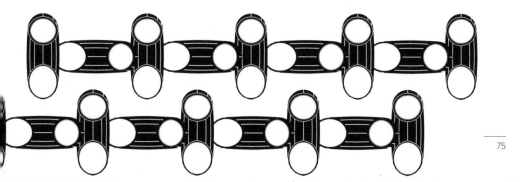

CONCHIGLIE RIGATE

Dimensions
Length: 1.26 in
Width: 0.94 in

Synonyms
arselle (type of clam),
abissini, coccioline (shards),
conchigliette ("small shells"),
tofettine

Also good with this pasta
arrabbiata; braised bacon
and peas; langoustines and
saffron; *puttanesca;* ricotta
and tomato; tomato sauce;
Treviso, speck, and fontina;
tuna belly and tomato

Master *pastai* (pasta-makers) can reproduce almost any type of shell with near-photographic precision. Indeed, there is some semblance between many pastas and shells, diatoms and microorganisms – looking through the illustrations for this book, I'm reminded of books with etchings of seashells and early microscope studies.

Whilst any shell-inspired pasta might be called *conchiglie*, the term primarily refers to a specific form, not unlike a stylised winkle or cowrie. With a ridged outside and smooth, deep bowl of an interior, *conchiglie rigate* cradle a sauce more than any other pasta. They are excellent with lighter sauces, such as light tomato (page 15) or *arrabbiata* (page 196), as well as with chunkier vegetables (such as in the two recipes that follow), where the vegetables might enter into the shell's cavity and make for easy eating.

CONCHIGLIE RIGATE CON FAVE E RICOTTA
Broad beans and ricotta

½ pound *conchiglie rigate*
1⅔ pounds broad beans in their pods (or ½ pound podded)
¾ cup sheep's milk ricotta
6 tablespoons extra-virgin olive oil
1 medium onion
3 tablespoons of your best olive oil, or a little grated pecorino Romano, to serve

Also good with this sauce
chifferi rigati, orecchiette

Pod the broad beans and blanch them for 2 minutes in boiling water, then refresh in cold water. Pop them out of their shells, unless very small (smaller than a fingernail).

Puree the ricotta with 4½ tablespoons water and 1½ tablespoon of the oil – either in a blender, or by forcing through a fine sieve. Put in a large bowl and set aside.

Now you need to exercise your judgement. Late in the season, broad beans will be large, starchy, and require longer cooking, in which case start to fry the onions about 10 minutes before you put the pasta on. Early in the year they will be small, sugary, and tender, in which case put the pasta on at about the same time as the onions. In either case, gently warm the bowl of ricotta sauce by perching it over the boiling pasta, stirring occasionally and removing before it curdles.

Finely chop the onion and fry in the remaining oil over a medium heat until soft and starting to turn pale golden – about 10 minutes. Add the broad beans and enough water to barely cover (⅓ cup or so), and simmer together to make the sauce – a couple of minutes for small, early spring beans or 20–25 minutes for starchy, late-summer ones. If cooking for a while you will need to add some more water from time to time, although be sure the sauce does not end up too wet.

When both the pasta and beans are cooked, drain the pasta and toss in the broad-bean mixture. When well coated, add to the ricotta and stir to coat. Serve with a drizzle of oil or grating of pecorino.

CONCHIGLIE RIGATE CON BROCCOLI ROMANESCO
Romanesco broccoli

⅓ pound *conchiglie rigate*

1 head Romanesco broccoli (14 ounces)

½ cup extra-virgin olive oil

1 large salted anchovy fillet, chopped (optional)

1 garlic clove, finely chopped

A pinch of crushed red pepper flakes (or ¾ teaspoon if you want it hot)

6 tablespoons chopped flat-leaf parsley, divided

A little grated pecorino Romano or Parmesan, or a few spoons of great oil, to serve

Also good with this sauce
casarecce, farfalle, farfalle tonde, linguine, orecchiette, penne, reginette, spaccatelle, spaghetti, spaghettini, tortiglioni, trofie

This is one of many dishes where you could cook the pasta and broccoli together (see *orecchiette* with broccoli rabe, page 173, and *farfalle* with broccoli, page 95). Indeed, it would seem ideal, as both take the same time to cook. Here I diverge from my usual principle of keeping everything as simple as possible – I prefer the broccoli to have had some time to marinate in olive oil before I make the sauce. This dish is one with a hundred variations — addition of pine nuts and/or raisins, serving with bread crumbs or pecorino or Parmesan, to anchovy or not to . . .

Cut the Romanesco broccoli into florets, discarding any dark leaves but keeping the tiny paler ones, which look so pretty and taste just as nice. You should end up with about ⅔ pound prepared weight. Boil in well-salted water (as for pasta, with about 2 teaspoons salt per quart) for 10–14 minutes, until so soft it melts in your mouth — nearly falling apart. Drain well, spread out on a plate, and drizzle with half the oil. Leave to marinate for at least 10 minutes before you put the pasta on.

Five minutes before the pasta is done, put the anchovy, garlic, and red pepper flakes in a cold frying pan with the remaining oil, and cook for 3–4 minutes over a very low heat, until the anchovy has completely disintegrated (the force of the back of a spoon might help with this). Add the broccoli, increase the heat, and sauté for a minute or 2 (don't let the broccoli colour at all — if it threatens to, add a splash of water). Add three-quarters of the parsley, then the drained pasta and a little of its cooking water. Sauté together for a minute before serving with the remaining parsley on top, and a drizzle of good-quality oil and a little grated cheese if you like.

CORZETTI

Dimensions
Diameter: 2.4 in
Sheet thickness: 1.5 mm

Synonyms
curzetti in Genovese dialect;
croset in Piedmont; *crosetti*
in Emilia-Romagna; *croxetti,
torsellini*

Also good with this pasta
pesto Genovese

Corzetti are large coins of pasta from Liguria, made from flour and water, sometimes with a little egg and oil. Rolled not-too-thick, they are cut into discs and embossed on both sides using a pair of cylindrical fruit-wood stamps, hand-carved on the end grain with a delicate pattern, normally the family coat of arms. Their name derives from an old Genovese money-piece via *crosets* – a pasta dating from the fourteenth century and as long as your thumb. Although *corzetti* did begin as ancient *crosets*, they are not to be confused with *crosets Piemontese* – of the same origins, but now the northern equivalent of *orecchiette* – thumbnail-sized pieces of pasta lightly indented with a finger.

Corzetti are a highly decorative pasta, and would have had some symbolical significance. As with all good pasta design, the decorative is also functional – the embossed pattern helps to hold scant oily sauces such as walnut pesto, or the classic marjoram and pine nuts.

CORZETTI ALLE NOCI
Walnut pesto

Serves 8 as a light starter or 4 as a main

CORZETTI
3 cups "00" flour
5 egg yolks or 2 whole eggs
½ cup white wine

WALNUT PESTO
¾–1 cup shelled walnuts
2 hefty slices day-old bread
(about 2 ounces, weighed
without crust)
6 tablespoons milk
1 garlic clove
A few fresh oregano
leaves – just shy of 1½
tablespoons
1 cup grated Parmesan,
divided
½ cup plus 1 tablespoon
extra-virgin olive oil

Also good with this sauce
*fazzoletti, pansotti, tortelloni,
trofie*

For the dough, knead the ingredients together well, then rest before rolling 1.5 millimeters thick. *Corzetti* are cut into discs (perhaps 2¾ inches wide), then stamped on both sides with carved wooden molds. Unless you happen to have one of these molds, see if you can't find something else with which to emboss the pasta. Discard the trimmings from between your discs – there's no use trying to re-roll them. Let the *corzetti* partially dry for an hour or so before using. (Or you could use ¾–1 pound dried *corzetti*.)

For the sauce, soak the walnuts in just-boiled water for 15 minutes, then drain and pick off any particularly dark pieces of skin. Soak the bread in the milk, and crush the garlic. Now combine all the ingredients in a food processor – save several tablespoons Parmesan to garnish – and work until relatively smooth. Season to taste. If too thick (you're looking for a spooning consistency), add a bit more water. At this stage, put the pasta on to boil.

Toss the cooked *corzetti* in the sauce with a little of the pasta's cooking water, just to thin it enough to coat. Serve plain or with a light sprinkling of extra grated Parmesan.

CORZETTI CON MAGGIORANA E PINOLI
Marjoram and pine nuts

1 recipe *corzetti* pasta
dough
1 cup pine nuts
½ cup butter
6 tablespoons fresh
marjoram leaves (or fresh
oregano)
Grated Parmesan or other
grana, to serve

Also good with this sauce
*caramelle, fazzoletti,
pansotti,* ravioli Genovese

This dish is equally good with olive oil as with butter. You can substitute a generous ⅓ cup of the best extra-virgin olive oil you have (Ligurian if possible), but then it is best not to cook the sauce at all, to leave the pine nuts raw and resinous, and simply to use the oil, nuts, and marjoram as a dressing for the cooked pasta, tossed together in a bowl.

Make the *corzetti* as per the recipe opposite.

Put the pasta on to boil. Fry the pine nuts in the butter until both turn a light golden brown (not too dark, mind). Add the marjoram, wait literally a second or 2 while the leaves sizzle, and add about ½ cup of the pasta water. The exact quantity of water is somewhat immaterial – you want there to be enough that the sauce can boil away for a couple of minutes, thickening and forming a sturdy emulsion as you shake the pan. If there's too much water, you can boil it more furiously – and if too little, you can add a bit more. When the sauce is as thick as heavy cream, and the pasta verging on done, combine the 2 and sauté together just for a few seconds until the pasta is well coated. Serve with Parmesan on top – I suggest using a potato peeler to make shavings, which somehow look good with the *corzetti*.

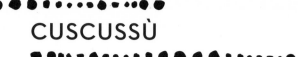

CUSCUSSÙ

Dimensions
Diameter: varies 1.5–3 mm

Synonyms
casca, cashca in Sardinia;
cuscussu in Tuscany

Cuscussù is of course famous for its origins in North Africa, but it is also a staple food in Sicily today – one of many gastronomic, architectural, and cultural vestiges in what was once an Arab land. That said, couscous recipes are still found across Italy – notably in Sardinia (in a dish of chicken cooked in saffron) and Tuscany (Livorno, with a soupy meatball accompaniment) – perhaps suggesting that its presence on the mainland dates back instead to times of Roman rule.

Cuscussù is made unlike any other pasta, where the flour is worked into a strong dough before forming. To make couscous, water is sprinkled on to a bed of semolina (not the finer *semola rimacinata*, but a reasonably coarse one) with one hand, and stirred and raked through with the other until tiny balls of moistened flour are formed. These are then normally dried before cooking over steam – careful work leading to a fluffy texture and a particular lightness, as almost no gluten is formed when the pasta is made (gluten is a product of gliadin and glutenin, which cross-link to form gluten when dough is kneaded). The tiny particles of pasta act to mop up a sauce when eaten, like a sponge with water (or rather a bed of sand), or as rice does.

CUSCUSSÙ TRAPANESE
Fish and almonds

½ pound *cuscussù*

⅔ pound small fish (red mullet, gurnard, and the like, weighed after gutting)

½ medium or 1 small onion, finely chopped

6 tablespoons extra-virgin olive oil, divided, plus a little extra if you like

1 small dried chili

1 bay leaf

1 small (¾-ounce) bunch flat-leaf parsley

3 tablespoons blanched almonds

1 garlic clove

1½ cups light fish stock

2 medium tomatoes (⅔ pound), finely chopped

This recipe is the most famous in Sicily and comes from Trapani.

The smaller the fish are, the better the dish will be, albeit more fiddly to eat. Cut any longer than a cigarette into appropriate chunks.

Fry the onion in 4½ tablespoons of the oil with the chili and bay leaf over a medium heat until soft and golden – about 10 minutes. Chop the parsley roughly, then pound to a paste with the almonds and garlic. Bring the stock to a boil, pour exactly half over the couscous along with another 1½ tablespoons of oil and salt to taste, and leave, covered, while you finish making the fish stew.

Add the tomatoes to the onion and fry for a couple of minutes, then add the fish (seasoned with salt and pepper) and turn once or twice in the pan, just to coat. Bring to a boil and stir in the pounded almonds, then simmer for a minute or 2 until the fish is just cooked. Taste for seasoning.

Fluff the couscous with a fork. Serve the fish stew spooned over a bed of couscous, with an optional extra drizzle of oil.

DISCHI VOLANTI

Dimensions
Diameter: 0.8 in
Thickness: 2 mm

Also good with this pasta
artichokes, peas, and broad
beans; braised bacon and
peas; ham, peas, and cream;
Hungarian fish soup;
langoustines and saffron;
lentils; rabbit and asparagus;
ricotta and tomato; warming
red pepper and whiskey sauce

Named flying saucers (literally, "flying discs"), *dischi volanti*
were designed shortly after the name was coined in 1947
following Kenneth Arnold's sighting in the United States. A
media frenzy cast these objects of dubious reality into the
forefront of the world's psyche. Martians or no, *dischi volanti*
do actually exist as a pasta, and a delicious one at that.

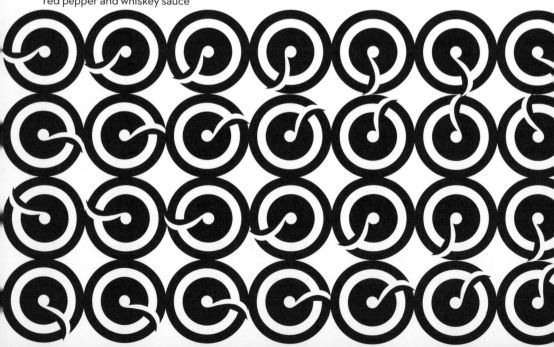

DISCHI VOLANTI CON OSTRICHE E PROSECCO
Oysters, prosecco, and tarragon

½ pound *dischi volanti*

1 dozen small, plump oysters

1 large shallot, finely chopped

2 tablespoons butter

⅔ cup prosecco or champagne, divided

½ cup heavy cream

1 tablespoon chopped tarragon

Also good with this sauce
ruote, tagliatelle, tagliolini

This recipe began in a distinctly different place, with Constance Spry and a decidedly retro 1950s dish involving canned smoked oysters, béchamel, and cayenne. Unfortunately, I found it impossible to make the dish suit my palate, and so it has evolved into a marriage of lighter flavours. No doubt my version will, in time, become so outdated it shall seem repugnant to future moderns, but hopefully it will do for the moment.

Shuck the oysters, catching all of their juices. Discard the shells.

Put the pasta on to boil.

Sauté the shallot in the butter for a couple of minutes over a low heat (you don't want any colour), then add 6 tablespoons of the prosecco. Allow it to bubble down, then add the cream and bring to a boil. When fairly thick, add the oysters and simmer very gently for just a minute, until they plump up. Remove them with a slotted spoon, and cut into quarters. Allow the sauce to reduce until quite thick and luscious.

Miraculously, or with some careful planning, your pasta will be ready now, still *al dente*. Drain it and add it to the sauce, along with the quartered oysters, tarragon, and the last dribble of prosecco. Add pepper and, if necessary, salt. Serve with a glass of the prosecco you cooked with.

DITALI AND DITALINI

Dimensions
Diameter: 0.24 in
Length: 0.28 in
Wall thickness: 1 mm

Synonyms
tubetti, tubettini, gnocchetti di ziti, ditaletti, coralli ("coral," like beads from a coral necklace); in Puglia and Sicily *denti di vecchia* ("old woman's teeth"), *denti di cavallo* ("horse's teeth"), *ganghi di vecchia, magghietti*

Similar forms
ditali rigati, ditalini rigati, ditaloni, ditaloni rigati

Also good with this pasta
anelletti al forno; chicken and prunes; lentils; macaroni salad

Ditali and their smaller brethren *ditalini* are short tubes of pasta whose diameter is about the same as their length. Their name stems from *ditale* ("thimbles"), and thus *dita* ("finger"). Among the numerous other names, *denti di vecchia* ("old folks' teeth") and *denti di cavallo* ("horse's teeth") stand out as amusing. Whilst they are an industrial pasta, *ditali* have been around since the 1800s. Small ones are usually served *in brodo*, larger ones in thicker soups. Both sizes come *lisci* ("smooth") or *rigati* ("ridged"), the latter pairing well with thicker sauces – such as Calabrese *pasta ca trimma*, the pasta cooked with potatoes and tossed in a sauce of beaten egg, pecorino, and parsley. Given their bead-like dimensions, they are one of the best for making necklaces, along with *sedanini* (page 224).

PASTA E FAGIOLI
Bean and pasta soup

3½ ounces *ditali rigati*
2 cups cooked, drained borlotti beans (1 pound)
1¼ cups bean cooking liquid (or water, if using canned beans)
½ small onion, very finely chopped
1 garlic clove, finely chopped
1½ teaspoons finely chopped fresh rosemary
1 pinch crushed red pepper flakes
½ cup extra-virgin olive oil, divided

Also good with this soup
chifferi rigati, maltagliati, pappardelle (broken up)

Puree two-thirds of the beans finely with the water (or their cooking liquid, if you cooked your own). Gently fry the onion, garlic, rosemary, and red pepper flakes with a good pinch of salt in all but 1½ tablespoons of the oil for a couple of minutes, until soft and starting to colour.

Add the beans, pureed and whole, and bring to a boil. Add the uncooked pasta and simmer until *al dente*, stirring gently. You may need to add a touch more water as it cooks, but you want to achieve a thick soup. Serve with the remaining oil drizzled on top.

DITALI CON CECI E VONGOLE
Chickpeas and clams

⅓ pound *ditali*
1⅓ cups cooked, drained chickpeas (⅔ pound)
1⅓ cups chickpea cooking liquid (or water, if using canned)
1⅓ cups extra-virgin olive oil, divided
1 pound live clams
2 garlic cloves, thinly sliced
A decent pinch of crushed red pepper flakes
A small bunch of flat-leaf parsley, chopped, divided
1½ teaspoons finely chopped fresh red chili (optional)

Also good with this sauce
chifferi rigati, farfalle, farfalle tonde, pasta mista, torchio

You need to start making the sauce about 10 minutes before your pasta is ready (just undercooked, probably a minute or so less than stated on the package), so time yourself accordingly.

Finely puree three-quarters of the chickpeas with their liquid. Heat a wide frying pan (large enough for the clams to fit in a single layer, with some space to spare). When very hot, add 9 tablespoons of the oil, the clams, and the garlic all at once. Fry until the garlic starts to colour, then add the red pepper flakes and half the parsley for just a second or 2 before the pureed and whole chickpeas. Let the sauce bubble away merrily. As the clams pop open, pick them out one by one (leave them in the shells), and set aside. When the last have popped, test the sauce for seasoning. Leave it to boil, if necessary, until the sauce has the consistency of light cream. Add the drained pasta, along with the cooked clams, back to the pan with the remaining parsley, and let everything cook together until the sauce is as thick as heavy cream but still somewhat soupy.

Serve immediately with the remaining oil drizzled on top, and a scattering of fresh chili if you like.

FARFALLE

Dimensions
Length: 1.56 in
Width: 1.1 in

Synonyms
fiocchetti ("little flakes");
stricchetti in Modena;
nocchette in Abruzzo and
Puglia.
For smaller versions see
canestrini; bigger ones,
farfalloni.

Also good with this pasta
artichokes, peas, and broad
beans; braised bacon
and peas; broad beans;
chickpeas and clams; ham,
peas, and cream; porcini
and cream; *puttanesca;*
Romanesco broccoli; salad
with prawns; scallops and
thyme; zucchini and prawns

Farfalle ("butterflies") are sometimes known as "bow-tie" pasta outside of Italy. They are one of the simplest shapes formed by manipulating a sheet of pasta. Rectangles, normally cut with frilly ends, as though by pinking shears, are pinched across the middle to make a bow shape.

A variation, *farfalle tonde* ("fat butterflies"), are made from an oval or disc of pasta rather than a rectangle. These hold more sauce but are less economical to make. The dough may be made of simple semolina, or flour and egg – the former being perhaps better suited to greens, the latter to mushrooms, meat, and cream sauces – but the choice is ultimately the cook's.

In general, more artisanal producers who command higher prices may choose to use an egg dough, whilst more industrial producers use the cheaper *semola*. Their form, inspired by the natural world, is one of a family of pastas including *cocciolette* ("sea-snails"), *conchiglie* ("shells," page 76), *lumache* ("snails," page 150), *coralli* ("coral"), and *vermicelli* ("worms," page 54). The pinched middle of *farfalle* helps keep them *al dente* when cooked and catches a little sauce. They are often dressed with light vegetable sauces as a summer pasta, to eat outside when the butterflies are in full swing.

INSALATA DI FARFALLE, ZUCCHINE E PINOLI
Salad of zucchini, lemon zest, and pine nuts

½ pound *farfalle*
3 smallish, firm zucchini (⅔ pound), thinly sliced in 2–4-millimeter rounds
6 tablespoons extra-virgin olive oil, divided
2 garlic cloves, thinly sliced
Zest and juice of 1 lemon
⅔ cup pine nuts
Oil for frying the pine nuts
A small handful each of basil and flat-leaf parsley leaves, finely shredded
Grated Parmesan, to serve (optional)

Also good in this salad
casarecce, fusilli, gemelli, sedanini

Boil the *farfalle* until cooked as you like them, then drain and cool under cold running water. Heat a frying pan until very, very hot over a high flame. Add the zucchini, then 1½ tablespoons of the olive oil and a little salt. Sauté for a minute or so. When half-cooked, a few nicely browned, add the garlic and cook for a minute more. When still just underdone, turn off the heat, and leave in the pan to finish cooking. The zucchini should be partly coloured, fully cooked but still slightly crunchy, and nicely dry.

Make a dressing of the lemon zest, juice, and remaining 4½ tablespoons of olive oil, and season to taste with salt and pepper. To toast the pine nuts cover them with oil in a small pan and fry over a medium heat until pale amber. When the zucchini and pine nuts have cooled to room temperature, toss with the pasta, herbs, and dressing. Best left to stand for 20 minutes before eating plain or with a light grating of Parmesan.

FARFALLE CON PROSCIUTTO CRUDO E PANNA
Prosciutto and cream

½ pound *farfalle*
5 tablespoons heavy cream
1¾ ounces prosciutto, sliced into ½-inch strips
Generous ½ cup grated Parmesan, plus extra to serve
2 egg yolks

Also good with this sauce
bucatini, fettuccine, rigatoni, tortiglioni

This recipe is a delightful medium between a cream sauce and *carbonara* (page 36) – quick and easy and both light and indulgent in flavour. Replace the prosciutto with crisp-fried pancetta and its fat, and you have something delicious that a Briton or American might call "carbonara," and a Roman certainly "a travesty."

Put the *farfalle* on to boil. In a bowl combine the cream, prosciutto, Parmesan, and egg yolks. Season with salt and lots of freshly ground pepper. Drain the *farfalle* when edible but still *al dente,* and toss into the sauce – serve with extra cheese.

FARFALLE AL SALMONE, ASPARAGI E PANNA
Smoked salmon, asparagus, and cream

½ pound *farfalle*
⅓ pound smoked salmon
A small bunch of asparagus
⅓ cup heavy cream
3½ tablespoons butter
A few gratings of nutmeg
A few sprigs of tarragon,
    dill, or basil, shredded

Also good with this sauce
fettuccine, gnocchi shells,
tagliatelle

Slice the salmon into strips about ¼ inch wide. Cut the asparagus in 1¼-inch lengths, discarding the tough stalk end.

Put the pasta on to boil. When they are a couple of minutes from being ready, add the asparagus to the boiling pot. In a smaller pan bring the cream and butter to a simmer, seasoned with nutmeg and black pepper (but no salt). Add a little ladleful of the pasta water as necessary. When the pasta is just on the firm side of *al dente*, drain and add to the sauce. Toss together and cook until well coated by the cream. At the last minute (and off the heat), stir in the salmon and your herb of choice. Season to taste.

FARFALLE CON BROCCOLI E ALICI
Broccoli, anchovy, and cream

⅓ pound *farfalle*
1 head broccoli (¾ pound),
    cut into florets
2 garlic cloves, thinly sliced
3 tablespoons extra-virgin
    olive oil
⅜ teaspoon crushed red
    pepper flakes
3–4 salted anchovy fillets
¼ cup heavy cream
Generous ½ cup grated
    Parmesan

Also good with this sauce
canestri, fettuccine, gnocchi
shells, *reginette, trenette*

This dish was first cooked for me by Sam and Sam Clark, of Moro restaurant, and was utterly delicious. It works well with the everyday broccoli we know and love (or hate) ourselves.

Cook the *farfalle* and broccoli together in plenty of well-salted water. In a wide pan, fry the garlic in the oil until starting to colour, then turn off the heat and add the red pepper flakes. When no longer sizzling, add the anchovies (chopped and moistened with a spoon of water), and crush with a wooden spoon to dissolve into the oil. When the pasta is almost ready, add the cream to the garlic mixture and return to the heat. Drain the pasta (it should be quite *al dente*, and the broccoli soft), and add to the sauce. Cook together until the sauce coats thickly, adding the Parmesan and plenty of black pepper at the end, and 1½ tablespoons of pasta water if it all gets a bit too sticky.

FAZZOLETTI

Dimensions
Length: 5 in
Width: 7.08 in
Sheet thickness: 0.5 mm

Synonyms
fazzoletti di seta ("silk
handkerchiefs") or *mandilli
di sea* in dialect

Also good with this pasta
artichokes, peas, and broad
beans; marjoram and pine
nuts; *tartufo dei poveri*;
walnut pesto; walnut sauce

Found around north-central Italy, and often a favourite of
contemporary chefs who enjoy the free-form way these fine,
almost transparent squares fall on a plate, *fazzoletti* derive their
name from handkerchiefs. They are particularly popular in
Liguria (where they are made from a flour and white wine
dough – elsewhere egg is used), called *fazzoletti di seta*, or
mandilli di sea in dialect, meaning "silk handkerchiefs." The
dough is so supple, the thickness so fine, the texture so smooth
that, when well-made, they do indeed seem silken. It was a
conceit of Renaissance cooking to elevate pasta-making to
such a high art. When working by hand, it is a rare skill to
roll dough so thinly. Just like chickpea-sized *tortellini* (page
262), rarely made by hand today, and *capelli d'angelo* (page
54), like long blonde hair and never made by hand in the
modern world, the finest *fazzoletti* require levels of artistry
that correspond with the Renaissance ideal of perfection.

These sheets take just a minute to cook and cannot trap
much sauce. Classic *pesto Genovese* (page 276) or walnut sauce
(page 19) are fine pairings.

FAZZOLETTI CON TARTUFO NERO
Truffled *fazoletti*

½ pound enriched egg
    pasta dough (page 13)
1 black winter truffle (1½–
    1¾ ounces)
5–6 tablespoons butter
Grated Parmesan, to serve

Also suitable for truffling
tagliatelle, pappardelle

Roll the pasta dough as usual, to make an elongated rectangle about 4¾ inches wide and about 2 millimeters thick. Shave half the truffle thinly – use a truffle shaver if you have one, but don't go running to the shops just for this dish. You could spend more on the truffle shaver than the truffle itself, and a humble potato peeler does just as good a job.

Lay the slices of truffle over half the rectangle of pasta, being careful not to let them overlap. Fold the other half of the pasta, to enrobe the fungus in your silky dough. Roll it out, first to the same thickness as before (if you are using a machine just leave it on the same setting), then thinner still until it is just under 1 millimeter thick.

If your pasta tears when you roll it with the truffle inside, don't fret. Minor tears can be patched up, and if it looks really bad fold the pasta up a few times and start rolling again – the truffle will mince itself into the dough, although in this case the end result won't be quite so pretty, and your dough will be a little wetter from the truffle and might need a dusting of flour on the outside as you roll.

Cut the pasta into rough squares, as big as the width of your sheet of pasta, and leave these *fazzoletti* to dry for a few minutes while the water boils.

When your pot of salted water has come to the boil, add the sheets of pasta one at a time, but in rapid succession. They will take just a minute or 2 to cook, barely long enough to make the sauce by grating the remaining half of the truffle into a saucepan in which you have melted the butter, and warming on the gentlest of heats to bubble slightly for a minute or so. It is into this sauce that you add the *fazzoletti*, along with a spoon or so of their cooking water. Toss gently to coat, and serve in crumpled heaps with a grating of Parmesan on top.

FAZZOLETTI CON LE FAVE FRESCHE
Pureed broad beans

½ pound egg pasta dough (page 13)
⅔ pound podded broad beans, fresh or frozen
3 green onions, cut in ¾-inch lengths
1 garlic clove, thinly sliced
½ cup extra-virgin olive oil
A small bunch of basil leaves
Grated pecorino (optional)

Also good with this sauce
campanelle/gigli, farfalle, farfalle tonde, fettuccine, orecchiette, pansotti, pappardelle, reginette, strozzapreti, tagliatelle, torchio, truffled *fazzoletti*

This dish sings of spring and summer. Whilst I am a great lover of fresh young broad beans, frozen ones work equally well with that little bit less effort, and are even better than the fresh ones as the season draws to a close. Being available all-year round, they can provide welcome relief if you start to tire of winter vegetables.

Roll the pasta as usual, to just under 1 millimeter thick or the second–finest setting on most machines. Cut it into rough 4¾– to 6-inch squares and set aside. If using fresh broad beans, blanch them for just a minute in boiling water, then refresh in cold – frozen ones may be defrosted in a bowl of cool water. Pop the beans out of their pods.

Put the green onions, garlic, and oil into a small pan with ½ cup water. Season with salt and lots of black pepper, cover tightly, and boil over a medium heat for 5 minutes or until the onions are tender. Add three-quarters of the shelled beans, and simmer until tender – just a minute if they're nice and young. Add the basil and puree whilst still hot – the resultant sauce should be thick but pourable.

As the sauce is blending, set the pasta on to boil. Taste 1 of the broad beans you've set aside. If cooked to your liking, put in a bowl set to warm over the pasta water; if under-done, add to the water with the pasta for a final minute's cooking. Drain the pasta, and transfer to the warmed bowl with the broad beans, pureed and whole. Toss together and serve quickly with a drizzle of extra-virgin oil (either 3 tablespoons, or 1½ tablespoons mixed with 1 tablespoon of truffle oil). Pecorino is delicious on top, but I prefer the simplicity of this dish without.

FETTUCCINE

Dimensions
Length: 10 in
Section: 0.5 in x 1 mm
Sheet thickness: 1 mm

Synonyms
fettucce (wider versions), *tagliatelle, ramicce, sagne*

Also good with this pasta
artichokes, peas, and broad beans; braised bacon and peas; broccoli, anchovy, and cream; *carbonara*; cream and prosciutto; ham, peas, and cream; langoustines and saffron; lentils; morels; porcini; pureed broad beans; rabbit and asparagus; *ragù Genovese*; scallops and thyme; smoked salmon, asparagus, and cream; Treviso, speck, and fontina; walnut sauce; white truffle; wild boar sauce

Fettuccine are the southern equivalent to *tagliatelle* (page 248). Although they hail from Rome (bang in the center of Italy), this is already considered "south" by northern *tagliatelle* eaters. Although these pastas can be used interchangeably, *fettuccine* would typically be 2–3 millimeters wider than *tagliatelle* and perhaps double the thickness. Meaning "ribbons" (from *affettare*, "to slice"), *fettuccine* are usually served with a creamy sauce, which they can absorb a little, and are thick enough not to become sticky and clump together in the process. Normally made with a simple egg dough (page 13), in Capranica Prenestina (a province of Rome) they make a version called *lane pelose* ("shaggy-wool pasta") with bran, whose name may derive from *lana*, "wool," or the diminutive of *lagane*, an early pasta.

FETTUCCINE AL TRIPLO BURRO
Alfredo

About ½ pound *fettuccine*
(less if dried, more if fresh;
if using fresh, make with
simple egg pasta dough,
page 13)
⅓ cup heavy cream
3½ tablespoons butter
A few gratings of nutmeg
1⅓–1½ cups grated
Parmesan, plus a little
more to serve
¾ teaspoon ground black
pepper
A touch of salt

This is surely the most famous recipe for *fettuccine*, originally served as *fettuccine al triplo burro* by Alfredo di Lelio at his restaurant, Alfredo alla Scrofa, in 1914. The dish had been invented for his wife who, having recently conceived a child, was having trouble keeping her food down. *Doppio burro* ("double butter") referred to the practice of adding butter before and after putting the pasta in its serving dish – to make *triplo burro*, he doubled the amount of butter in the bowl before adding the pasta. The baby, when born, must have been of a decent size. At any rate, the dish became popular with Americans, particularly after Mary Pickford and Douglas Fairbanks became fans on their 1927 honeymoon. The dish has now become a staple of Italian American restaurants Stateside, where vegetables and chicken or seafood are also added. It barely exists in Italy, at least in the form below, although *pasta al burro* remains a well-liked luxury in the south as an alternative to the usual olive oil.

With the *fettuccine* on the boil, warm together the cream, butter, and nutmeg until they simmer. Add the Parmesan, in 2 or 3 additions, along with 4½–6 tablespoons of the pasta's cooking water, pepper, and salt. Drain the *fettuccine* when still just a little too firm for you, then toss in the sauce over a medium heat until it coats the pasta well.

FREGOLA

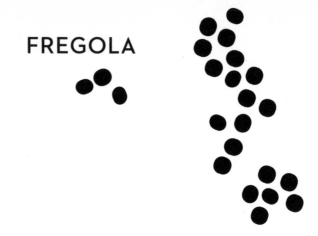

Dimensions
Diameter: 4–5 mm

Synonym
fregula

Koiaimi ca sciu fai fregula.
("Marry me as I know how to make *fregola*.")
—Sardinian proverb

Fregola is, in essence, Sardinian *cuscussù* (page 84), although actual *cuscussù* is also found in Sardinia. Made in essentially the same manner, but rubbed in a wide ceramic or wooden bowl (the name stems from the Latin *fricare*, "to rub") to create larger, more regular spheres about ¼ inch across. These are lightly toasted to aid drying, so if you buy a packet you'll notice a few that have been toasted brown, and you'll taste a certain nuttiness like the crust of a good loaf. Saffron (along with *bottarga*, page 232) is the flavour of Sardinia – as with *malloreddus* (page 164), it sometimes makes its way into the dough of the pasta as well as the sauce.

Due to the large size and fierce drying over fire, *fregola* is cooked by boiling (often in a stew, sauce, or broth) unlike its sister, *cuscussù*, which is steamed.

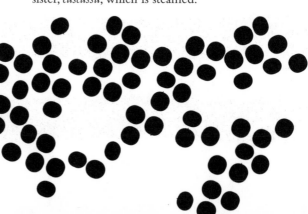

FREGOLA IN CASSOLA
Clams and tomato

½ pound *fregola*

4 garlic cloves

½ cup extra-virgin olive oil, divided

1 large tomato (½ pound), diced

½ cup chopped flat-leaf parsley, divided

⅜ teaspoon crushed red pepper flakes

1⅔ cups light fish stock

⅔ pounds Manila clams

Break the cloves of garlic with the flat of a knife or your palm. Fry in all but 1½ tablespoons of the oil over a medium heat until browned, then discard the garlic. Add the tomatoes, all but 1½ tablespoons of the parsley, and the red pepper flakes, and fry for 2 minutes. Add the *fregola*, stir to coat, then add the stock, and salt and pepper to taste. Simmer, uncovered, for 15 minutes (depending on the grade of *fregola*), until the *fregola* is still slightly too chewy and almost all the stock absorbed. Add the clams, submerge them in the juices, and cook until all have opened. Serve with the remaining oil and parsley atop.

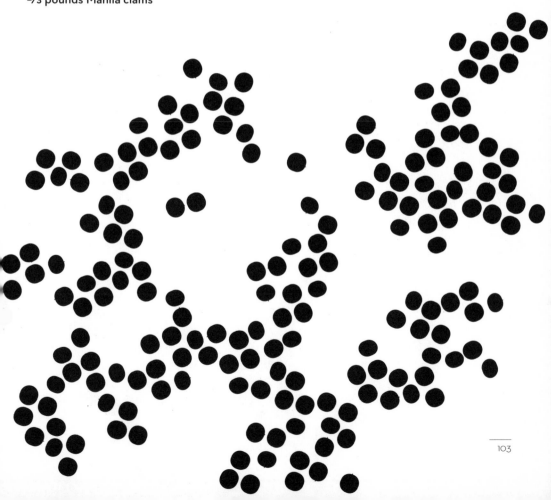

FUSILLI

Dimensions
Length: 2.1 in
Width: 0.3 in

Similar forms
rotini, eliche

Also good with this pasta
al forno; arrabbiata;
braised bacon and peas;
bread crumbs and sugar;
frankfurters and fontina;
garlic sauce; green beans;
green olives and tomato;
lentils; *ragù Napoletano;*
ricotta and tomato; salad of
zucchini, lemon zest, and pine
nuts; raw tomato; warming red
pepper and whiskey sauce

Fusilli ("spindles") are an industrial semolina pasta, a triple helix, like an elongated propeller or fan blade. They are just over 1 inch long, and are made of up to four entwined layers, which catch sauce between them. Similar are *rotini* (tighter spirals that hold sauce better) and *eliche* (looser screws for a lighter texture). The design is not only great for holding sauces, but is delightful to behold and has an unmistakable mouthfeel.

MAKING FUSILLI FATTI A MANO

Good with *fusilli fatti a mano*
broccoli rabe; broccoli rabe and sausage; green olives and tomato; *pesto Genovese; pesto Trapanese; puttanesca; ragù Napoletano;* sausage sauce; sausage, tomato, and saffron; *secchio della munnezza;* squid and tomato; tuna belly and tomato; *vincotto*

Again, a confusing term. *Fusilli fatti a mano* are handmade *fusilli* — and this can mean one of two things: a delicate hollow helix, like a telephone wire (also called *busiati*, and described on page 40); or a chunkier pasta related to *trofie* (page 274), like the thread of a screw — a helix with a solid axis.

These are made quite easily, by taking a quantity of semolina pasta dough (page 10), rolling to the thickness of a cigarette, and cutting into 1⅔-inch lengths. Place one of these on a wooden or marble worktop, with the ball of the palm at one end of the pasta at a 45° angle to the thumb. The form is made in a single action: With considerable pressure, the hand is drawn towards the body, with the pasta rolling long the length of the hand and thumb to make a deep, chunky spiral.

There is a thin line between where *fusilli* stop and *trofie* begin, but *fusilli fatti a mano* are more substantial, with more eccentric ridges, and go well with both pestos and pungent meaty or tomato sauces, either of which may be caught in the grooves.

FUSILLI AL VINCOTTO
Vincotto and bread crumbs

½ pound *fusilli*
4½ tablespoons *vincotto*
6 tablespoons extra-virgin olive oil
½ garlic clove, crushed
⅓–½ cup toasted fresh bread crumbs, to serve

Vincotto, mosto cotto, or *saba* is reduced grape must, southern Italy's answer to balsamic vinegar. Here it is used to make a pasta sauce that is nothing more than a simple dressing.

Boil the *fusilli* until exactly as *al dente* as you like — they will not cook further in the sauce. When done, toss in a dressing

Grated pecorino Romano,
to serve

Also good with this sauce
fusilli fatti a mano

made of the *vincotto*, oil, and garlic, seasoned with salt and pepper. Serve with the bread crumbs scattered on top and a grating of cheese.

FUSILLI "GREEK SALAD"

½ pound *fusilli*
1 cup finely diced cucumber
1 small red pepper, seeds removed, finely diced
3½ ounces cherry tomatoes, cut into eighths
12 kalamata olives, pitted and quartered
¼ pound feta, finely diced
½ cup extra-virgin olive oil
1 tablespoon chopped fresh oregano leaves

Also good in this salad
fusilli bucati, gemelli

It seems many are tired of picnic pasta salads of *fusilli*, red peppers, zucchini, and maybe corn. This one (a more substantial twist on a classic Greek salad) at least is delicious and different. As with all pasta salads, it must not be refrigerated, but instead served at room temperature.

Before cooking the pasta, make the salad: Toss together all the ingredients except the oregano, season well with salt and pepper, and leave to macerate for as long as the *fusilli* take to cook. Boil the *fusilli* until just done (a little less firm than if serving hot, as they will stiffen ever so slightly when cool), drain, refresh under cold running water, and drain again. Toss into the salad along with the oregano. Serve straightaway, or allow to stand at room temperature until ready to do so.

FUSILLI BUCATI LUNGHI E CORTI

Dimensions

fusilli bucati lunghi
Length: 4.8 in
Diameter: 3.5 mm
fusilli bucati corti
Length: 1.6 in
Width: 0.42 in

Synonyms

busiata, maccaruna di casa, pirciati, filato cu lu pirtuso; busiati ribusiati in Pantelleria

Good with this pasta

broccoli rabe; garlic sauce; "Greek salad"; *pesto Genovese; pesto Trapanese;* pork and pigskin; *ragù Napoletano*

There is some confusion around certain ancient pastas' names, because over time several pastas have come to share the same name or because pastas still referred to by one name have evolved into a number of distinct species. The inverse is true of some modern pastas, such as the present subject, where a new but popular name has been attributed to a number of forms. *Fusilli bucati* are a case in point:

- They may be long, spiralled, narrow, hollow tubes, like spiralled *bucatini* (page 34) or smooth, vastly elongated, narrowed *cavatappi* (page 68) – here termed *fusilli bucati lunghi*.

- They may be shorter versions of the above (i.e., smooth, narrowed *cavatappi* or shortened helical *bucatini*), here referred to as *fusilli bucati corti*.

- They may be like normal *fusilli*, but with the flat fins of the double-helix replaced by tubular ones. You might call these *fusilli bucati gemellati* (twinned hollow spindles), but as with the other suggested names above this is artificial – all you'd likely see on the packet is *"fusilli bucati."*

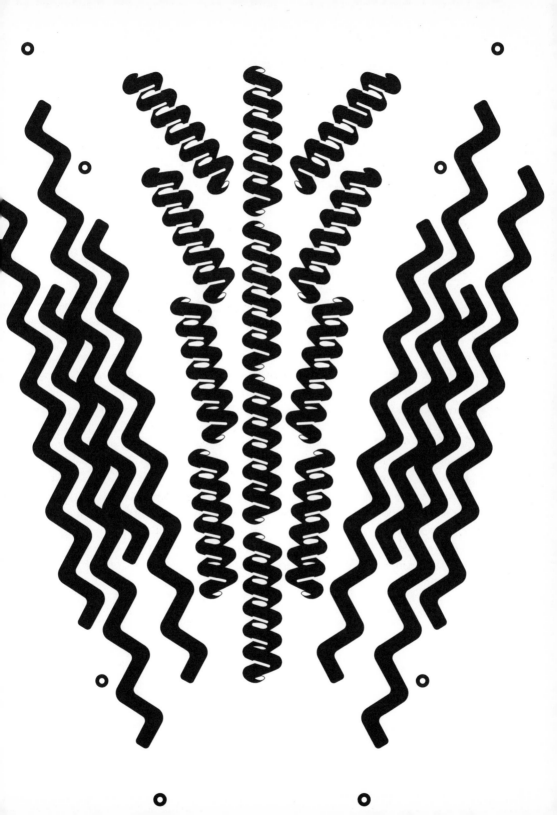

GARGANELLI

Dimensions
Length: 2.6 in
Width: 0.56 in

Synonyms
maccheroni al pettine; in
Le Marche *fischioni "paglia
e fieno"* (straw and hay), a
culinary term for green and
white mixed pasta

Also good with this pasta
artichokes, peas, and broad
beans; arugula, tomato, and
onion; braised bacon and
peas; chicken and prunes;
rocket, tomato and onion;
scallops and thyme; Treviso,
speck, and fontina

These thin ridged tubes closely resemble that oft-unidentified
tube in the neck end of a chicken — the esophagus, which
translates as *garganel* in Emilia-Romagna, hence the name
garganelli. The shape is formed by wrapping small (roughly
1⅔-inch) squares of egg pasta diagonally around a wooden
dowel, then rolling over a *pettine del tessitore* ("weaver's comb")
or basket to give the signature ridges around the tube of pasta.
Legend tells of a poor *massaia* near Ravenna (the heartland of
this pasta) who, having rolled out the pasta and cut squares for
making *tortellini* (page 260), discovered her cat had eaten all
the filling. As her guests were at her door, she quickly rolled
the pasta up and over a loom comb, likely to be found in
the house of any *Romagnola* housewife back in the old days.
Garganelli are made by no accident, however — they were
traditionally boiled in a rich capon broth and served *in brodo*
(page 46) — today they are more often eaten *asciutta* (literally,
"dry," meaning "in sauce" as opposed to soup), especially in a
creamy sauce of ham and peas.

GARGANELLI, CONIGLIO E ASPARAGI
Rabbit and asparagus

Serves 6 as a starter
or 3 as a main

½ pound dried *garganelli*,
  or about ¾ pound fresh
½ a farmed rabbit, or a
  whole wild one (with offal,
  about 1½ pounds)
2 celery stalks
1 large carrot, halved and
  peeled
1 medium onion, halved
5¼ tablespoons butter,
  divided
3 tablespoons extra-virgin
  olive oil
10 juniper berries
20 black peppercorns
2 garlic cloves, broken but
  whole
2 bay leaves
3 sprigs thyme or oregano
7 tablespoons white wine
2 cups chicken stock (or
  water in a pinch)
⅔ pound asparagus
Grated Parmesan, to serve

Also good with this sauce
*cavatappi, dischi volanti,
farfalle tonde, fettuccine,
pappardelle, pici, radiatori,
spaccatelle, strozzapreti,
tagliatelle*

Farmed rabbit, with its milder flavour, is preferable for this dish.

Bone the rabbit, keeping all the offal you can stomach (I use the liver, lungs, kidney, and heart). Dice the meat and offal 1 inch, cutting kidney and heart into quarters – you should have about 14 ounces meat and 10½ ounces bones. Cut the bones into about a dozen chunks.

Separate your celery, carrot, and onion into 2 equal piles. Cut one into biggish chunks, the other dice finely (2 inches).

Heat 1¾ tablespoons of the butter and the oil in a medium pot over a medium heat. Fry the bones in this until well browned (15 minutes), then add the larger chunks of celery, carrot, and onion, and fry for 5 minutes more. Add the aromatics (juniper, peppercorn, garlic, and herbs), and fry for a minute, then deglaze the pan with the wine. After the alcohol has evaporated, add the stock and bring to a boil. Reduce the heat and cook at a bare simmer for roughly an hour, until well reduced and slightly thickened. Strain through a fine sieve, but don't skim it – you should have ¾ cup of rich stock.

In the water which will shortly cook your pasta, boil the asparagus (unless it's muddy, best to do this still held in a bunch by an elastic band) for a minute or until cooked but crunchy. Refresh in iced water, drain, and remove the elastic before cutting into 2–3 centimeter lengths, discarding the woody ends of the stalk.

Set a wide frying pan over a high heat, and fry the rabbit meat and diced vegetables (seasoned with salt and pepper) in the remaining 3½ tablespoons of the butter for 10 minutes, or until the vegetables are completely tender and the meat lightly browned. Reduce the heat to medium-low. Now put the pasta in the again-boiling water.

A couple of minutes before the pasta is done (remembering it must be drained when still more *al dente* than you like), add the asparagus to the frying pan and sauté with the meat for a minute, then add the reduced stock, which should boil immediately. Let it bubble for a minute (add a touch of the pasta water if it gets too dry), then add the drained pasta and cook together until well coated in an intense *jus*, and the pasta cooked to your liking. Serve with grated Parmesan.

GARGANELLI CON PROSCIUTTO COTTO, PANNA E PISELLI
Ham, peas, and cream

About ½ pound (less for dried, more for fresh) *garganelli*
½ pound fresh podded peas
¾ cup chicken stock (optional)
1¾ tablespoons butter
¼ pound thickly sliced cooked ham, cut into strips the size of the pasta
7 tablespoons heavy cream
Nutmeg to taste
Grated Parmesan, to serve

Also good with this sauce
dischi volanti, farfalle, farfalle tonde, fettuccine, gnocchi shells, maccheroni alla chitarra, strozzapreti, tagliatelle

Prosciutto cotto, cooked ham, is quite prevalent in northern Italy — even if we do consider it to be a northern European/American thing. In this recipe, it marries beautifully with sweet summer peas and cream. Any kind of cooked ham will do, but a smoked one is best.

The peas can simply be boiled until tender and drained, in which case you can omit the stock. However, they become sweeter and softer when braised: Put the peas and stock in a smallish saucepan, cover with parchment paper and a tight lid, and cook over a low heat until completely soft — about 15 minutes. Remove the cover, and boil until the remaining stock starts to thicken — it is this sweet liquid which will add the extra depth to your sauce.

When the peas are done, add the *garganelli* to a pot of boiling, well-salted water. A few minutes before the pasta is ready, heat the butter in a pan until it foams. Add the ham, fry for a minute, then add the cream and cooked peas. Season with nutmeg, salt, and pepper, and cook until just starting to thicken. Add the drained pasta and cook until well coated in thickened cream. If it goes too far, just add a bit of the pasta water. Serve with grated Parmesan.

GEMELLI

Dimensions
Length: 1.68 in
Width: 0.28 in

Also good with this pasta
aglio e olio; arrabbiata;
braised bacon and peas;
chicken and prunes;
"Greek salad"; *Norma;*
pesto Trapanese; pork and
pigskin; salad of zucchini,
lemon zest, and pine nuts;
tomato sauce

Gemelli, "the twins," are related to *fusilli* (page 104) as another complex helix – in this case, always with two blades, but the blades are curved until they almost enclose themselves to make tubes, somewhat like twisted *casarecce* (page 66). They are an example of pasta architecture at its best and, as with all good architecture, not only for adults to enjoy – children just love *gemelli* and other entwined pastas.

GEMELLI AI FAGIOLINI
Green beans

⅓ pound *gemelli*
⅔ pound green beans
⅓ cup heavy cream
Scant ¾ teaspoon ground cinnamon
½ garlic clove

Also good with this sauce
busiati, campanelle/gigli, cavatappi, cavatelli, fusilli, fusilli bucati, maccheroni inferrati, torchio, trofie

This dish has been done before, but I break with tradition by adding cinnamon. Sam and Sam Clark, of Moro restaurant, introduced me to the rather wonderful combination of green beans and cinnamon, describing it as "naturally perfect." They served green beans with a walnut and cinnamon *tarator*. The recipe below would be lovely with walnuts, too — but here it is without.

Trim the tops from the green beans, but leave the tails which are rather attractive. Boil two-thirds of them in salted water until completely cooked (no crunch, but not overdone). Drain and puree in a blender whilst still hot with the cream, cinnamon, and garlic, then season with salt and pepper.

Put the pasta on to boil. About 4 minutes before it is done, add the remaining beans (cut in half to a similar length as the pasta). When moments from being perfectly cooked, drain and put in a frying pan with the pea-green sauce and a splash of pasta water. Cook together until *al dente* and well coated in the sauce. Serve with either a sprinkling of *grana* cheese (Parmesan or the like) or a drizzle of extra-virgin olive oil. A scattering of chopped toasted walnuts would be a nice way to evoke the flavours of Moro.

GNOCCHI

Dimensions
Length: 0.6 in
Width: 0.4 in
Depth: 0.28 in

Synonyms
topini ("little birds" or "sandmartins")

Also good with this pasta
al forno; braised bacon and peas; *pesto Genovese; sugo di coda;* tomato sauce; Treviso, speck, and fontina

Gnocchi are little dumplings, normally made of potato, boiled and served in a sauce. Their name may derive from *gnocco* ("idiot"), but seems more likely to stem from *nodo* ("node," or "knot" as in wood). This refers to an ancient folktale about a poor wife who laments she has nothing to cook for her husband as he returns from war. She is overheard by a kindly old tree who offers her its knots to boil for him; she accepts, and the gnarled bits of wood turn into fluffy dumplings when the wife lifts the lid from the pot.

They are made by rolling out a sausage of soft potato dough and cutting it into sections. These are already *gnocchi*, but these can be modified by:

- Dimpling them by pressing with your thumb when on the work surface, to give a smooth exterior and make a hollow that catches sauce.

- Performing the same action over the back of the tines of a fork, to give a similar hollow thumbprint, with a ridged outside to trap even more sauce.

This process is well-demonstrated in a rather sexy scene between Andy Garcia and Sofia Coppola in *The Godfather: Part III*. It is well worth practising at home – *gnocchi* are perhaps the easiest pasta to make, one of the quickest, and can be truly delicious, unlike the tasteless, almost bouncy balls that industrial manufacturers package under the same name.

MAKING POTATO GNOCCHI

1 very large floury potato
(about 14 ounces), such
as Russet or Idaho
1 egg
½ cup all-purpose flour
A few gratings of nutmeg

These little dumplings are many people's favourite. Store-bought versions have to withstand the rigours of packaging, transport, and supermarket checkouts, so they are made firm and rubbery. This recipe, instead, is much more ethereal.

Boil the potato whole, skin on, in salty water. When cooked all the way through (test with a skewer or toothpick), drain and let cool for a few moments until you can handle it. Peel off the skin with your fingers, and put through a ricer/food mill.

Weigh out ⅔ pound (about three-quarters) of the riced potato. When cool enough to handle, but still warm, add the egg, flour, and nutmeg.

Mix just as well as you need to make an even blend, but work as little as possible or the texture will become doughy. Take a small lump, roll on a well-floured surface, cut off a little nugget, and test in boiling water to make sure it will withstand cooking. If it falls apart, a judicious addition of flour should fix the problem. If it persists even after this, adding a little more egg and yet more flour will certainly resolve it, but it is important to add the minimum amount necessary to ensure the lightest of textures.

Shape your *gnocchi*: On a well-floured board, roll a sausage of the dough to become as thick as a finger (up to you whether you use thumb, index, or little as your guide). Use a table knife to cut the sausage into little dumplings, as long as they are wide. A little flick of the knife as it hits the board will move one just aside before you cut the next.

Handle very gently – drop them into boiling salted water, and cook for 2 minutes (start timing when they bob to the surface).

Once cooked, they can be used immediately, or spread out on an oiled plate to chill, and reheat in water or directly in a sauce when you're ready to eat.

GNOCCHI CON GORGONZOLA
Gorgonzola

14 ounces (1 recipe) potato *gnocchi*
⅓ cup cream
1½ cups crumbled Gorgonzola (skin removed)
Nutmeg to taste
A handful of lightly roasted walnuts (optional)

Also good with this sauce
chifferi rigati

Put the *gnocchi* on to boil; they won't take long, but neither will the sauce.

Heat the cream and Gorgonzola, stirring with a spoon until unified. Season with nutmeg and black pepper; taste also for salt, which may not be necessary. Drain the *gnocchi*, add to the sauce along with a dribble of their water, and cook together until well coated.

A topping of chopped walnuts is by no means necessary.

HALÁSZLÉ
Hungarian fish soup

Serves 4

13 ounces canned tuna in vegetable oil (not olive oil)

2 medium onions, finely chopped

4 garlic cloves, chopped

3 tablespoons concentrated tomato paste

Scant ½ cup best sweet Hungarian paprika (*különleges* or *édesnemes*), mixed with hot paprika (*erös*) to taste

Cayenne pepper or crushed red pepper flakes to taste

A bouquet garni (containing at the very least thyme and bay, possibly also celery and parsley)

7 cups vegetable or fish stock, hot

3 medium waxy potatoes (red bliss or creamer), cut into small chunks

1 pound skinless cod fillet, pin-boned and cut into cubes

NOCKERLI
3 eggs
1⅓ cups flour

Also good in this soup
campanelle/gigli, chifferi rigati, dischi volanti, gomiti, penne, pennini rigati, torchio

This recipe is provided by David Kenedy, my father. We both remember it as a childhood favourite, and it is a family adaptation of a traditional Hungarian dish (*hal* meaning "fish"). In Hungary, a landlocked country, this soup would normally begin with the purchase of a live female carp full of roe. This version instead uses cod, with canned tuna added to give the soup some body. *Nockerli* (the Hungarian version of Italian *gnocchi*) are made from a runny batter like *spätzle* and have such an irregular shape that I used to call them "snotballs." If you don't want the hassle of making them, you can substitute dried pasta like *dischi volanti* (page 86) or *gigli* (page 42) and cook them directly in the broth, adding the cod a few minutes before the pasta is done. This substantial soup is a meal in itself.

Drain the oil from the canned tuna into a suitable saucepan (set the tuna aside for later), add the onions and a pinch of salt, and fry for 10 minutes over a gentle heat. Add the garlic and cook for 5 minutes more, until the mixture is soft and golden. Add the tomato paste, paprika, cayenne, and bouquet garni. Remember you can always add extra hotness later, but you cannot take it out, so go easy on the cayenne at first. Add a little of the stock, to make the spice mixture into a paste, then gradually stir in the rest. Season with salt to taste, add the potatoes, and simmer until they are done – about 10–15 minutes.

To make the *nockerli*, have ready a separate pan of boiling well-salted water. Beat together the eggs and flour to make a smooth, thick batter that finds its own level – it will take some elbow grease to work any lumps of flour out. Spoon a manageable quantity (one-third) on to a flat wooden board or ceramic tile – it should spread out a little but not run off the edges. Use a flat-bladed knife to cut little sections of this viscous mix and slide them off the tile into the water (it is best to separate a strip of paste 6 inches wide on the tile, and then cut little 4- to 6-inch strips off this one). Boil in tile-sized batches until they rise to the surface of the water, and then a minute more until they puff up. Drain and set aside in a bowl, covered with a cloth to keep the heat in while you make the next batch.

If you have been organised, you should have got the *nockerli* ready in the time the potatoes have cooked. As the last batch of *nockerli* are about to meet their fate, add the tuna (broken up) and cod to the soup for a brief, 3–4 minute poaching. When this last batch is done, you should drain and add all the *nockerli* to the soup, which is now ready to serve with warm country bread and butter.

1¾ pounds (2 recipes)
    potato *gnocchi*

SAUSAGE SAUCE
¾–1 pound Italian sausage
    (fennel-seedy and slightly
    spicy if possible)
6 tablespoons extra-virgin
    olive oil, divided
3 garlic cloves, sliced
¾ teaspoon crushed red
    pepper flakes
About 2⅔ cups chopped
    canned tomatoes (1⅓
    pounds)
2 teaspoons finely chopped
    fresh rosemary

Also good with this sauce
*bigoli, casarecce, fusilli fatti
a mano, gnudi, lumache,
orzo, radiatori, spaghetti,
tortiglioni*

GNOCCHI IN RAGÙ DI SALSICCIA
Sausage sauce

This recipe is not easily halved, but can be scaled up without difficulty, and the sauce keeps well refrigerated or frozen.

Cook the sausages in 1½ tablespoons of the oil – in either a frying pan or a hot oven. They don't need to be cooked through, but set and slightly coloured. Cut into ¾-inch chunky rounds, and keep any pan juices.

In a fairly small pan, fry the garlic in the remaining oil until browned, but nowhere near burned. Add the red pepper flakes, then the tomatoes, sausages, and their juices. Cook at a bare simmer (either on stove top or in a slow oven) for 50 minutes until rich, condensed, and delicious. Add the chopped rosemary as you remove from the heat.

GNOCCHI SHELLS

Dimensions
Length: 1.2 in
Width: 0.68 in

Synonyms
gnocchetti

Also good with this pasta
al forno; broccoli, anchovy, and cream; ham, peas, and cream; ricotta and tomato; smoked salmon, asparagus, and cream; tomato sauce; Treviso, speck, and fontina

These are an industrial, dried semolina pasta that take their name and image from the famous, freshly made *gnocchi* dumplings (page 116). Rather like an open shell (these are relatives of *conchiglie*, page 76) with a series of bulbous, rounded ridges, this is the pasta the Michelin man would make. They are good baked (see *pasta al forno*, page 196), as well as with wet sauces.

GNOCCHI CON PISELLI E PANCETTA BRASATA
Braised bacon and peas

½ pound *gnocchi* shells
½ pound sweet-cured streaky bacon, thickly sliced
1 cup good dark chicken stock
⅓ cup heavy cream
2 tablespoons butter
1⅓ cups frozen peas, or blanched fresh ones (½ pound)
3 tablespoons chopped flat-leaf parsley
Grated Parmesan to serve

Also good with this sauce
bavette, casarecce, cavatappi, chifferi rigati, conchiglie, dischi volanti, farfalle, farfalle tonde, fettuccine, fusilli, garganelli, gemelli, gnocchi, gomiti, linguine, lumache, radiatori, strozzapreti, tagliatelle, torchio

Perhaps a Westernised version of peas and cooked ham (page 113), this sauce is sweeter and more indulgent. It is perhaps as distant from the Italian original as are the "*gnocchi*" pasta shells from their dumpling inspiration.

Preheat the oven to 425°F (or 390°F for convection ovens).

Next, braise the bacon. Cut it into ½-inch strips and cover with the chicken stock in an ovenproof dish only just large enough to accommodate both. Place in the oven and leave to simmer for 2–3 hours, stirring every half-hour until the juices are thick, more fat than water, and deliciously unctuous, unhealthy, and sweet. This is a highly uneconomical use of an oven – therefore advisable to undertake when you have something else baking away. The braised bacon will keep in your fridge for a week at least.

The *gnocchi* shells take a little while to cook, so put them on before making the rest of the sauce. About 5 minutes before they are done, bring the cream to a simmer with the butter and the peas, and cook for 5 minutes, or until slightly thickened, the peas tender and the cream sweet. Add the bacon (and all its juices) and the parsley, and season with plenty of pepper and a touch of salt. Drain the *gnocchi* shells when just on the hard side, and stir through the cream still on the heat for a few moments. You may need to cook them together for a minute more – some water often gets trapped in shell-shaped pastas, diluting the sauce, which will need to thicken again.

GNUDI AND MALFATTI

These are, perhaps, two distinct pastas. *Gnudi* ("nudes") are smaller (about ¾ inch in diameter) and almost perfectly round, being made from a fairly firm dough that is easy to mold. *Malfatti* ("badly made") are, as their name suggests, more irregular as they are made from a softer dough that is hard to shape. They are also larger, about 1½ inches across.

Both are simple types of dumpling, normally based on ricotta bound together with egg and flour or bread crumbs. They represent the origins of *ravioli* (page 208): They are essentially *ravioli* without wrappers, the filled pasta having come about as a marriage of pre-existing dumplings with the newer invention of pasta. These early dumplings, made from ground meat, were a popular first course in Renaissance Italy. Their modern counterparts are found across the country (*gnudi* particularly in Tuscany and *malfatti* in Lombardy), and are best in the springtime when ricotta is at its peak.

RICOTTA GNUDI

1 cup sheep's milk ricotta
½ cup grated pecorino
   Romano (or Parmesan),
   plus extra to serve
1 egg
5–6 tablespoons fresh
   bread crumbs
Grated nutmeg to taste
All-purpose flour for rolling

Served with lamb *ragù*, this dish is based on a recipe by Simon Hopkinson. It is certainly no improvement on his, but is the way we have come to make these lovely little dumplings at Bocca di Lupo. The name, pronounced "nudie," means just that — these are little naked pastas, like balls of *ravioli* filling with nothing on the outside.

If your ricotta seems wet, let it drain in a sieve for a while. Mix together all the ingredients, season and then let sit for half an hour for the bread crumbs to thicken the mixture. Roll a small ball in flour, and test for integrity (by boiling in water — it should just hold together) before rolling the dough into 20–30 small balls with well-floured hands. You want plenty of flour on the outside of each ball, each the size of a large marble, as this will help make a protective skin on the naked pasta.

Boil in well-salted water (wait for them all to bob to the surface, then cook for 2 minutes more), and serve immediately. If you want to avoid the hassle of shaping dough just before dinnertime, roll and cook them in advance, then keep on a well-oiled tray until ready to reheat in hot salted water.

GNUDI AL RAGÙ D'AGNELLO
Lamb sauce

LAMB SAUCE
1 carrot, finely chopped
1 onion, finely chopped
1 or 2 sticks celery stalks,
    finely chopped
2 garlic cloves, sliced
1 bay leaf
1/3 cup extra-virgin olive oil
1 pound leftover slow-roast,
    braised, or pot-roasted
    lamb meat, diced, plus its
    cooking liquid (reduced if
    watery)
1 pound canned chopped
    tomatoes
1½–2 tablespoons finely
    chopped fresh rosemary

1 recipe ricotta *gnudi*
Grated pecorino Romano,
    to serve

Also good with this sauce
campanelle/gigli,
maccheroni alla chitarra,
orecchiette, pici, torchio

This recipe should be scaled up or down depending on the amount of meat you have. If cooking lamb especially for this recipe, best to use shoulder, and slow-roast it with rosemary, juniper, and plenty of white wine. A large shoulder will yield about 3⅓ pounds of cooked meat, or 3 times the recipe below (which is itself enough for about 8 servings, yielding about 4–4¼ cups).

Sweat the vegetables, garlic, and bay with a good pinch of salt in the oil until translucent and soft, 10–15 minutes on a medium heat. Add the lamb, cooking liquid, and tomatoes, and simmer for an hour, or until reduced, the oil having risen to the top. Remove from the heat, stir in the rosemary, and season with salt and pepper.

The freshly cooked or reheated *gnudi* (see opposite page) should be served on a bed of 1 cup of the lamb *ragù*, with a good grating of pecorino Romano to finish – sheep milk with sheep meat with more sheep milk on top.

MALFATTI

Serves 3–4 as a main course

**2–2¼ cups fresh spinach
(½ pound)**
**1 cup ricotta (sheep's or
mixed milk is best)**
½ cup grated Parmesan
1 egg
**Generous ⅓ cup all-
purpose flour, plus plenty
extra for rolling**
A few gratings of nutmeg

These misshapen green dumplings are another favourite of mine and my father's. There is some confusion as to the correct name — some insist they should in fact be called *gnudi*, and that *malfatti* are instead stuffed parcels akin to *tortelloni* (page 266), or flat misshapen pasta (aka *maltagliati*, page 166). It is our considered opinion that *malfatti* are distinct, and here is how to make them.

Boil the spinach in well-salted water until tender, refresh under cool running water, and squeeze as dry as you can. Chop finely (either in a food processor for evenly green dumplings or with a knife for a speckled appearance). Mix together with the ricotta and other ingredients to make a very soft dough. Season with salt and pepper, but not a heavy hand — the flavours are very subtle, and so too should be the salt.

Roll 1 golf-ball-sized lump as round as you can in plenty of flour. The dough is so soft you will never manage a sphere, but that is why they are called *malfatti* – "badly made."

Bring a pot of salted water to the boil (the spinach water is fine if you still have it), and drop in the ball to make sure it is strong enough not to break up. If it is OK, roll the rest of your dough to make about a dozen dumplings. If it isn't, mix a bit more flour in and then roll your balls.

Cook at a gentle simmer for 10–15 minutes, counting from when they rise to the surface. You can take them out sooner if you like an oozing middle.

These are best served with either:

BURRO E SALVIA
Butter and sage

Fry ½–⅔ cup butter with 24 leaves of sage until the leaves are crispy and the butter nutty; pour directly on top of the *malfatti*. Serve with a generous amount of grated Parmesan.

Or

AL POMODORO
Tomato sauce

Heat 1¼ cups light tomato sauce (page 15), or 1 cup medium tomato sauce (page 15), and serve on warm plates under the *malfatti*, over which either Parmesan or pecorino is grated at the table.

GOMITI

Dimensions
Length: 1.32 in
Width: 0.8 in
Diameter: 0.5 in

Synonyms
elbow macaroni

Also good with this pasta
braised bacon and peas;
chicken and prunes;
frankfurters and fontina;
Hungarian fish soup;
puttanesca; ricotta and
tomato; Treviso, speck, and
fontina

Gomiti means "elbows" or "crank-shafts." It is unclear whether their inspiration was in fact anatomical or industrial. In either case, the resultant curved, ridged tube is a versatile one, functioning both as a cup and a tube, and excellent at trapping chunky, heavy, and oily sauces.

GOMITI CON SCAMPI E ZAFFERANO
Langoustines and saffron

½ pound *gomiti*
1 pound small raw
    langoustines
5²/₃ tablespoons butter,
    divided
1 bay leaf
⅓ cup white wine
A small pinch of saffron
    (about 30 strands)
1½ tablespoons chopped
    flat-leaf parsley (optional)

Also good with this sauce
*conchiglie, dischi volanti,
fettuccine, maltagliati,
pappardelle, tagliatelle,
trenette*

The cooked langoustine tails bear a vague similarity in shape to the *gomiti*, which is pleasing. Tubular *festoni*, ruched tubes looking somewhat segmented, are a better visual homonym of the langoustine tails but have been omitted from this book as they no longer seem as available as they once were. Alternative pairings might involve richer egg pastas.

Here I use small langoustines, which are cheaper and sweeter than big ones. They also allow for a larger number of little bites, perfect for mixing into a pasta.

If the langoustines are alive (best if they are), put them out of their misery by splitting their heads in half with a knife, leaving the tails intact. Blanch immediately in boiling water for literally 3 seconds (this leaves them raw, but makes them easier to peel), and refresh in iced water. Peel the tails, reserving the shells and leaving the end tail-fin attached for presentation. If you are lucky enough (and the prawns unlucky enough), you might have a few gravid females. Pick off their eggs and add to the tail meat — they make a pretty addition to the sauce.

Fry the shells in a small pan in half the butter with the bay, crushing them with the butt end of a heavy, blunt instrument (a rolling pin). Fry until they have started to brown, with an unmistakable smell of grilled seafood. Add the wine and barely cover with water (½–¾ cup). Boil furiously for 10 minutes.

Put the pasta on to boil.

Strain the winey liquid, and wipe its pan clean. Return it to the pot, add the saffron strands and remaining butter, and reduce until the sauce just begins to have some body, but is neither thick nor smelling of over-reduced fish stock (a common crime). Season with salt and a little pepper — this is one occasion I might use white.

The pasta should now be moments away. Add the langoustine tails to the sauce, and gently poach for about a minute. Drain the pasta (still ever so slightly under-done), add to the sauce, and cook together until the sauce coats and the pasta has just the right amount of bite. Stir in some parsley, but only if you like.

GOMITI CON VENTRESCA
Tuna belly, tomato, and *ricotta salata*

½ pound *gomiti*
2 garlic cloves, thinly sliced
6 tablespoons extra-virgin olive oil
3 tablespoons salted capers, soaked in water until tolerably salty, then drained
2 medium fresh tomatoes (²/₃ pound), chopped
6–7 ounces canned tuna belly (*ventresca*), torn into chunks
3 tablespoons chopped basil or parsley
Plenty of coarsely grated *ricotta salata* to serve

Also good with this sauce
bucatini, busiati, conchiglie, fusilli fatti a mano, linguine, bavette, maccheroni alla chitarra, maccheroni inferrati, malloreddus, penne, pennini rigati, pici, spaghetti, torchio, tortiglioni, trenette

Fry the garlic in the oil until golden in a wide pan over a medium flame, then add the capers and tomatoes.

Cook for a further 10 minutes; meanwhile, add the *gomiti* to a pot of boiling, well-salted water. When the tomatoes have turned a dark concentrated red, add a few spoonfuls of the water from the pot in which the pasta is already boiling, as well as the *ventresca*, just to warm through.

Drain the pasta when *al dente,* and stir into the sauce along with the basil or parsley. Serve with a mound of crumbly, milky, and salty *ricotta salata* atop.

GRAMIGNE

Dimensions
Length: 0.48 in
Width: 0.74 in
Diameter: 2.8 mm

Synonyms
gramignoni, spaccatelle

Also good with this pasta
artichokes, peas, and broad beans; broccoli rabe and sausage; sausages and cream; sausage, tomato, and saffron; tomato sauce

These tiny pastas, like enlarged commas or young grass shoots in fact take their name from the latter – *gramigne* means "little weeds." They may be made with a plain semolina-and-water dough or with an egg dough. In either case, they are an industrial form that is likely to have evolved from a fairly stiff dough that could have been grated to produce little wormy shapes.

They are served with tasty, savoury sauces, often with a base of sausage. Because of their diminutive size, they tend to almost become a part of the sauce, rather than a vehicle for it. In fact, in summer they might be actually cooked in a light tomato sauce and served, hot or at room temperature, with plenty of refreshing basil and oil.

GRAMIGNE CON VERZA E SALSICCIA
Cabbage and sausage

½ pound *gramigne*
½ pound Italian sausage, skin removed
1½ cups finely chopped white cabbage (7 ounces or so)
3½ tablespoons butter
1 bay leaf
½ cup plus 1 tablespoon chicken stock
½ cup plus 1 tablespoon milk
Grated Parmesan, to serve
1½–3 tablespoons chopped flat-leaf parsley (optional)

Also good with this sauce
spaccatelle

In a fairly small pan, fry the sausage meat and cabbage with the butter and bay over a low heat. Break the meat up with a spoon, cooking until the cabbage is sweet, soft, and partly caramelised – around half an hour. Add the stock and milk, and simmer gently until the sauce is thick and creamy, a further 20 minutes.

As mealtime approaches, put the pasta on to boil as usual. Drain when slightly more *al dente* than entirely pleasant, and add to the sauce with a small ladle (about ¼ cup) of the pasta water. Cook together over a medium heat until the sauce coats the pasta.

Delicious with a grating of Parmesan. You can garnish with a little chopped parsley just before serving, if brown food isn't your thing.

LASAGNE

Dimensions
Length: 7.4 in
Width: 3 in
Sheet thickness: 0.6 mm

Synonyms
bardele/lasagnoni in
Veneto; *capellasci* in Liguria;
sagne in Salento; *lagana* in
Puglia.
Also in smaller sizes:
*mezze lasagne, mezze
lasagne ricce* (with ruffled
edge).

Similar forms
lasagne ricce

Also good with this pasta
eggplant *lasagne*

*Chi guarda a maggioranza spesse volte s'inganna: granel di pepe
vince per virtú lasagna.*
("He who looks at magnitude is often mistaken: A grain of
pepper conquers lasagna with its strength.")
—Jacopone da Todi

The above quartina dates from the thirteenth century, proof
that *lasagne* are indeed one of the earliest types of pasta; also
mentioned in medieval texts are *gnocchi* (page 116), *ravioli* (page
208), *maccheroni* (see *maccheroncini*, page 152), and *vermicelli*
(page 54). *Lasagne* are rectangular sheets of pasta dough, and
are always layered with a sauce to make the familiar baked dish.
Their name may derive from *laganum*, a Greco-Roman word
for an unleavened cake of dough that would have been baked
on hot stones or fried, then used as a dumpling in soups. It has
also been attributed to the Latin *lasanum* or Greek *lasonon*, a
tripod-like cooking vessel. One of the earliest recipes (in *Liber
de coquina*, an anonymous fourteenth-century cookbook from
the Angevin court in Naples) is for *lasagne a vento* – thin sheets
of leavened dough, cut in 1¼-inch-wide strips and boiled
before being sprinkled with cheese and spices and eaten with
a pointed stick.

Lasagne is the plural of *lasagna,* and so whilst the latter could
refer to a single sheet of pasta, it more normally refers to the
finished dish of the same name – and the former, the pasta
itself. Francesco II, the last king of Naples, was nicknamed
"Lasa" by his father, in recognition of his fondness for it. From

the early nineteenth century, as houses began to have their own ovens, *lasagne* became a popular dinner party dish as a way of showing off – and it still enjoys a place of honour at Italian family meals along with other baked pastas (see *timballo,* page 284). Perhaps because of their long history, *lasagne* come in a variety of guises. In the south, they are thicker and made with semolina dough (page 10) and then dried (they may also have ruffled edges, *lasagne ricce,* as on the following pages). In the north, they would be made with an egg dough or even, in Bologna, a green one made with eggs and spinach. The type of dough has a profound effect on texture and taste, so make sure you know what you're buying if you're purchasing a packaged, dried product (not that one is better than the other, but they are different). *Lasagne* are quite versatile – there are plenty of vegetarian preparations, and recipes range from the modern (deconstructed *lasagne,* layered directly on the plate instead of in an oven dish), to the arcane (such as *lasagne de fornel,* a Christmas dessert from the Dolomites in the Veneto of layered pasta with apples, raisins, poppy seeds, butter, and sugar). Here are two traditional, meaty recipes.

LASAGNE ALLA BOLOGNESE

Serves 6–8

1 pound enriched egg pasta dough (page 13), rolled just under 1 millimeter thick (or the second-thinnest setting on most machines)*
1½–3 tablespoons olive oil
1½ quarts *ragù Bolognese* (just under 1 recipe, page 250)
3½ cups grated Parmesan

Béchamel
7 tablespoons butter
¾ cup plus 2 tablespoons all-purpose flour
Freshly grated nutmeg
4¼ cups milk

*You can use store-bought pasta instead — see package for instructions. Note also that you can make this dish without blanching the pasta if your *ragù* is wet enough to moisten it. Mine isn't.

This dish is rich — typical of Bologna, the lovely medieval city known by Italians as *La Grassa* ("the fat lady"). Though it is traditionally made with green pasta, I prefer it with a yellow dough (use the enriched egg one, page 13).

Preheat the oven to 425°F (or 390°F for convection ovens).

Lightly butter a baking dish, about 8 by 12 inches, and 2½ inches deep. Cut your pasta to size — you should have enough for 9 layers in my book (which this is). Blanch small batches of the pasta for 30 seconds in boiling, well-salted water with the oil to keep it from sticking. Layer the sheets of partly cooked pasta between clean cloths to blot dry.

Make a béchamel by melting the butter and cooking the flour in it for a minute along with a generous grating of nutmeg. Add the milk slowly, stirring constantly with a wooden spoon and allowing the mixture to come back to the boil before each addition of milk.

In building this dish, it is important to remember that it is a dish of pasta with sauce — very thin layers of sauce and lots of layers of pasta will result in the best eating. Spread a small amount of *ragù* on the bottom of the baking dish, then your first layer of pasta. Spread thinly with a little *ragù*, then some béchamel and a good sprinkling of Parmesan. It is OK if you can see areas of pasta through the sauces. Repeat until the top layer, which should be a little thicker with both sauces (especially the béchamel) and the Parmesan. Bake for about 40 minutes, until well browned.

Leave to cool for 15 minutes or so before serving.

VINCISGRASSI

Serves 6–8

1 pound egg pasta dough
(page 13)
3½ cups grated Parmesan

GIBLET SAUCE
1½ pounds chicken giblets
(supposed to include
cockscombs and testicles,
but the usual liver,
heart, and gizzard to be
found in the bag inside
supermarket birds will do
fine)
6 tablespoons olive oil,
divided
²/₃ pound veal sweetbreads
or brains or both
2 slices lemon
2 medium onions, finely
chopped
3 celery stalks, finely
chopped
1 large carrot, finely
chopped
3 garlic cloves, finely
chopped
¼ pound prosciutto, sliced
and chopped
3½ tablespoons butter, plus
more to grease the pan
²/₃ pound minced veal
³/₈ teaspoon grated nutmeg
³/₈ teaspoon ground
cinnamon
2 bay leaves

The name of this dish has been spuriously attributed to an Austrian general called Windisch Graetz, who fought against Napoleon in the siege of Ancona in 1799. However, a recipe from Le Marche called *princisgrass* had already been described in a cookbook in 1781, and was substantially similar to the one below. It is perhaps the most famous from the region and something of a delight to the offal-eater. The apparently indiscriminate use of wobbly bits from chicken and calf results in a delicate taste, thanks to a careful balance of otherwise powerful flavours.

Prepare and blanch the pasta as per the *lasagne alla Bolognese* recipe on page 139.

To make the next step less grisly, fry the giblets in half the oil over a high heat until cooked through and starting to brown. Remove from the heat and chop finely (do the livers by hand; the rest are easier in a food processor).

Poach the veal sweetbreads/brains in salted water with the slices of lemon until just cooked through. Leave to cool in their water, pull off any membranes, drain, and dice (about ½ inch).

In a wide frying pan, sweat the vegetables, garlic, and prosciutto with a good pinch of salt in the butter and remaining oil until soft but not coloured. Add the minced veal, and cook over a medium-high heat until thoroughly cooked and starting to sizzle, breaking up any lumps of meat with a spoon. Add the chopped giblets to the pan, the spices, and the bay. Fry until lightly browned, 10–15 minutes. Add the porcini (finely chopped), their soaking water, and the wine, and let bubble for a minute or 2. Transfer to a suitable saucepan, add the stock and *passata*, and simmer until very thick and dry – about 2 hours. Add the milk and the sweetbreads/brains, and simmer

1½ ounces dried porcini, soaked for 20 minutes in ¾ cup boiling water (reserved)
1 cup plus 2 tablespoons dry white wine or dry marsala
2¼ cups chicken stock
⅓ cup tomato *passata*
¾ cup milk

BÉCHAMEL
3½ tablespoons butter
7 tablespoons all-purpose flour
Freshly grated nutmeg to taste
1¾ cups plus 2 tablespoons milk

for a further 10–15 minutes, until the sauce has a thick coating consistency.

Make a béchamel by melting the butter, and cooking the flour in it for a minute along with a generous grating of nutmeg. Add the milk slowly, stirring constantly with a wooden spoon and allowing the mixture to come back to the boil before each addition of milk, as per the *lasagne alla Bolognese*.

Indeed, from here on in, make the *vincisgrassi* exactly as per the *lasagne alla Bolognese* described on page 139.

LASAGNE RICCE

Dimensions
Length: 5.68 in
Width: 1.44 in
Sheet thickness: 1 mm

Synonyms
doppio festone (scalloped),
sciabo, sciablo

Lasagne ricce are crimped, wavy, or ruffled *lasagne* – *lasagne* with wavy edges – that are decorative and may allow lighter sauces to infiltrate the dish better. Like the preceding *lasagne*, there are regional variations: In Campania and Lazio *lasagne ricce* would be made with semolina, but no egg, while in Emilia-Romagna a flour-and-egg dough would appear. This shape of pasta is, however, primarily a southern thing. Across Sicily, baked *al forno* with layers of a rich *ragù* and ricotta, it is a staple of the Christmas table. In Caltanissetta, in the center of Sicily, it is layered with a pork *ragù*, crispy fried broccoli, and egg. In Palermo, on New Year's Day, they serve *lasagne cacati* ("shit *lasagna*," rather charmingly), where the ricotta is dropped from a height in a big SPLOT, redolent of certain Catalan scatological festive traditions (*Caga Tió*). Meanwhile, in Campania, they serve it as described on page 144.

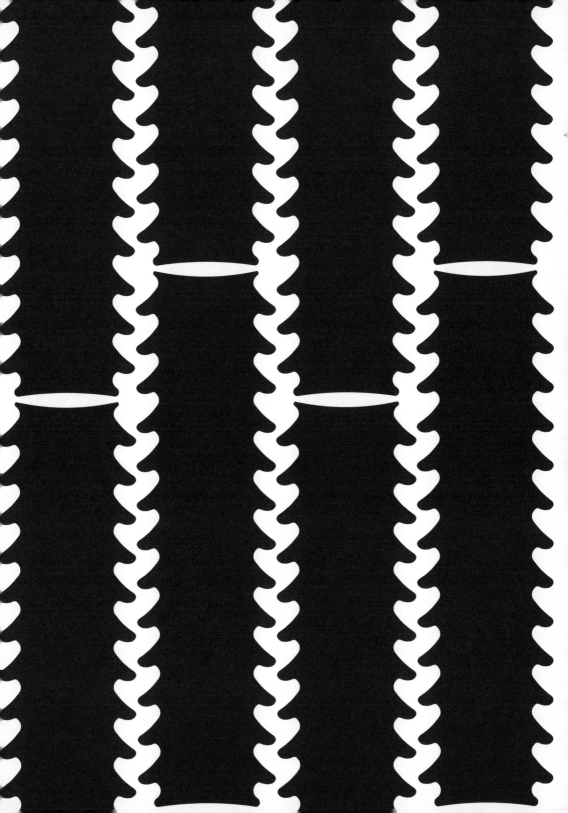

LASAGNE RICCE NAPOLETANE

Serves 6

¾–1 pound dried *lasagne ricce*, or 1–1¼ pounds fresh *lasagne* (simple or enriched egg pasta dough, page 13), prepared as for *lasagne alla Bolognese*
4½ tablespoons olive oil

MEATBALLS
½ pound minced beef or veal
½ pound minced pork
1 egg
4 cups plus 1 tablespoon grated pecorino Romano (or Parmesan), and more to serve if needed
3 tablespoons fresh bread crumbs
4½ tablespoons olive oil

THE DISH
2 cups plus 3 tablespoons *ragù Napoletano* (page 216)
¾–1 pound mozzarella (buffalo or *fior di latte*, or half mozzarella and half ricotta), cut into small chunks and set to drain
3½ cups grated Parmesan

This dish proves that one is allowed, even in Italy, pasta with meatballs (although perhaps not served with *spaghetti*). The following recipe is traditional and delicious. Hard-boiled egg is often added. Being a bit of a fop, I might add 18 boiled quails' eggs to the recipe below, as they are only a little larger than the meatballs, but here it is without.

Preheat the oven to 425°F (or 390°F for convection ovens).

Lightly grease a baking dish about 8 by 12 inches, and about 2½ inches deep, with 1½ tablespoons oil. Blanch the pasta (leaving it more or less raw) in boiling, well-salted water with 1½–3 tablespoons of oil to keep it from sticking. Refresh in cold water, then layer between clean cloths to blot dry.

Make the meatballs by kneading together the minced meats, egg, pecorino Romano, and the bread crumbs with salt and pepper to taste. Make tiny meatballs (the size of a hazelnut) and fry in a hot, wide pan in the 4½ tablespoons of oil until just browning on the outside. This is fortunately not a huge quantity of meat, as the process of forming such small spheres is laborious and repetitive (much like trying to find a hundred ways of saying "now boil the pasta").

Spread a few tablespoons of the *ragù* on the bottom of the dish, then cover with a slightly overlapping layer of pasta. Spread sparingly with the *ragù*, dot with meatballs and mozzarella, and sprinkle generously with Parmesan. Ration yourself so that the process can be repeated until all the pasta has been used with no meatballs on the very top layer, but instead a slightly more generous quantity of *ragù*, mozzarella, and Parmesan.

Bake for about 30–40 minutes, until hot through and browned on top. Leave to stand for 10–15 minutes before serving.

"MELANSAGNA NAPOLIGIANA"
Eggplant lasagne

Serves 6

¾–1 pound *lasagne ricce*
2 medium eggplants,
   sliced no more than 5
   millimeters thick
Flour for dusting
Oil for frying
2 cups *arrabbiata* sauce
   (page 196) or light tomato
   sauce (page 15) with a
   little red pepper added
1 small (¾- to 1-ounce)
   bunch basil, roughly
   chopped
½ pound buffalo mozzarella,
   chopped or torn
2⅓ cups grated Parmesan

Also good in this dish
lasagne

This dish is the bastard son of *melanzane parmigiana* and *lasagne Napoletane* — both its progenitors hark from Naples. Their offspring was conceived far away, however (I must confess I had something to do with it), and you're as likely to find this dish in Naples as you are a curry.

Preheat the oven to 425°F (or 390°F for convection ovens).

Blanch the pasta until quite flexible but still pretty raw in the middle, refresh in cold water, and blot dry. Salt the eggplant slices with a sprinkling of fine sea salt (not so much to remove bitterness as excess water), stack them up, and leave to stand for 30 minutes. Rinse and squeeze dry. Set your widest pan over a high heat with a half-centimeter depth of oil. As it just starts to smoke, flour the eggplant slices lightly, and fry in batches, as a single layer in the pan, for a minute on each side until a light golden brown. Drain well.

Take a suitable baking pan (around 8 by 12 inches) and smear the base with a little of the tomato sauce. Cover with a scant layer of eggplant, then one of pasta. Top this with a generous sprinkling of basil, mozzarella, and Parmesan, then drizzle with more sauce and cover with a sheet of pasta followed by eggplant. Continue to stack in this order (pasta, eggplant, cheese, basil, and sauce) so your finished dish has eggplant on both the bottom and top layers. On the uppermost layer you should aim to have no basil, but extra Parmesan. Bake for 40 minutes or until bubbling and well browned.

LINGUINE, BAVETTE, AND TRENETTE

Dimensions
Length: 10.4 in
Width: 3 mm
Thickness: 2 mm

Synonyms
lingue di passero ("sparrow's tongues")

Also good with these pastas
arrabbiata; bottarga and bread crumbs; braised bacon and peas; broccoli, anchovy, and cream; langoustines and saffron; lentils; lobster, mussels, and ginger; *pesto Genovese; pesto Trapanese; puttanesca;* Romanesco broccoli; scallops and thyme; *tartufo dei poveri; tocco;* tomato sauce; tuna belly with tomato; zucchini and prawns; zucchini and their flowers

Bavette and *linguine*, two near-identical pastas, are oral delights even in their names. *Bavette* is probably the more ancient. Its name stems from *sbavare* ("to drool"), or *bava* ("a dribble"), itself stemming from the French (in which a bib is called a *bavette*). *Linguine*, the more common name, has a less obscure etymology – it simply means "little tongues." This describes the shape – as long as *spaghetti* (page 230), but flattened to an ellipse in cross-section, like your own tongue. The pasta has some of the sturdiness of a cylinder and some of the folding properties of flat noodles. It is commonly used, especially with seafood- and tomato-based sauces.

Trenette are typical of Liguria, and Genoa in particular. Somewhat like square-cut *linguine*, they are made from a simple semolina and water dough, and while best fresh, they are also delicious dry. As with the similar *maccheroni alla chitarra* (page 156), *trenette* possess two great qualities: They are blessed with a larger surface area than *linguine* or *spaghetti*, so they get coated in that little bit more sauce, and they are slightly chunky, so they retain a marvellous bite when cooked properly.

Traditionally, they would be served with pesto, green beans, and potato (page 276) or with *tocco* (page 212) – Liguria's answer to *ragù:* Use ⅓ cup *tocco* per ½ pound *trenette* to serve two as a main course or four as a starter.

LINGUINE ALLE VONGOLE
Clams

½ pound dried pasta
(*linguine/bavette/
spaghetti/spaghettini*)
½ cup extra-virgin olive oil
1¼ pounds Manila clams
(*vongole veraci*), or ¾–1
pound *tellines* if you can
get them
1 garlic clove, thinly sliced
A good pinch of crushed red
pepper flakes
A handful of flat-leaf
parsley, chopped
6 tablespoons white wine

Also good with this sauce
spaghetti, spaghettini

Almost everyone's favourite, and one of the simplest things to make.

While your pasta is cooking, heat a wide frying pan over a high heat. When smoking hot, add the oil and then, quickly and all at once, the clams, garlic, and red pepper flakes. Fry for a few moments (I like my garlic to just start to colour at the edges, but this is a matter of taste), then add the parsley and then the wine. Let the pan bubble away – the clams will let out some liquid as they begin to cook. Once they have started to open, they shouldn't fry – if your pan gets too dry, add a little water, but remember that in the finished dish the sauce should be about 1:1 oil to water.

When most of the clams have opened, add the drained pasta and cook together until the last ones pop. Serve immediately.

If you want your sauce to emulsify, add a pinch of flour to the oil before the clams. This makes the dish somehow taste heavier, so I prefer not to.

LINGUINE ALL'ASTICE
Lobster

1/2 pound dried *linguine*
1 small live lobster (about 1 pound)
6 tablespoons extra-virgin olive oil
1 garlic clove, thinly sliced
3/8 teaspoon crushed red pepper flakes
3 tablespoons white wine
3/4 cup light tomato sauce (page 15), or tomato *passata* or pureed raw tomato in a pinch

Also good with this sauce
bavette, malloreddus, spaghetti, spaghettini

Kill the lobster by splitting it down the middle – head end first, then the tail. If you're squeamish, numb it in the freezer for 15 minutes, then plunge into boiling water for 3 minutes to half-cook it, but the apparently brutal method with a knife is actually the more merciful (especially if you use the freezer trick first). And you'll still have to split the lobster in half, anyway.

Prepare and cut the lobster: Rinse out any brown meat under cold running water, pulling out the sac behind the eyes and discarding it. Trim off the front 3/4 inch of shell (with eyes and antennae attached) and discard. Also throw away the gills (dead man's fingers), which you can pull out with your fingers from between the tops of the legs and the outer shell. Cut the body (aka the "head") and tail into nice chunks. Pull off the claws and the "knuckles" that attach them to the body, and crack open with a knife to make eating easier a little later on. Do not peel the flesh from the shell – the shell not only adds to the look of the dish, but flavours the sauce.

Put your pasta on to boil. About 4 or 5 minutes before it's done, heat a wide pan, add the oil, and fry the lobster for 2 minutes without stirring much. Add the garlic and red pepper flakes, and fry for 30 seconds more, then add the wine, followed by the tomato sauce. Cook together, stirring around, until the lobster is cooked through. The sauce should stay a little saucy – add a splash of the pasta water if it dries out. Drain the pasta (slightly under-done, as ever) and add to the sauce. Cook together until the sauce coats and the pasta is only pleasantly *al dente*. Serve immediately.

LUMACHE

Dimensions
Length: 1.08 in
Width: 0.6 in
Diameter: 0.5 in

Synonyms
chifferini, ciocchiolette,
cirillini, gomitini, gozziti,
lumachelle, pipe, pipette
("little pipes"), *tofarelle*

Also good with this pasta
braised bacon and peas;
puttanesca; ricotta and
tomato; sausage sauce;
Treviso, speck, and fontina

Lumache ("snails") are much like *gomiti* (page 130), but often larger and with one end crimped so as to be partially closed – better to impersonate the model snail shell, and better too to hold the sauce once it gets into the pasta. "Average" ones are the size of a thumb joint (indeed, the size of an average snail), but giant versions best used for stuffing like *cannelloni* (page 50) or *manicotti* (page 168) exist too. Whilst most versions are clearly modified but basic tubes of pasta, others are tightly spiralled and look alarmingly like the recently raided snail shells you might find in your garden after an attack of starlings.

LUMACHE ALLE LUMACHE
Snails

Serves 8 as a starter or 4 as a main course or light meal

¾–1 pound *lumache*
1 medium onion, red or
  yellow
3 garlic cloves
¾ cup chopped flat-leaf
  parsley, divided
¾ cup extra-virgin olive oil
¾ pound cooked shelled
  snails (canned are just fine)
4 large ripe tomatoes (1¾
  pounds), pureed
6½ tablespoons white wine
6 tablespoons chopped
  fresh basil leaves
4½ tablespoons chopped
  fresh mint leaves
To serve:
6 tablespoons fresh bread
  crumbs, toasted with 1
  tablespoon extra-virgin
  olive oil, cooled and mixed
  with 6 tablespoons grated
  pecorino Romano

Snails with snails — but this *ragù* is also nice (if less fun) with other pastas, too . . .

Finely chop the onion, garlic, and half of the parsley together. Fry in a tall-sided saucepan in the oil with a pinch of salt for 10 minutes over a medium heat or until soft, then add the snails and cook together for a few minutes. Add the tomato and wine, and simmer for 45 minutes, until the sauce is thick and the oil has risen to the top. Taste for seasoning — it is now ready to serve, or refrigerate until you wish to do so.

When you're hungry enough to eat, put on the pasta. Toss it (drained) in the hot sauce over the heat for a minute or two, stirring in the basil, mint, and remaining parsley. Serve with the bread crumbs and pecorino for a crunchy pep.

MACCHERONCINI

Dimensions
Diameter: 0.24 in
Length: 1.8 in
Wall thickness: 1.5 mm

Also good with this pasta
chicken and prunes;
macaroni salad; tuna and
eggplant

This is a tubular pasta, quite narrow, 1¼–2 inches in length – and would be called macaroni outside of Italy (the name clearly derives from *maccherone*, itself probably stemming from the Greek *makaria*, "food of the blessed"). In Italy, *maccherone* is the generic term for all dried alimentary doughs cooked in broth or water (i.e., dried pasta) – and until recently, this was also true Stateside. Only in 1981 did the National Pasta Association acquire its new name, previously the National Macaroni Institute.

The shape of *maccheroncini* was born in Naples. Neapolitans were once known across the land as *mangiafoglie* ("leaf-eaters") for their love of greens. The eighteenth century saw a boom in pasta production centered in Naples, with its climate so suited to drying the dough. Street sellers made steaming hot plates of pasta with cheese, and served them to the local working classes and the young aristocracy of England on Grand Tour alike. These street vendors became a tourist attraction and a symbol of Neapolitan exuberance. Neapolitans were rebranded *mangiamaccheroni* ("pasta-eaters"), and the name has stuck to this day – pasta is almost synonymous with the city, even if Naples accounts for less than a quarter of Italian production.

PASTA ALLA NORMA
Eggplant and tomato

½ pound *maccheroncini*
1 medium eggplant
¾ teaspoon fine sea salt
Oil for deep-frying (corn,
　sunflower, or rapeseed)
½ medium onion, finely
　chopped
2 garlic cloves
A small pinch of crushed red
　pepper flakes
4½ tablespoons extra-virgin
　olive oil
⅓ cup medium tomato
　sauce (page 15)
8-10 basil leaves, torn or
　roughly chopped
2¾-3 ounces *ricotta salata*
　(grated), or 4-4¼ ounces
　smoked ricotta (crumbled)

Also good with this sauce
*bucatini, cavatappi, gemelli,
paccheri, penne, pennini
rigati, rigatoni, sedanini,
spaccatelle, spaghetti,
tortiglioni, ziti/candele*

One of Sicily's most famous dishes, this is named after Bellini's *Norma*. There is a (likely apocryphal) story that a chef, enraptured after hearing a rousing performance of the opera, rushed back to his kitchen and immediately concocted this dish in its honour. The recipe pre-dates the work, however, and it is likely that the name of the dish was changed after some of Bellini's compatriots started using the term *una vera Norma* to extol the merits of a remarkable product or deed. So delicious is the sauce – *una vera Norma* indeed – that it became synonymous with its praise.

Cut the eggplant into rough ¾-inch dice. Season with half the salt, and deep-fry in plenty of very hot oil until browned and soft all the way through. Drain on absorbent paper. It is best to do this before you cook your pasta, in case you splash any water into the oil (just about the worst thing you could do).

When you start to cook the pasta, gently fry the onion, garlic (cloves gently crushed but otherwise whole), and red pepper flakes in another pan with the remaining salt and the olive oil. After 5–8 minutes, the onion should be soft and golden. Remove and discard the garlic, then add the tomato sauce and about 3 tablespoons of the pasta's water. Add the eggplant and stir gently, then add the drained and marginally undercooked pasta. Cook together for a minute or so (you may need to add a splash more water), then stir in the basil at the last moment. Serve with the ricotta on top.

MACARONI AND CHEESE

*Serves 2 as a main or
4–5 as a side dish*

½ pound *maccheroncini* or
   cavatappi (page 68)
3½ tablespoons butter,
   plus extra for the dish
4½ tablespoons all-purpose
   flour
1 bay leaf
A few gratings of nutmeg
1 cup plus 2 tablespoons
   milk
1¾ cups grated Parmesan,
   divided
3½ ounces cheddar or
   fontina, diced
4½ tablespoons fresh
   bread crumbs (optional)

Also good in this dish
*cavatappi, chifferi rigati,
sedanini*

Thomas Jefferson is reputed to have brought this recipe back to the States after a sojourn in Italy in the early nineteenth century. It is, of course, not an Italian recipe (Jefferson probably returned with a recipe for *pasta al forno*, page 196, which evolved into the present dish) but you can use fontina instead of cheddar cheese for the illusion of authenticity.

Preheat the oven to 465°F (or 425°F for convection ovens).

Butter a suitable ceramic baking dish (about 8 by 5 inches for this quantity). Boil the pasta for half the time stated on the package, in salted water as usual. Drain, and don't worry that it's still crunchy.

Next, make a roux. Melt the butter, adding the flour, bay leaf, nutmeg, and a little salt and pepper. Fry for a few moments (don't let the flour brown), then gradually add the milk, stirring manically with a wooden spoon. A judicious addition of milk will result in a smooth sauce. Stir in two-thirds of the Parmesan, then the pasta. When the pasta is well-coated, add the cheddar or fontina, stir to just mix, and transfer to your baking dish. Flatten as best you can with the back of a spoon, and top with the remaining Parmesan (mixed with the bread crumbs, if you want them).

Bake for around 20 minutes until well-browned and piping hot. Let it sit for 10 minutes before serving, or someone will get hurt.

MACCHERONI ALLA CHITARRA

Dimensions
Length: 4 in
Width: 3 mm
Depth: 2 mm

Synonyms
caratelle, tonnarelli in Lazio;
crioli in Molise; *stringhetti* in
Le Marche

Also good with this pasta
anchovy; duck sauce; garlic
sauce; ham, peas, and cream;
lamb sauce; *pesto* Genovese;
scallops and thyme; *tocco*;
Treviso, speck, and fontina;
tuna belly and tomato;
zucchini and their flowers

Typical of the region of Abruzzo, this is a long egg noodle made by pressing a thick sheet of pasta dough through a *chitarra* – a "guitar" of tightly stretched strings or wires. It may be surprising to find a long noodle called *maccheroni* but this is historically correct – indeed, the word is still in use as a general term for pasta in the south. Traditionally served with a sauce of hot peppers and diced lamb, this pasta has recently broken out of its original *terroir* and gone global – a favourite among chefs for the ease with which it is made (if you have the equipment) and the way it marries so well with julienne vegetables. Sauté it with thin strips of raw zucchini and peeled red prawns, and you're in heaven. The recipe given on page 158 is for another local concoction.

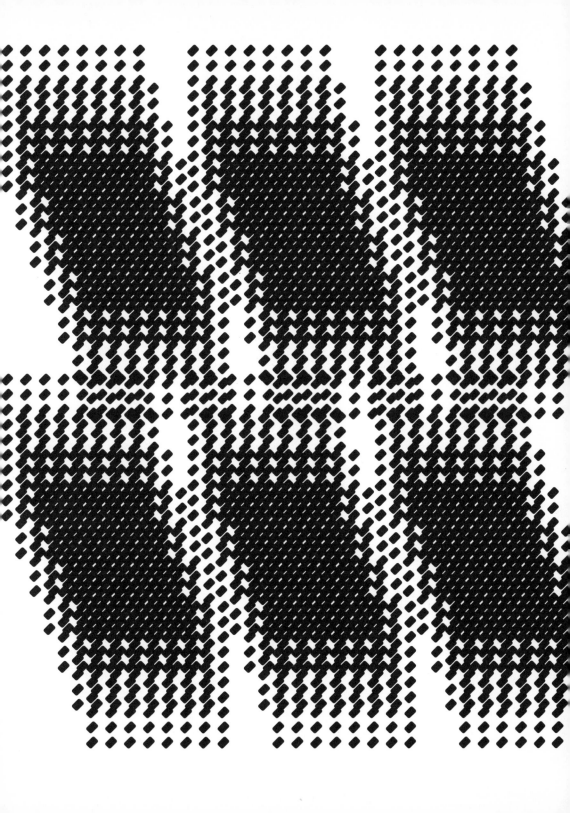

MACCHERONI ALLA CHITARRA CON TARTUFO DEI POVERI
Poor man's truffle

½ pound fresh *maccheroni alla chitarra* (or a little less dried)
½ pound mushrooms (cremini or button)
20 pit-in, wrinkly dried black olives
2 anchovy fillets
6 tablespoons extra-virgin olive oil
A pinch of crushed red pepper flakes

Also good with this sauce
bigoli, fazzoletti, pici, spaghetti, trenette

Despite its name, this sauce does not exactly taste of truffles, although it does share their earthy complexity. In this day and age, truffles being the price they are, "middle-class truffle" would be just as apt — none but the über-rich can afford the real deal.

This sort of dryish sauce goes so well with the chewy texture of fresh pasta that it is one of the few recipes for which I would recommend fresh spaghetti (available at many supermarkets) as a suitable alternative pasta.

Cut off and discard the protruding stems of the mushrooms, and wipe the caps clean with a damp cloth only if necessary. Pit the olives. Combine mushrooms, olives, anchovies, and red pepper flakes in a food processor, and process until fine.

Assuming fresh pasta is used, cook the sauce at about the same time as the pasta goes into the water.

Fry the processed mushroom mixture in the olive oil over a medium heat until the mixture is the colour of dark soil and looks oily. Add about 6 tablespoons of the pasta water along with the drained, ever-so-slightly undercooked, pasta and stir together over the heat until well coated. The sauce should be quite dry, but you may need to add a touch more water if overly so.

MACCHERONI ALLA CHITARRA CON GAMBERI E ZUCCHINE
Zucchini and prawns

About ½ pound (less for dried, more for fresh) *maccheroni alla chitarra*
2–3 zucchini (⅔ pound)
4½ tablespoons extra-virgin olive oil
1 garlic clove, cut into matchsticks
⅔–½ pound raw shell-on prawns, shelled (you should end up with ⅓–½ pound shelled meat)
3½ tablespoons butter
10 basil leaves, torn or shredded

Also good with this sauce
farfalle, farfalle tonde, maltagliati, pappardelle, spaghettini, tagliatelle, trenette

This dish is a cinch to make — and delicious, provided the prawns are of the highest possible quality. I use Sicilian red prawns — a rare delicacy, and scrumptious. Substitutes could be Poole prawns (the lovely, transparent shrimp landed in the south of England in late autumn and winter), rock shrimp, or shelled langoustines or lobster.

Top and tail the zucchini, then cut across into half to make them of manageable length. Slice each section lengthways in thin, 1- to 2-millimeter slices, then stack the slices and cut into julienne strips the same width as the pasta will be when cooked. You could lightly season these with salt a few minutes before cooking, but it isn't really necessary. Put the pasta on.

A few minutes before the *maccheroni* are cooked, heat a wide saucepan over a medium heat (you need some room to cook the sauce — a wok will work well, too). Add the oil and the garlic, which should fry a little but not colour. Add the zucchini, prawns, and salt and pepper to taste. Fry until the prawns are half-cooked, then add the butter. Sauté together until the sauce is luscious and the zucchini wilted — definitely cooked but with some bite. Drain the pasta and toss into the sauce, increasing the heat to high for this last 30 seconds. Stir in the basil, taste one last time, and serve quickly.

MACCHERONI INFERRATI

Dimensions
Length: 5 in
Width: 5 mm

Synonyms
busiati or *firrichiedi*,
maccheroni chi fir,
maccheroni al ferro

Also good with this pasta
amatriciana; broccoli rabe;
cacio e pepe; *carbonara*;
garlic sauce; green beans;
gricia; *pesto Genovese*;
pesto Trapanese; rabbit and
spicy tomato; sardines and
fennel; sausages and cream;
tocco; tuna belly and tomato

The terms *busiati* (page 40) and *maccheroni inferrati* are used interchangeably to describe two distinct forms of pasta made in almost identical manners. For some semblance of clarity they have been listed separately – under *busiati* you will find a description of a telephone-wire shape. Here is a different, almost tubular version. Both are specialities in Sicily and Calabria.

Maccheroni inferrati are made traditionally by wrapping a strand of pasta dough around an iron rod (an old, thin knitting needle), although a wooden one works at least as well. Where the strand is wrapped diagonally to make the *busiati*, for *maccheroni inferrati* the length of the pasta is parallel to the rod, which it encloses to make a tube. Here we are describing the handmade equivalent to *bucatini* (page 34).

There are two ways to make these, both using a plain dough of *semola* (page 10).

MAKING MACCHERONI INFERRATI

METHOD ONE

Roll out a cigarette-width cylinder of dough, and cut into cigarette lengths. Lay a piece flat on a board and lay your rod along its length. Press down, then roll rapidly back and forth on the board with the palms of your hands, moving your hands apart to extend the pasta along the length of the rod. The rolling action will also loosen the pasta, the diameter of the hole running its length becoming greater than that of the rod, which can then be removed.

METHOD TWO

Roll out a strand of pasta about 3 millimeters wide, and cut into 6-inch lengths. Take 1 and lay it out straight on a board. Use a straight edge (such as a plastic ruler) to form the pasta. Put the edge against the board parallel to the pasta, with the pasta between the ruler and your body. Keeping the ruler angled at about 45° to your body, draw it towards yourself across the pasta. The ruler should stretch out the pasta, which will then curl up to form an almost complete tube.

MACCHERONI INFERRATI CON RAGÙ DI COTICA
Pork and pigskin

Serves 4 as a main

Maccheroni inferrati freshly
  made with 2⅓ cups plus
  4 teaspoons semolina, or
  14 ounces dried ones
1 pound skin-on, boneless
  pork belly
6 tablespoons extra-virgin
  olive oil
1 celery stalk, finely
  chopped
½ carrot, finely chopped
1 medium onion, finely
  chopped
2 garlic cloves, chopped
2 bay leaves
¾ teaspoon crushed fennel
  seed (optional)
1¾–2 cups red wine
14 ounces canned chopped
  tomatoes, or fresh ones
1 cup milk
20 basil leaves
Grated Parmesan or
  pecorino Romano,
  to serve

Also good with this sauce
*bucatini, cavatelli, fusilli
bucati, gemelli*

This recipe serves four, but half the sauce can easily be set aside if two are dining. Pigskin is too often discarded, or fed to the dogs. It is a delicious and nutritious food, full of gelatin, and makes delicious sausages, sauces, and stews — something not to turn one's snout up at.

This sauce takes a good three hours to make, but can be left pretty much unattended and made in advance if desired.

Start by cutting the skin from the belly meat. Dice the meat quite finely, ⅓–½ inch. Plunge the skin into boiling water for 5 minutes to make it easier to cut (it's very tough raw), then cut into strips 1½ inches long and ¼ inch wide. Heat the oil in a medium saucepan over a medium heat. Fry the pork meat until quite well browned (10–15 minutes), then add the vegetables, garlic, bay, and fennel seed (if using) along with a generous measure of salt. Sweat together for a further 10–15 minutes until tender and starting to colour. Add the pigskin, wine, tomatoes, and milk, and bring to a simmer, then reduce the heat to low and leave to gently bubble until the sauce has thickened and the skin is silky and soft. This is the point to stop if cooking in advance — carry on if you're ready to eat.

Cook the pasta, still just too hard for your taste, and drain. Add it to the hot sauce, increase the heat for a few moments and stir together until the pasta is ready and well coated. Stir in the basil leaves as an afterthought, and serve with the Parmesan grated on top.

MALLOREDDUS

Dimensions
Length: 1.2 in
Width: 0.42 in

Synonyms
caidos, macarones cravaos, maccarronis de orgiu. Industrial ones are called *gnocchetti sardi.*

Also good with this pasta
bottarga and bread crumbs; *cacio e pepe*; lobster; salad with prawns; tomato sauce

The diminutive of *malloru* ("bull" in Sardinian dialect), *malloreddus* are therefore "fat little calves." Made from a semolina dough (page 10) normally coloured with a little saffron, these tiny dumplings have an elongated, elegant conch shape that is ridged on the outside to catch sauce. This was once impressed upon the dough by rolling against a wicker basket – nowadays a specially made grooved piece of glass (*ciuliri*) is used for home production. Outside of Sardinia, one is more likely to buy *malloreddus* packaged and dried – and the same is true on the island for most occasions. On her wedding night, a Sardinian bride will parade through town wearing silver jewellery and carrying a large basket of *malloreddus* made by her own hand. She is closely followed by her family until she reaches the doorstep of her betrothed, who will scare off her entourage with rifle shots. The bride will then enter, to dine on her *malloreddus* off the very same plate as her new husband.

Saffron is, to us, by no means the cheapest of materials; but where crocuses grow, the only investment needed to obtain it is one of time and patience. The addition of saffron to the dough was probably in order to give poor man's flour-and-water dough the appearance of pasta rich with egg yolks, a privilege of the wealthy. It is reminiscent of the centuries-old practice of decorating food with gold leaf as a sign of prestige – still commonly undertaken today by *chocolatiers*. Once upon a time Italian butchers would hang their fillets of beef up for display completely enrobed in gold.

MALLOREDDUS ALLA CAMPIDANESE
Sausage, tomato, and saffron

½ pound *malloreddus*
1 medium onion, finely chopped
4½ tablespoons extra-virgin olive oil
½ pound Italian sausage, skin removed
1 small pinch saffron strands
¾ cup tomato *passata*
5 basil leaves, torn
Plenty of grated pecorino (a good, hard one), to serve

Also good with this sauce
fusilli fatti a mano, gramigne, spaccatelle

This sauce can be made in advance and even frozen if you make a large batch.

Fry the onion gently in the oil with a pinch of salt until translucent. Add the sausage meat and continue to fry over a medium-low heat, breaking up with a spoon until the mixture sizzles and just starts to colour — around 15 minutes. Add the saffron and *passata*, and cook at a gentle simmer until thick, the oil having risen to the surface (about 30 minutes more).

Boil the *malloreddus* until *al dente*. Heat the sauce with a splash of pasta water, then add the drained pasta. Cook together for perhaps 30 seconds, stir in the basil, and serve with grated pecorino on top (pecorino Sardo is best).

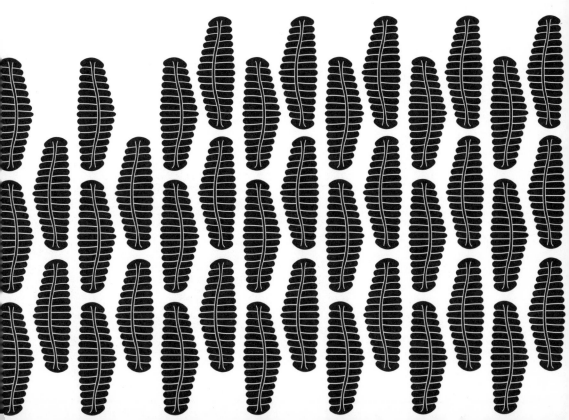

MALTAGLIATI

Dimensions
Length: 2.4 in
Width: 0.64 in
Sheet thickness: 1 mm

Synonyms
malmaritati ("badly married"),
or *blecs* (made with
buckwheat flour); tiny ones
in Valtellina are called
pizzoccherini; in Mantova
straciamus or *spruzzamusi*
(literally: "splatter-mouth");
in Liguria *martaliai*; in Emilia-
Romana *bagnamusi* ("wet-
mouth") and *sguazzabarbuz*;
in Le Marche *strengozze*;
in Lazio *sagne 'mpezze*; in
Puglia *pizzelle*

Also good with this pasta
artichokes, peas, and broad
beans; *cacio e pepe*; duck
sauce; langoustines and
saffron; morels; *pasta e fagioli*;
porcini and cream; scallops
and thyme; white truffle;
zucchini and prawns

Meaning "badly cut," these should be just that – fairly random shapes. Shop-bought ones are usually depressingly identical rhombi, usually made from an egg pasta but occasionally made from a plain semolina dough. Originally they would have been made from the leftover scraps of a *tagliatelle* cutting session, but their shapes may nowadays be more stylised. In Piedmont, they are also called *foglie di salice*, cut to resemble willow leaves and served in bean soup, while in Emilia-Romagna they are roughly cut from a roll of pasta and served simply with grated pecorino and oil. They go well with many a sauce; the one given here a simple affair with a luxurious mushroom – fresh young porcini.

MALTAGLIATI AI FUNGHI PORCINI
Porcini

About ½ pound (less for dried, more for fresh) *maltagliati*
½ pound fresh, young, firm porcini (caps no more than 2 inches across)
5½ tablespoons butter
2 garlic cloves, thinly sliced
Grated Parmesan, to serve

Also good with this sauce
fregola, pappardelle, tagliatelle

A simple sauce with the king of wild mushrooms — earthy and heavenly all at once. This sauce is quick to make and can be done as the pasta cooks.

Clean the porcini (wipe the caps with a damp cloth, and carefully pare the skin from the stalks) and slice ½ inch thick. Heat the butter in a wide pan over a high heat, and brown the mushrooms for 2 minutes on each side; add the garlic as you turn the slices. Add the *maltagliati* to a pot of boiling, well-salted water while the mushrooms cook. Add about ¼ cup of the pasta's water to emulsify the butter, shaking the pan until you're satisfied. Drain the pasta, marginally undercooked, and toss in the pan until the sauce is thick enough to coat. Serve with a little Parmesan and a glass of red.

MANICOTTI

Dimensions
Length: 5 in
Width: 1.2 in
Wall thickness: 1 mm

Also good with this pasta
ground veal stuffing (page 52)

Manicotti ("sleeves") are the subject of some confusion. In the USA, where *manicotti* probably originate, the term often refers to a baked dish of stuffed tubular pasta rather than the pasta itself. Dried tubes of pasta are often sold as *cannelloni* (page 50) although *cannelloni*, at least originally, are sheets of pasta rolled around a filling, rather than extruded tubes that need to be stuffed from the ends. Whilst these dried smooth tubes are not normally named as such, they are likely the original *manicotti*. There is no doubt that the ridged versions, like ruffled sleeves of fabric, are indeed *manicotti*. These in turn should not be confused with the Italian pasta *maniche*, which are similar to *rigatoni* (page 218) and served only occasionally baked, and never stuffed.

BAKED MANICOTTI

¼ pound *manicotti*
1¾ cups spinach (½ pound)
1 generous cup ricotta
1 cup grated Parmesan, divided
2 egg yolks
Freshly grated nutmeg
3 tablespoons all-purpose flour
1½ tablespoons butter
¾ cup milk
¾ cup medium tomato sauce (page 15)
Grated Parmesan or *grana*, to serve

Also good with these fillings
ricotta (page 267); spinach and ricotta (page 210); veal and spinach (page 52)

So very, very American . . .

Preheat the oven to 425°F (or 390°F for convection oven).

Boil the *manicotti* in salted water until *al dente*, drain (reserving the water), refresh in cold water, and drain again. Use the pasta water to blanch the spinach until tender, which is also drained, refreshed, and drained – but this time also squeezed as dry as you can manage.

Finely chop the spinach and mix with the ricotta, half the Parmesan, the egg yolks, and some nutmeg. Season with salt and pepper, and stuff the *manicotti*.

Make a béchamel with the flour, butter, and milk (if you need help, see page 155).

Spread the tomato sauce on the bottom of a suitable baking dish. Arrange the *manicotti* on top, then cover with the béchamel. Sprinkle with the remaining Parmesan, and bake until browned on top, about 20–25 minutes. Leave to stand for 10–20 minutes before serving this perilously hot meal with additional grated cheese on top.

ORECCHIETTE

Dimensions
Length: 0.68 in
Width: 2.5 mm at thickest
point, tapering to 1 mm

Synonyms
orecchini in Rome;
recchietelle in Campania,
Molise, and Basilicata;
orecchie di prete ("priest's
ears") in Abruzzo and
Basilicata; *cicatelli* and
recchie di prevete in Foggia;
cagghiubbi or *fenescecchie*
in Bari; little ones are
chiancerelle, and larger
are *pochiacche* in Taranto;
stacchiodde in Lecce

Similar forms
crosets

Also good with this pasta
broad beans and ricotta;
broccoli rabe with sausage;
lamb sauce; lentils; pureed
broad beans; Romanesco
broccoli

Widely available in their dried form, these "little ears" of pasta are quite unappetising unless fresh. *Orecchiette* are made from semolina dough and are fairly thick, so that by the time their interior is cooked from dry, the outside will be over-done. Freshly made, however, their cooking time is reduced to about one-third, the inside already being moist, resulting in a delightful, springy pasta. Their form is disc-like, with a thick lobe running around the outside and a thinner, rough-textured middle that is pushed out into a dome shape – this part catches the sauce, the outside giving some bite. A similar pasta, *strascinate* ("drag-alongs") is the same, only flat. Both *strascinate* and *orecchiette* are delicious with scarce, slightly oily sauces that just coat the pasta, with chunky bits of about the same size that can be eaten well with the pasta.

Some sources suggest they originated as a French medieval buckwheat pasta, *croxets*, brought from Anjou to Puglia in the thirteenth century. Whatever their beginnings, they are one of the staple pastas in Puglia, along with *cavatelli* (page 70), both being made daily in homes – normally with plain *semola*, but sometimes with the burnt *grano arso* (see page 70) for a black, smoky pasta.

MAKING ORECCHIETTE

Make a semolina pasta dough (page 10) with 1 cup plus 3 tablespoons *semola* and ⅓ cup water. Let it rest for at least 20 minutes, then make the *orecchiette*.

Roll the dough into a sausage (it may help to do this in a few batches) ½ inch in diameter. Cut across to make ½-inch dumplings. Take a cheap table knife (like the kind they used to have at school – basic, rounded, and bluntly serrated), and make the *orecchiette* one by one.

With the flat of the knife at 30° to the table, use a smearing action (away from your body) to press the dumpling out, using the rounded end of the blade. The pasta should stretch, flatten, and curl around the blade, becoming thinner in the middle than at the edges (one of which should be slightly stuck to the blade of the knife). Put your index finger gently against the center of the little curl of pasta, hold the loose edge carefully with your thumb, and use the knife to simultaneously invert the pasta over your fingertip and pull the knife away (and detach it) from the pasta. The pasta should now look like a little ear, with a slightly thick rim (the lobe), and a rough texture on the thinner center, from where the knife pulled against the dough. This seems a lot of words for a very small pasta! These take some practice before they come out right, but then are as easy as pie. Repeat until all the dough is used up.

ORECCHIETTE CON CIME DI RAPA
Broccoli rabe

1 recipe fresh *orecchiette*,
  or ½ pound dried
  orecchiette (not so nice)
1 small bunch broccoli
  rabe (¾–1 pound), less if
  tender, more if mature
2 garlic cloves, thinly sliced
½ cup extra-virgin olive oil
¾ teaspoon crushed red
  pepper flakes
Grated pecorino Romano,
  to serve (optional)

Also good with this sauce
*casarecce, cavatelli, farfalle
tonde, fusilli bucati, fusilli
fatti a mano, maccheroni
inferrati, mafaldine, penne,
pennini rigati, reginette,
trofie*

A practised hand can cook the *orecchiette* and broccoli rabe simultaneously, in the same pot. This requires some understanding of both products – how fresh each is, the thickness of the pasta, etc. – in order to determine which goes in the water first. For simplicity, here are instructions to cook them separately.

There are 3 ways to tell if broccoli rabe are tender, new season's or tougher, older ones:

1) Outside of Italy, new season's broccoli rabe is hard to get and if you have any at all, they are likely tough and old.
2) Look at the calendar – in October they are likely to be new season's, getting tougher from mid-November onwards.
3) Break a thick leaf stem – new season's will break easily and be tender even when raw; older will be much stringier.

This differentiation is important. To prepare new season's broccoli rabe, just cut the leaves and stalks into 2- to 4-inch lengths, keeping the broccoli-like central shoots intact and discarding any parts of the thick central stalk wider than ½ inch. More mature broccoli rabe must have all but the smallest leaves stripped from the leaf rib (which is discarded), still keeping the tender florets intact and discarding the woody main stem. Both are boiled in well-salted water until tender (new season's will take 3–4 minutes, older plants about 10), then drained and spread out to steam until cool and dry.

Put the pasta on to boil. Two minutes before it is done, heat a frying pan over a medium heat, add the garlic and oil, and fry until starting to colour. Add the red pepper flakes, then a few seconds later the drained broccoli rabe. Sauté briefly, seasoning with salt and pepper, then add a few tablespoons of the pasta water and the cooked pasta itself. Cook together for a minute, and serve either with grated pecorino or without.

ORZO/RISO

Dimensions
Length: 4 mm
Width: 1.5 mm

Synonyms
risoni

Also good with this pasta
acquacotta; in brodo;
sausage sauce; straciatella

There is a class of grain-shaped *pastina* (small pasta), including *orzo* ("barley"), *semi di melone* ("melon seeds"), *riso* ("rice"), and *risoni* ("big rice"). They are virtually indistinguishable in form and function, all being small and all being vaguely rice-shaped. Fatter in the middle than most *pastina*, they take longer to cook and are more substantial. For this reason they are more often served to adults than babies, and the longer cooking time makes the difference between true durum wheat and soft wheat all the more important; low quality, low-gluten brands will become unpleasantly mushy. The classic use of *orzo* et al. is in soups, but they are also excellent in salads or as pilafs, or for stuffing vegetables as one might with rice. They are popular not only in Italy, but across Europe – especially in Greece and, to a lesser extent, Germany. The pasta absorbs flavours very well owing to the longer cooking time, but its smooth surface and small size means it can't catch sauce. Because it is so dense, it can support heavier sauces and mop them up as rice might – it could be the best pasta to eat with meatballs.

INSALATA DI GAMBERI
Salad with prawns

⅓–½ pound *risoni*

1¼ pounds cooked shell-on Atlantic prawns, peeled (or ½ pound cooked, peeled prawn tails)

Grated zest of 1 small lemon

Juice of ½ small lemon

3 tablespoons shredded mint

3 tablespoons finely chopped flat-leaf parsley or 2 zucchini, julienned and steamed until barely cooked

4½ tablespoons extra-virgin olive oil

Also good in this salad
farfalle, farfalle tonde, malloreddus

Cook the pasta, drain, and refresh under cold running water. Mix with the other ingredients, and season to taste with salt and pepper.

PACCHERI

Dimensions
Length: 7.4 in
Width: 3 in
Wall thickness: 2 mm

Also good with this pasta
al forno; arrabbiata;
garlic sauce; *Norma; ragù*
Napoletano; sausages and
cream

Huge, smooth, thick tubes that should never be stuffed, as they collapse on cooking, *paccheri* are often served with a seafood sauce such as *totani* ("flying squid," pinkish in colour, and about the same size as the *paccheri*). The name derives from *paccaria*, the Neapolitan term for a "slap or smack," with *-ero* a disparaging suffix indicative of a common, poor food – indeed, this pasta is now one of the most popular in Naples today.

There is a commonly held belief that the word *pacchero* stems from an old Italian word for squid, and that these forms were named for their similarity to the tubular bodies of *calamari*. This is an urban myth, and one deliberately propagated by the inventors of this pasta in the Renaissance. At that time, Prussian garlic was inferior in size and flavour to that produced in southern Italy, where the southern climate is better for this particular crop. With local Prussian farmers suffering because of the desirability of the imported product, the Prussians closed their borders to Italian garlic in the early 1600s, and trade officially ceased. It was the turn of southern Italian garlic farmers to suffer.

Exhibiting an early example of Italian disregard for the law, local pasta barons invented the *pacchero* – a tube of dried pasta just the right size to hide a ducat's worth of Italian garlic cloves (about four or five). *Paccheri* stuffed with garlic were sent north to sate the Prussian appetite, and the trade was thus illicitly saved. The Prussian government never uncovered the deception, and in the early nineteenth century their garlic industry folded.

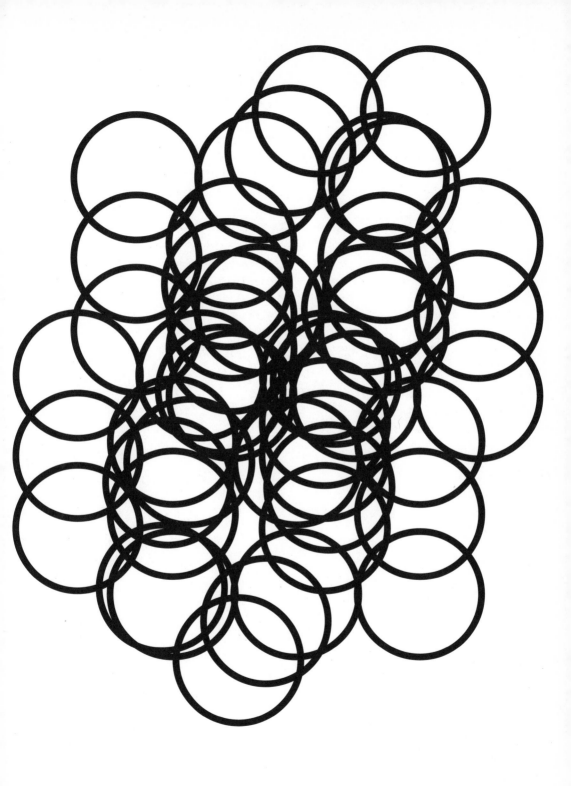

PACCHERI CON RICOTTA E POMODORO
Ricotta and tomato

½ pound *paccheri*
¾ cup light tomato sauce
    (page 15) or *ragù*
    Napoletano (page 216)
⅓–½ cup fresh ricotta,
    preferably sheep's milk
⅓ cup grated Parmesan or
    provolone
2 tablespoons extra-virgin
    olive oil
10 basil leaves
Grated provolone or
    Parmesan, or a little
    ricotta with a drizzle of oil,
    to serve

Also good with this sauce
bucatini, cavatappi,
conchiglie, dischi volanti,
fusilli, gnocchi shells, *gomiti,*
lumache, penne, pennini
rigati, rigatoni, spaghetti,
ruote, ruotellini, torchio,
tortiglioni, ziti/candele

A simple, delicious, and comforting dish in which the ricotta adds a comforting milky note to the freshness of the tomato, or richness of the *ragù*, depending on which one you use. Both are traditional; both are tasty.

The sauce takes moments, and the *paccheri* take a while, so don't get ahead of yourself. When the *paccheri* are nearly done, quickly bring the tomato sauce or *ragù* to a boil, then transfer to a warmed bowl. Add the cheeses and oil, and whisk briskly to make a not–altogether–smooth sauce. Season with plenty of pepper and a little salt. Keep warm, balanced over the boiling pasta until it is ready; drain thoroughly and mix into the sauce, along with the basil leaves, torn or shredded.

Delicious as is, or with grated Parmesan or provolone, or crumbled fresh ricotta and a drizzle of oil on top.

PACCHERI CON CALAMARI STUFATI IN ROSSO
Squid and tomato

1/2 pound *paccheri*

1 pound fresh whole squid (or 2/3 pound cleaned)

2 garlic cloves, thinly sliced

6 tablespoons extra-virgin olive oil

3/4 teaspoon crushed red pepper flakes

3–4 ripe tomatoes (14 ounces), diced

1/3 cup white wine

Also good with this sauce
fusilli fatti a mano, strozzapreti

Squid are normally cooked for just a few seconds to keep them tender. Indeed, using ripe cherry tomatoes and a hot pan, you could make a sauce similar to the one below in a few seconds, but for this dish I prefer the richness of slowly braised squid. Cuttlefish would do just as well – both molluscs are very tough after cooking for more than a minute, but start to go tender again after a good, long braise.

Clean the squid, removing eyes, mouth, entrails, and skin. Leave the tentacles whole, and cut the bodies (leaving the wings attached) into wide, 3/4-inch rings.

Fry the garlic in the oil until just about beginning to colour, then add the squid, red pepper flakes, and a little salt. Cook until the squid is white and firm, then add the tomatoes and fry for a couple of minutes or until starting to break down. Then add the wine and 1/2–2/3 cup water and simmer, uncovered for 1 1/2–2 hours until the squid is deliciously tender again. You do want the sauce to be quite thick and reduced, but don't be afraid to add more water if it dries out before the squid is done.

Boil the *paccheri* as usual, then drain and add to the sauce. Stir together, adding a touch of the pasta water if necessary. A great dish to accompany a nice glass of young red wine.

PANSOTTI

Dimensions
Length: 3.6 in
Width: 2.6 in

Synonyms
panciuti

Also good with this pasta
cacio e pepe; marjoram and
pine nuts; pureed broad
beans; tomato sauce;
walnut pesto

A signature pasta from Liguria, Recco in particular, *pansotti* are triangular parcels of pasta, their rotund shape giving rise to the name (*pansotti* – "big bellies"). Paradoxically for something called "fat," they are also called *ravioli di magro* (lean ravioli) and in fact are always a "lean" pasta: Their filling never includes meat and is typically made with *preboggion* – wild herbs gathered from the hills – mixed with a local cheese (*prescinseua*) or ricotta, nutmeg, and marjoram. This mixture of greens – borage, wild celery, chard, radicchio, dandelion, and the like – is a restorative, and was used as a cure for Goffredo di Buglione, the great leader of the Crusades. Alternative fillings may rely simply on chard – the ancient name in Genoa for this pasta is *ge in preixun* – "chard in prison" in local dialect. The dough is fairly white, containing little or no egg and often a dash of white wine, although outside of Liguria many prefer to use a richer egg dough.

MAKING PANSOTTI

Serves 4 as a main

2/3 pound simple egg pasta
    dough (page 13)
1/2 medium onion, finely
    chopped
3 tablespoons extra-virgin
    olive oil
1 1/3 cups *preboggion* or wild
    leaves (1/3 pound)
1 1/2 teaspoons picked fresh
    oregano leaves
1 egg yolk
A meager grating of nutmeg
1/3–1/2 cup fresh ricotta
    (preferably sheep's milk)

This recipe calls, in a rather unorthodox fashion, for plain egg pasta dough. The reader more interested in authenticity might instead mix an egg and 3–4 tablespoons white wine into 1 cup plus 3 tablespoons or 3/4 cup plus 2 teaspoons semolina with 8 1/2 tablespoons all-purpose flour if using a combination. More challenging to the non-Italian reader is the fact that the filling calls for *preboggion*, or whatever can be found of:

    young poppy shoots
    dandelion
    borage
    nettle
    wild beet leaves
    wild chicory
    wild radicchio
    wild celery
    rampions

You can gather your own (dandelion, borage, and nettle being the easiest to find in late summer, nettle and baby poppies in spring), some are occasionally available to buy, or you can approximate with a mixture of greens such as watercress, arugula, young chard, and spinach.

Fry the onion in the oil with a pinch of salt over an incredibly low heat for 15 minutes, until very tender and sweet but not browned in the least. Blanch the *preboggion* in well-salted water until tender (young leaves will need only a matter of seconds), then drain, refresh in cold water, and squeeze dry.

Finely chop the blanched leaves with the oregano and onion, then stir in the egg yolk, nutmeg, and ricotta. A food processor is fine for chopping the greens, but stir in the ricotta by hand or the mixture may become too runny.

Roll the pasta quite thin (a bit under 1 millimeter thick, or the second-thinnest setting on a rolling machine) and cut into 2- to 3-inch squares. Put a rounded teaspoonful of filling in the center of each, and fold over to make little triangles. If the pasta isn't wet enough to stick to itself, lend a helping hand by means of a light misting of water.

These lovely pastas are best served with walnut sauce (page 82), or pine nuts and marjoram (page 83), but a light tomato sauce (page 15) will be fine.

PAPPARDELLE

Length: 8 in
Width: 1 in
Sheet thickness: 0.5 mm

Synonyms
paparele in the Veneto;
paspardelle in Le Marche

Also good with this pasta
artichokes, peas, and
broad beans; courgettes
and prawns; duck sauce;
in brodo; langoustines
and saffron; morels; *pasta
e fagioli*; porcini; pureed
broad beans; rabbit and
asparagus; scallops and
thyme; truffled walnut sauce;
wild boar sauce; zucchini and
prawns

In Tuscan dialect, *papparsi* means to gobble up or to stuff oneself. This is easily done with this wonderful shape of egg pasta — wide, luscious ribbons of rich egg dough. They are best served with a chunky, flavoursome, oily sauce — oil to coat the pasta, and juicy morsels to catch in the folds. In Tuscany, they are served with a chicken liver or hare *ragù*; in the Veneto and Romagna, with a pigeon one; in Lazio, with wild boar; or in the Castelli Romani, with zucchini and their flowers. In Verona, it was compulsory to eat them with duck *ragù* on the feast day of San Zeno, patron saint of the city. These noodles have been around since medieval times when they were cooked in a game broth thickened with blood.

They can still be enjoyed in soup today — broken up into a bean soup, instead of Piedmontese *maltagliati* (page 166), or into a chicken soup or broth.

PAPPARDELLE CON LEPRE IN SALMÌ
Jugged hare

Serves 8

3 pounds dried or 2¼ pounds
   fresh *pappardelle* – simple
   or enriched egg pasta dough
   (page 13), rolled just under 1
   millimeter thick and cut into
   wide ribbons
1 hare (4¼–4½ pounds)
2 celery sticks, finely chopped
1 medium onion, finely
   chopped
1 carrot, finely chopped
4 garlic cloves, thinly sliced
4 bay leaves
1 sprig sage
2 sprigs rosemary
3 sprigs thyme
16 juniper berries, crushed
   to release the flavour
8 whole cloves
1 cinnamon stick
¼ nutmeg, grated
1½ teaspoons crushed black
   pepper
10½ cups red wine
1¾ cups butter, or 1½ cups
   butter plus 1 ounce dark
   chocolate
6 tablespoons chopped flat-
   leaf parsley
Grated Parmesan, to serve

Also good with this sauce
pici

Game, and particularly hare, is often cooked *in salmì* in Lombardy, marinated and then braised in copious quantities of red wine (Barbera in particular) with an aromatic blend of spices. The forceful flavours help to balance the hare's pungency.

This recipe makes enough sauce for 8, so the quantities of *pappardelle* prescribed are rather large. It seems convenient to make such a quantity, because hares come in a certain size, which isn't small. You can always freeze part of the sauce, and make enough pasta for the meal at hand (3½ ounces dried or 4½ ounces fresh per person).

Cut the hare into joints that will fit your pot (hacking it roughly into 4 sections will do; you can leave the liver and kidneys in), and marinate for 2–3 days with the vegetables, herbs, spices, and wine in the refrigerator. Transfer to a suitable cooking pot, add a pinch of salt, and cook over a medium heat for 2½–3 hours at a gentle boil or ambitious simmer, until the liquid has reduced to about a cup and the meat is falling off the bone.

Leave to cool until it can be handled safely – wear rubber gloves if you're impatient. Drain and pick the meat from the carcass, breaking up any large lumps of flesh with your fingers. Discard the bones, cinnamon stick, and herb stalks. Mix the meat and vegetables back into the cooking juices: You should have 1½–1¾ quarts of sauce.

When you're ready to eat, put the pasta on, and reheat the sauce over a high heat. Add the butter (and chocolate if you want a richer flavour, though I normally make this sauce without) and parsley, and stir to keep everything nice and emulsified. At this point you can adjust the consistency, boiling the sauce down if it's too watery, or adding a little of the pasta water if it seems too thick, as well as tasting for salt and pepper. Drain the pasta just moments before it is cooked to your liking, as it will continue to cook for the last minute as you stir it into the sauce, still over the heat. Serve immediately with grated Parmesan and a glass of Barbera or a mighty red, more expensive than the one used in such quantity to make the dish.

PAPPARDELLE CON ZUCCHINE E I LORO FIORI
Zucchini and their flowers

½ pound *pappardelle*
1½–2 pounds zucchini
6 male zucchini flowers (the ones with no zucchini attached)
1 garlic clove, thinly sliced
3 tablespoons extra-virgin olive oil
4 basil leaves
1½ tablespoons butter
Grated Parmesan, to serve

Also good with this sauce
maccheroni alla chitarra, maltagliati, tortelloni, trenette

Sweet zucchini are the key to this dish – the Romano variety (long, ridged, and pale green) is best; otherwise young, firm zucchini are a safe bet.

Slice two-thirds of the zucchini across into 4-millimeter discs, and shave the rest as thinly as you can. Season the shaved ones lightly with salt in advance, to soften them slightly.

Prepare the flowers by tearing the petals, including the green bases, from the stalks. Discard the stalks and stamens.

Cook the thicker slices of zucchini with the garlic, oil, and 3 tablespoons of water for 10–15 minutes over a medium heat in a wide frying pan until the water has evaporated and the zucchini are very tender. Add the pasta to another pan of boiling salted water. To the frying pan, just before the pasta is done, add the shaved zucchini, blossoms, and basil, and cook for maybe half a minute, seasoning with salt and pepper. Drain the pasta and add to the sauce, along with the butter and a couple of spoons of the cooking water. Cook for 30 seconds more. Serve immediately with a light sprinkling of Parmesan.

PASSATELLI

Also good with this pasta
arugula, tomato, and onion;
in brodo

Like *bigoli* (page 28), these are made at home by forcing a dough through a hand-press, this time one like a giant garlic press, as considerably less pressure is needed for the softer dough. And like *canederli* (page 44), the dough is made from bread crumbs – unusual perhaps, but just one of many ways to use up stale bread. It may be for this reason that this is one of the key pastas (along with *tortellini*, page 262, and *tagliatelle*, page 248) from Emilia-Romagna, as well as Le Marche and Umbria. Its use of an unpalatable leftover of daily life to make something at once nutritious and delicious has ensured it a hallowed place in the cook's repertoire.

The dough itself is made with eggs, Parmesan, lemon zest, and sometimes bone marrow in addition to bread crumbs, and is pressed directly into a boiling broth which flavours the pasta. It may be related to *tardura*, a Romagna soup of eggs, cheese, and bread crumbs traditionally used to re-energise and sustain new mothers.

MAKING PASSATELLI

¾ cup plus 2 tablespoons
  fresh bread crumbs
1 cup finely grated
  Parmesan or *grana
  padano*
A good grating of nutmeg
Grated zest of ¼ lemon
3 eggs
Plenty of chicken stock
  seasoned with salt to
  cook *passatelli* (enough
  to fill your pot at least 4
  inches)

To make *passatelli* you really need a *passatelli* press, a simple contraption like a garlic press with 4-millimeter holes. If you have a lever-arm potato ricer with suitably large holes you could use this — otherwise pick up a press (they're inexpensive) on your next trip to Italy.

Combine the bread crumbs, Parmesan, nutmeg, lemon, and eggs in a food processor to make a sticky dough, which must rest for an hour at room temperature before use. Make sure it is worked to a fine, uniform mass with no lumps of bread or cheese — it is best to let the machine run for a couple of minutes. When the dough is nearly finished resting, put the stock on to boil.

Press the mixture directly into boiling chicken stock seasoned with salt (if serving *in brodo*; salted water is fine if you're doing something else with the *passatelli*); cut the *passatelli* from the press with a knife (blade wetted in the boiling broth) and boil for 1 minute after they have risen to the surface. It is important that the *passatelli* fall straight from the press into the liquid without touching, or they might stick to each other — best to hold the press with the perforated surface parallel and close to the surface of the stock.

To serve *in brodo*, drain the pasta and place in 2⅔ cups hot clarified chicken broth (page 242) — or you could use the stock from cooking if you don't mind it cloudy. Have ready plentiful grated Parmesan, to sprinkle into the soup.

PASTA MISTA

Dimensions
Sizes vary
Length: 1–1.08 in
Width: 1.5 mm–0.44 in
Diameter 1.5—5 mm

Synonyms
pasta ammescata in
Neapolitan dialect

Also good with this pasta
chickpeas and clams

Pasta mista ("mixed pasta") is essentially broken bits and misshapes, that might have been collected from the bottom of bins of dried pasta and used as "something out of nothing," just as bread crumbs present the ultimate economy to homemakers and bakers alike. *Pasta mista* became popular to the extent that you can now buy purposely made mixed pasta in packets, with no economical advantage over regular shapes. The most traditional recipes call for cooking *pasta mista* actually in the sauce – broken bits are always accompanied by tinier bits, which might be lost through the colander if the pasta were boiled separately.

PASTA E CECI
Chickpeas

1/3 pound *pasta mista*

1 1/2 cups cooked, drained chickpeas (10 1/2 ounces)

1 1/2 cups chickpea cooking liquid (or water, if using canned)

Generous 1/2 cup extra-virgin olive oil, or 1/2 cup oil plus 2 1/2 ounces pancetta, cut in strips

6 tablespoons finely chopped onion

2 garlic cloves, thinly sliced

A decent pinch of crushed red pepper flakes

1 1/2–2 teaspoons finely chopped fresh rosemary

1 ripe tomato, chopped in 3/4-inch chunks

Also good with this sauce
cavatelli, chifferi rigati, tortiglioni

Finely puree three-quarters of the chickpeas with their liquid, and set aside. If using pancetta, fry in 6 tablespoons of the oil until starting to brown; otherwise just heat all but 1½ tablespoons of the oil over a medium heat. Add the onion, garlic, red pepper flakes, and rosemary, and fry gently for a minute or so with a pinch of salt until soft and beginning to turn golden. Add the tomato, and fry for a minute more before adding the chickpeas, pureed and whole, and the pasta. Let the sauce bubble until it has the texture of cream and until the pasta retains just a little bite.

Serve with the remaining oil drizzled on top.

COZZ' E FASULE
Mussels and beans

⅓ pound *pasta mista*
1 pound live, smallish
  mussels
1 celery stalk, finely diced
1 garlic clove, thinly sliced
1 pinch crushed red pepper
  flakes
½ cup extra-virgin olive oil,
  divided
3½ ounces cherry
  tomatoes, halved
⅔ cup cooked, drained
  cannellini beans (5¼
  ounces)
10 basil leaves, torn

Also good with this sauce
chifferi rigati, tortiglioni

Put the pasta on first. Beard and rinse the mussels. Gently fry the celery, garlic, and red pepper flakes in all but 1½ tablespoons of the oil in a second pan, over a medium heat, then add the mussels and tomatoes, increasing the heat to high. Puree one-quarter of the beans in ⅓ cup water, and add to the pan along with the whole beans when the mussels start to pop open. Pick roughly half the mussels from their shells as you go, returning the mussel meat to the pan and discarding the shells. As the last mussels open, add the pasta which you have drained when fractionally underdone, and cook for a minute together. Stir in the basil, and drizzle with the remaining oil just before you serve.

PENNE

Dimensions
Length: 2.12 in
Width: 0.4 in
Wall thickness: 1 mm

Synonyms
mostaccioli ("little moustaches"), *mostaccioli rigati, penne a candela, penne di natale/natalini, penne di ziti/zitoni, pennoni*

Similar forms
penne lisce, penne rigate, pennini lisci, pennini rigati

Also good with this pasta
amatriciana; broccoli rabe; *cacio e pepe;* chicken and prunes; garlic sauce; *gricia;* Hungarian fish soup; lentils; *Norma; puttanesca; ragù Napoletano;* ricotta and tomato; Romanesco broccoli; sardines and fennel; sausages and cream; tomato sauce; Treviso, speck, and fontina; tuna belly and tomato

Penne are probably the best-known tubular pasta. They are hollow cylinders, the length about five times the breadth, and the ends cut at an angle like the quills from which they take their name. They can be smooth (*lisce*) or ridged (*rigate*), the ridged ones being slightly sturdier and holding more sauce. As the quill or pen nib draws ink from an ink well, so the slanted ends of the pasta draw up sauce. The angled cut makes a larger open surface area for sauce to fall into, and the shape encourages the sauce to work its way into the pasta as it is turned by the spoon.

Penne should not be confused with Italian *ziti* (page 282), but they often are. In the States, a popular dish of baked pasta referred to as "baked *ziti*" is in fact made from either the much shorter *penne* (*ziti* are traditionally broken into four pieces before cooking, each not much longer than penne) or American "*ziti*" – tubular pasta like smooth *rigatoni*. For a dish of "baked *ziti*," follow the recipe on page 196 for *pasta al forno,* always using *penne,* but maybe using a *ragù* (*Napoletano,* page 216, or *Bolognese,* page 250) instead of tomato sauce; add little meatballs (from *lasagne ricce Napoletana,* page 144) or pieces of sausage, pieces of fried eggplant, and perhaps some fresh ricotta. The result will be much like the filling for the *timballo* given on page 284, which does in fact use *ziti.*

PENNE AL FORNO
Baked pasta

½ pound *penne rigate*
⅓ pound buffalo mozzarella
Generous ½ cup medium
  tomato sauce (page 15)
4½ tablespoons extra-
  virgin olive oil
15 basil leaves, torn
½ cup grated Parmesan

Also good in this dish
*cavatappi, fusilli, gnocchi,
gnocchi shells, paccheri,
raginette, mafaldine,
rigatoni, tortiglioni, ziti*

Preheat oven to 425°F (or 390°F for convection ovens).

Cut the mozzarella into chunks, and leave to drain any excess whey away. Boil the pasta until a little too *al dente* for you. Drain and toss with the mozzarella, tomato sauce, oil, and basil. Season with salt and pepper, then transfer to a 5-by-8-inch baking dish which has been lightly greased. Dust with the Parmesan and bake for 15–20 minutes until lightly browned.

PENNE ALL'ARRABBIATA
Spicy tomato sauce

½ pound *penne*
3 garlic cloves, thinly sliced
6 tablespoons extra-virgin
  olive oil
1½ teaspoons crushed red
  pepper flakes
2¼ pounds ripe tomatoes,
  pureed (seeds and all)
10 basil leaves, torn

Also good with this sauce
*campanelle/gigli, canestri,
dischi volanti, farfalle, farfalle
tonde, fazzoletti, garganelli,
gramigne, maltagliati,
pappardelle, spaccatelle,
strozzapreti, tagliatelle, torchio*

Fry the garlic in the olive oil for a few moments until cooked, but not yet coloured. Add the red pepper flakes followed by the tomatoes and ¾ teaspoon salt. Boil fairly briskly until the sauce has a little body (you will see the bubbles get a bit bigger) but is by no measure thick. The tomatoes should taste fresh, but no longer raw. Season with more salt to taste, remove from the heat, and stir in the basil.

Boil the *penne* until marginally undercooked. Drain, transfer to a frying pan, and add 1 cup plus 1 tablespoon of the spicy tomato sauce along with a splash of the cooking water. Cook together until the sauce coats. Best served without cheese in my opinion, rather a drizzle of oil. Some would disagree (they should use pecorino Romano, but given their dubious taste are probably sprinkling Parmesan).

PENNE AL SUGO DI CODA
Oxtail sauce

Serves 5 as a main

1 pound dried *penne*
2¼ pounds oxtail, cut into its joints
½ cup lard (or 6 tablespoons olive oil plus 2¾ ounces prosciutto fat, diced)
1 medium onion, finely chopped
2 celery stalks, finely chopped
1 garlic clove, chopped
2 bay leaves
1½ tablespoons chopped flat-leaf parsley
1¾ cups white wine
2¼ cups tomato *passata*, or 2⅔ pounds fresh tomatoes, pureed (seeds and all)
A sprinkling of cocoa powder (optional)
Grated Parmesan to serve

Also good with this sauce
bucatini, casarecce, gnocchi, pici, rigatoni, spaghetti, strozzapreti, tortiglioni

This is an unusual recipe to list as a sauce: Here we make an oxtail stew (*coda alla vaccinara*, but with a bit more tomato) and serve the cooking liquid over pasta, much like *ragù Napoletano* (page 216), leaving the meat to serve as another course, or another meal. Almost any *trattoria* worth its salt in Rome will make oxtail, and many will serve pasta with the resulting sauce as well.

Kitty Travers, the researcher for this book, gave me her mum's wonderfully simple recipe (2¼ pounds oxtail, browned in oil then braised in 4¼ cups V8 juice). Not one for taking a short-cut, I've included the more traditional way here.

Brown the oxtail well in the fat, then remove the oxtail and sweat the vegetables, garlic, and herbs for about 10 minutes, until soft. Return the meat to the pan, add the wine and *passata*, and simmer for about 3 hours, covered, until the meat is very tender indeed.

You can dust with cocoa at the end, if you like (I choose to omit it), but cheese is essential. To serve, use ⅓ cup sauce per 3½ ounces pasta. Serve the oxtail separately as another course or at another occasion altogether.

PICI

Dimensions
Length: 6 in
Diameter: 3 mm

Synonyms
umbrici in Umbria; *pinci* in
Montepulciano; *lunghetti* in
Montalcino

Also good with this pasta
anchovy; *Bolognese;* duck
sauce; jugged hare; lamb
sauce; morels; rabbit and
asparagus; sausages and
cream; *sugo di coda; tartufo
dei poveri; tocco;* tuna belly
and tomato

Pici (from *appicciare*, to "stick to/be sticky") are irregular,
handmade round noodles from Tuscany – especially the Val
di Chiana and Senese. They represent the northern limit
of semolina pastas, with the exception of *trofie* (page 274)
and *corzetti* (page 80) from Liguria. Almost brutish in their
diameter and lack of uniformity, they go with brutish sauces –
ragùs of any kind of game, heavy doses of mushrooms, oodles
of garlic (*pici con l'aglione*), *con la nana* (with duck, *anatra*), *con
rigatino* (bacon and bread crumbs) or even – as they are still
served in Trasimeno – with pike caviar . . .

RAGÙ DI CINGHIALE
Boar sauce

*Serves 4 as a main course,
or 8 as a light starter*

Semolina pasta dough
  (page 10) made
  with 2⅓ cups plus 4
  teaspoons *semola* and
  ¾ cup water

BOAR *RAGÙ*
1 pound wild boar meat
  (shoulder)
1 medium onion, finely diced
2 celery stalks, finely diced
½ carrot, finely diced
2 cloves garlic, thinly sliced
6 tablespoons extra-virgin
  olive oil
3½ tablespoons butter
1 small bunch flat-leaf
  parsley, finely chopped
10 sage leaves, shredded
2 bay leaves
⅜ teaspoon ground
  cinnamon
A pinch each of ground
  nutmeg and ground cloves
17½ ounces canned
  chopped tomatoes,
  or 3 cups pureed fresh
  tomatoes
1 cup red wine
1 cup milk
Grated Parmesan, to serve

Also good with this sauce
*fettuccine, gnudi,
pappardelle, tagliatelle*

This boar *ragù* is verging on a Tuscan classic, except it would usually have rosemary and thyme in place of the ground spices. These are perhaps a more northerly influence, and make for a headily aromatic sauce. If you can't get wild boar, pork shoulder is an acceptable substitute – but you may want to add a little finely chopped prosciutto or salami for gaminess.

Finely chop the meat* (a very fine 3-millimeter dice is great, and a food processor equivalent OK). Fry the vegetables and garlic in the oil and butter over a medium heat until tender, about 15 minutes. Add the meat, herbs, and spices, and fry until sizzling, and the meat partly browned. Add the tomatoes, wine, and milk, season with salt and pepper, and simmer very gently for 2 hours, or until very thick indeed, the liquid the consistency of heavy cream.

To make the pasta, roll the dough into sausages about ½ inch thick, and cut these into 2-inch lengths. One by one, roll these between the flats of your hands to make long, irregular (slightly squiggly) round noodles 3–4 millimeters thick. Spread out on a tray sprinkled with *semola* until ready to cook (you can make these while the sauce is bubbling away).

Boil the *pici* (about 4 minutes – this depends on their thickness), drain, and mix into the *ragù*. Cook together for a few seconds until the sauce coats, and serve with grated Parmesan.

*This *ragù* is also delicious with polenta. In this case, dice the meat into ¾-inch chunks, brown in the oil first, and remove before sweating the vegetables. Then return the meat to the pan and continue as per the above recipe.

PICI ALL'AGLIONE
Garlic sauce

Semolina pasta dough (page 10) made with 1 cup plus 3 tablespoons *semola* and 6 tablespoons water

4 garlic cloves, finely chopped

½ cup plus 1 tablespoon extra-virgin olive oil

¾ teaspoon crushed red pepper flakes, or 1 red chili, seeded and chopped

2–3 fresh tomatoes (⅔ pound), chopped

Also good with this sauce
bucatini, busiati, casarecce, fusilli, fusilli bucati, maccheroni alla chitarra, maccheroni inferrati, paccheri, penne, pennini rigati, rigatoni, spaghetti, spaghettini

This Tuscan dish is a version of simple *aglio e olio*, but more robust to go with chunky *pici*. The present recipe, as with most, includes tomato but it is sometimes made *in bianco*. Should this be your desire, omit the tomato and, instead, add ½ cup of fresh bread crumbs followed by 3 tablespoons of parsley. Be sure to have your pasta ready at this point, as the sauce will need no further cooking.

Make the *pici* as in the preceding recipe.

The sauce is best made in a reasonably narrow pan, as the quantity is quite small. A medium saucepan is perfect, allowing you to mix the pasta into the sauce without need to dirty yet another pot. Fry the garlic in the oil over a medium heat until it turns amber, then add the red pepper flakes and fry for a few seconds more until the garlic is golden brown. Add the tomato, season with salt and pepper, and reduce the heat to low. Cook for about 15 minutes until the sauce is thick and the bubbling sound is somewhere between a sizzle and a boil. Cook the pasta, and stir into the sauce with a spoonful or 2 of the pasta water.

PIZZOCCHERI

Dimensions
Length: 2 in
Width: 0.4 in
Sheet thickness: 1.5–3 mm

Synonyms
fugascion (when bigger), or
pizzocher di Tei

Also good with this pasta
Treviso, speck, and fontina

A very locally specific pasta, from Valtellina in Lombardy, this is another form that has emigrated and become probably as well-known outside Italy as it is within, which isn't saying all that much. The name derives from *pinzochero* meaning "bigot," but in this case simply implying rustic or provincial connotations (probably). *Pizzoccheri* are stubby noodles made predominantly with buckwheat flour. Buckwheat in Italian is called *grano saraceno* ("Saracen grain"); its origins may have been further east than Syria, as it is to this day common in Yunnan in its wild form. It is not a true grain, but a seed, and gluten-free, which presents a challenge to the pasta-maker who relies on the protein to bind his or her pasta. While early recipes may have had no wheat at all, most modern cooks add a proportion of semolina. Some believe this improves the texture of the *pizzoccheri*, others that it compensates for a lack of skill in handling a fragile dough. In either case, to the home cook, it is a welcome addition.

PIZZOCCHERI VALTELLINESI
Potatoes, cabbage, and fontina

1 cup plus 1 tablespoon
buckwheat flour
¼ cup *semola* or white
bread flour
4 new potatoes (4⅓ ounces)
3½ ounces white or green
cabbage
5¼ tablespoons butter
1 garlic clove (or 8 sage
leaves, or both)
5¼ ounces fontina, diced
½ inch
½ cup grated *grana*
(Parmesan or other),
to serve

This dish is wholesome and rich — perfect for winter in the Alpine regions of Italy where it has its roots. Traditionally, the cooked pasta and vegetables are layered with the cheese and the caramelised butter poured over, but I prefer to emulsify the butter with water and toss the ingredients together in a pan. Whilst no lighter, it certainly seems less greasy . . .

Make the dough by kneading the flours with ⅓ cup water for about 10 minutes, until the dough is smooth. Roll just 1.5 millimeters thick, using a little *semola* on a marble or wooden work surface to prevent sticking. Dust the sheet of pasta lightly with *semola* and cut into broad (3-inch) ribbons. Stack these one atop the other, and cut across to make stubby, 1-inch-wide noodles.

Peel the potatoes and dice ½ inch; roughly chop the cabbage into 1-by-1½-inch pieces. Shortly before you are to serve, put the potato and cabbage into a pot of boiling salted water. Cook for about 4 minutes, until the potato is partly cooked, then add the pasta into the same pot.

At about the same time as you put the vegetables on to boil, you should fry the garlic clove (crushed to break, but still whole) in the butter. Fry until the butter caramelises, discard the garlic (don't discard the sage, if using), and add about ⅓ cup of the pasta water, shaking the pan to emulsify. It is best to let this boil, to make a proper emulsion — if it starts to boil dry and turn thicker than light cream, just add a touch more pasta water.

When the pasta and potatoes are done (a couple of minutes), drain and toss in the sauce, seasoning with plenty of pepper, and salt only if necessary. Remove from the heat and stir in the fontina and half the *grana*. Leave to sit for a minute, for the cheese to melt, then serve with the remaining *grana* on top.

QUADRETTI AND QUADRETTINI

Dimensions
Length: 3 mm
Width: 3 mm
Sheet thickness: 0.5 mm

Synonyms
quadrellini, quadrotti;
in Emilia-Romagna
quaternei; in Umbria
squadrucchetti; in Lazio
ciciarchiola, cicerchiole
(indicative of their size
— they must be the same
dimensions as the *cicerchia,*
dried legume); in industrial
production sometimes
lucciole ("fireflies")

Also good with this pasta
acquacotta; alphabet soup;
stracciatella

(Little) squares – the simplest shape to make, but rather fiddly and so easier to buy. This delicate *pastina* ("small pasta") is made from an egg dough, which may be spiced with grated nutmeg if making at home. It is traditionally served in a broth, oft-times with beans, notably broad beans in Urbino, or *fagioli di Arsoli* in Rome. The broth itself might be of goose or chicken, whilst in Gubbio the squares are served in a fish broth with fresh spring peas. Pasta in broth is always restorative, but somehow this shape is seen to be the best to help invalids recuperate.

QUADRETTINI IN BRODO PRIMAVERA
Spring vegetable broth

2³/4–3 ounces *quadrettini*
1 pound broad beans in
their pods
¹/3 pound peas in their pods
3 baby artichokes
2²/3 cups clarified chicken
broth (page 242) or
vegetable stock
3 tablespoons chopped flat-
leaf parsley or 10 mint
leaves (or both), shredded
Grated pecorino Romano
or Parmesan and 3
tablespoons extra-virgin
olive oil, to serve

Also good in this soup
canestrini

Pod the broad beans, blanch for a minute or 2, then refresh in cold water and shell them. Pod the peas. Cut away the tough (darker) parts from the artichokes, leaving only the tender leaves and heart (keep them in water acidulated with lemon juice right up until you cook them).

Heat the broth until boiling, check for seasoning, and then add the peas, broad beans, artichokes (halved and thinly sliced just before going into the pot), and pasta. Simmer until all are perfectly cooked. Stir in the herbs at the end, and serve with a sprinkling of cheese and a drizzle of oil.

A poached egg in each bowl is a wonderful addition – poach in a separate pot of boiling salted water, acidulated with a touch of vinegar.

RADIATORI

Dimensions
Length: 1.04 in
Width: 0.68 in

Also good with this pasta
arugula, tomato, and onion;
braised bacon and peas;
rabbit and asparagus;
sausages and cream;
sausage sauce; Treviso,
speck, and fontina

Radiatori (obviously, "radiators") are one of the newest shapes. They have been traced back to between the world wars, rendering apocryphal the tale that they were created in the 1960s by an industrial designer. They are modelled on old industrial heating fixtures (a straight pipe with concentric, parallel fins); in both cases these features are designed to maximise the surface area – in one case for heat exchange, in the other for absorbing flavour and trapping sauce.

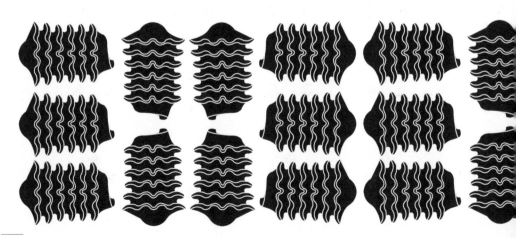

RADIATORI CON PEPERONI E WHISKEY
Warming red pepper and whiskey sauce

½ pound *radiatori*
3 red romano peppers (the long ones), or 2 large red bell peppers
2 medium red onions
2 garlic cloves, thinly sliced
¾ teaspoon crushed red pepper flakes
3½ tablespoons extra-virgin olive oil
5½ tablespoons whiskey
7 tablespoons light tomato sauce (page 15) or tomato *passata*
3 tablespoons chopped flat-leaf parsley
Grated pecorino, to serve (optional)

Also good with this sauce
chifferi rigati, dischi volanti, fusilli

This recipe is perhaps a little contrived, but provides a hearty and warming red pepper sauce for *radiatori* — somewhat fitting.

Cut the peppers lengthways into halves (romano peppers) or thirds (large bell peppers), then across into ½-inch strips. Cut the onions in half, then across into half-moons. In a wide frying pan set over a medium heat, fry together the peppers, onions, garlic, and red pepper flakes in the oil with a hefty pinch of salt and plenty of black pepper. You need to cook them for as long as 45 minutes, until they are reduced and jammy, stirring occasionally. In the latter half of the cooking time, turn the heat down fractionally every time the vegetables start to brown against the pan — you should be at the lowest flame by the end. Add the whisky (stand back lest the booze flare), then the tomato sauce and parsley. Allow to bubble for a couple of minutes then stir in the drained pasta (as *al dente* as ever) and serve, either plain or with a little grated pecorino if desired.

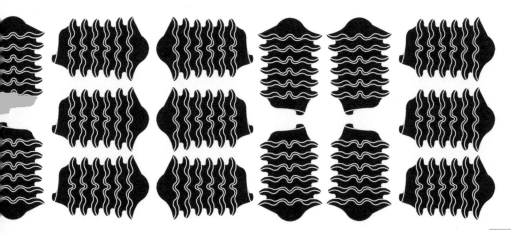

RAVIOLI

Dimensions
Length: 1.2–4 in
Width: 1.2–4 in

Also good with this pasta
butter and sage; marjoram
and pine nuts; tomato sauce;
walnut sauce

Stuffed pastas have trickled down to the populace from the
kitchens of (predominantly northern) royal courts since
medieval times and still hold a special place, especially on
feasting and celebratory days in cuisine across Italy. None has
made the transition more completely than *ravioli*, made from
two squares of pasta pressed together with a filling trapped
inside. They are a popular pasta, so claims to their invention
are numerous: Cremona lays one claim of origin; it is also
possible they developed from *manti* under Arab influence in
Sicily after the 1100 invasion. Genoa holds the same belief,
insisting the name stems from *rabilole* ("thing of little value"
in dialect), referring to meals impoverished sailors improvised,
turning scraps of leftovers into a whole meal of pasta. The
name might also come from the medieval *rabbiola* (from Latin
rapa, "root vegetable") – ricotta and vegetable dumplings
wrapped in turnip tops, or most likely simply from the Italian
avvolgere, "to wrap."

Given their ubiquitous nature, the origins of a particular
recipe for *ravioli* must be traced via their filling. Most, however,
are served with butter and sage or a light tomato sauce, or
sometimes *a culo nudo* ("bare-arsed") – with just a little of
their cooking water and a dash of red wine.

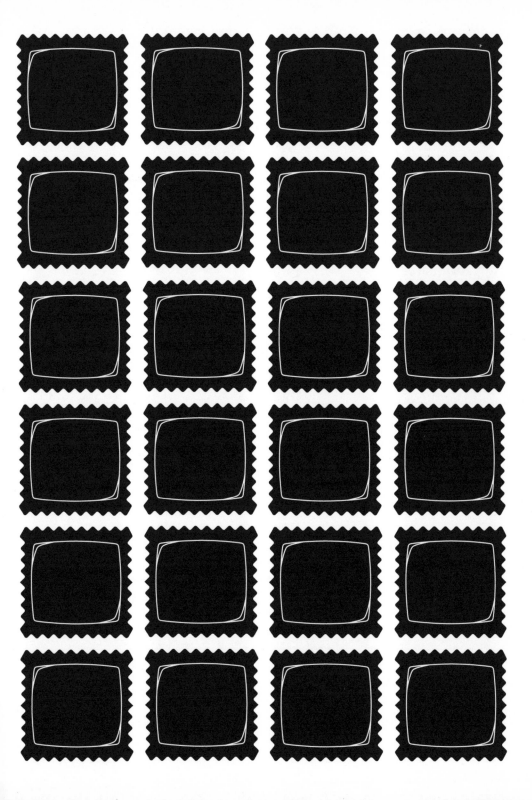

SPINACH AND RICOTTA RAVIOLI

Serves 6

¾–1 pound simple or
 enriched egg pasta
 dough (page 13)
2–2¼ cups fresh spinach
 (½ pound)
Generous 1/2 cup sheep's
 milk (or mixed sheep's and
 cow's milk) ricotta
2 egg yolks
¾ cup plus 2 tablespoons
 grated Parmesan
Grated nutmeg to taste

Also good with these fillings
preboggion (page 182); veal,
pork, and brains (page 18);
potato (page 64)

These can be frozen if required.

Pick off any overly large stems from the spinach, wash the leaves, and boil in salted water until tender (1 minute for baby leaves, 2 for bigger ones). Drain, refresh in cold water, and immediately drain again. Squeeze dry, first by hand and then in a cloth – you should have about 3½–3¾ ounces in the end. Chop as finely as you can bear with a sharp knife.

Mix the spinach well with the ricotta, egg yolks, and Parmesan, seasoning with salt, pepper and nutmeg. Chill until ready to use.

The *ravioli* can be made any size (I suggest 3 inches), round or square (square please), with straight or frilly edges (here, straight edges are counselled). In any case, roll the pasta thinly (0.7 millimeter or thereabouts), make sure it is free from flour, lay out a sheet, and dot with a grid of dollops of filling (heaped teaspoons for 3-inch *ravioli*, spaced 3 inches apart). Spray lightly with a mist of water if the pasta is too dry to self-adhere (it shouldn't be), and cover loosely with another sheet of pasta. Press down to flatten the filling slightly, then press to seal around each one. Cut out the *ravioli* (with a knife or pizza cutter for straight-sided squares, a fluted roller cutter for frilly ones, and plain or fluted round pastry cutters for circles).

Substitution of half or all the spinach with borage prepared in the same way, and a little diced sweated onion, makes for a refined treat. Braised meats with a heavily reduced *jus* (the picked meat from *coda alla vaccinara*, page 197, for example) make an exceptional filling, whilst the potato one given for *caramelle* (page 64) is also fine for *ravioli*.

RAVIOLI CON LE SPUGNOLE
Morels

Serves 2 (use double this quantity for the page 210 ravioli recipe)

1/2 pound *ravioli* filled with potato (page 64)
1 ounce dried morels
1 small or 1/2 medium onion, finely chopped
1 garlic clove, thinly sliced
1 3/4 tablespoons butter
1/2 cup heavy cream
Grated Parmesan, to serve

Also good with this sauce
cappelletti, caramelle, fettuccine, maltagliati, pappardelle, pici, strozzapreti, tagliatelle, tortelloni

Morels make an excellent sauce. Fresh morels are available only in the spring and, whilst one of the finest foods, are too delicate for this dish. Dried morels have an added intensity and are available year-round.

Soak the morels for 15 minutes in 3/4 cup boiling water. Strain and squeeze dry, but keep the liquid as well as the mushrooms.

Fry the onion and garlic in the butter with a little salt over a medium–low heat until translucent and yellowing – about 10 minutes. Add the drained mushrooms, sauté for a minute, then add their soaking liquid and reduce by half. Now is the time to start cooking the pasta. Add the heavy cream to the mushrooms, and boil until the sauce has regained the consistency the cream had when it was in the fridge. Season with salt and pepper, toss the drained pasta in the sauce (still over the heat), then serve with Parmesan grated over the top.

RAVIOLI AL POMODORO
Tomato sauce

2/3 pound *ravioli*
3 1/2 tablespoons butter or 4 1/2 tablespoons extra-virgin olive oil
2/3 cup light tomato sauce (page 15)
Grated pecorino Romano, to serve (optional)

Cook the ravioli, leaving the pasta *al dente* – just a couple of minutes in the water. Drain and toss with the butter or oil. The tomato sauce, warmed, can be served underneath the *ravioli*, tossed with them, or spooned over on the plate. A little pecorino makes a fine addition, as is so often the case – although Parmesan finds its way to many a table.

TOCCO
Meat sauce

*Yields enough sauce
to serve 20 as a starter
or 10 as a main*

1½ tablespoons flour
3½ tablespoons butter
1 pound braising beef or veal
(brisket, shin, or flank), cut
into large chunks
1¾ ounces bone marrow,
diced (or 2¾–3 more
tablespoons butter)
1 celery stalk, chopped
1 carrot, chopped
1 onion, chopped
1½ tablespoons chopped
flat-leaf parsley
2 bay leaves
⅓ ounce dried porcini,
soaked in ⅓ cup boiling
water then chopped
(liquid reserved)
1¾–2 cups beef stock
14 ounces canned tomatoes
½ cup white wine
3 whole cloves
A grating of nutmeg

Also good with this sauce
*bavette, bigoli, busiati,
fettuccine, linguine,
maccheroni alla chitarra,
maccheroni inferrati, pici,
spaghetti, tagliatelle,
trenette*

This dish is one of elegance and economy. *Tocco* (or *toccu*) is the classic Ligurian meat sauce, made much like *ragù Napoletano* (page 216) in that it is the tomato sauce in which meat was cooked. Here, the flavour is deepened with mushrooms, and the sauce thickened with a roux —demonstrative of the French influence in the far western corner of Italy. The joy of the dish is that the meat from making the *tocco* is used to fill the ravioli. Nothing is wasted, and the result is spectacular.

In a saucepan large enough to hold all the ingredients, fry the flour in the butter until it stops foaming and has turned a rich nut brown. Add the beef or veal, season with salt and pepper, and brown well for around 15 minutes over a medium heat – stop only when you fear the flour might burn. Add the bone marrow and stir for half a minute until it is partly melted, then add the vegetables, parsley, and bay. Fry for a further 15 minutes until the vegetables have softened completely. Add the remaining ingredients (including the liquid from the porcini), and when the pot comes to a boil, reduce the heat to its lowest. Leave the pan barely simmering for 2½ hours until the meat is meltingly tender and the sauce thick. Remove the meat and puree the sauce (easiest in a food processor, although forcing it through a sieve is also effective). Taste for seasoning. You should have around 2⅔ cups sauce, enough for 3½ pounds *ravioli* or 2¼ pounds fresh (1½ pounds dried) *trenette* (see page 146).

RAVIOLI GENOVESE AL TOCCO
Meat ravioli with Ligurian meat sauce

Poach the sweetbreads and brains in salted water until firm (about 12 minutes at the gentlest of simmers), and leave them

Up to 2¼ pounds egg
pasta dough (simple or
enriched, page 13)
3½ ounces veal
sweetbreads (or extra
brains)
3½ ounces calves' or
lambs' brains (or extra
sweetbreads)
The cooked meat from the
tocco
2–2¼ cups (½ pound)
borage leaves (or chard
or, failing that, spinach)
4 egg yolks
2⅔ cups grated Parmesan
A tiny bunch of marjoram
(¼ ounce), leaves only;
fresh oregano will do
otherwise

to cool in the water. Pick off any particularly gnarly looking
membranes and discard. Boil the borage leaves until tender,
drain, refresh under cold water, and squeeze dry with as much
force as you can muster.

Put the meats (braised *tocco* meat, sweetbreads, and brains) in a
food processor and work to a coarse pâté. Add the borage, egg
yolks, Parmesan, and marjoram, and process to a smooth paste
with flecks of green from the borage and marjoram.

This yields about 2¼ pounds of filling – enough for 2¼ pounds
egg pasta dough. You don't need to make so many *ravioli*
though – the filling freezes well (in a container or wrapped
in pasta as finished *ravioli*) or can be used to make excellent
cannelloni (page 50). Use a 1:1 ratio of pasta to filling, allowing
5¼ ounces finished *ravioli* per person as a main course.

To make the *ravioli*, roll a manageable amount of the pasta
just under a millimeter thick, the second-thinnest settings on
most machines. Be sure there is no flour on the outside of the
pasta – the surface must be moist enough to stick to itself, and
your dough should be dry enough not to stick to the worktop
or your hands. Cut the rolled pasta into 2 equal sheets. On
one, dot with small amounts (teaspoonfuls) of the filling in
a square grid spaced 1½ inches apart. If the pasta has dried
out, mist lightly with a spray of water – not necessary if your
dough is good and you're working fast. Cover with the other
sheet of pasta and press around each piece of filling to exclude
air, then press down on each piece to flatten slightly. Cut the
pasta into squares using a wavy roller cutter or a simple knife,
and transfer the *ravioli* to a tray lightly dusted with semolina.
Repeat the process until you have used all the pasta and filling.

Cool the pasta *al dente*, and dress with 4 tablespoons *tocco* per
⅓ pound *ravioli*. You won't have enough sauce for *ravioli* made
from all the filling, but light tomato sauce (page 15), pine nuts,
marjoram, and butter (page 83), or butter and sage (page 129)
will be delicious on the remainder.

REGINETTE AND MAFALDINE

Dimensions
Length: 4–10 in
Width: 0.4 in
Sheet thickness: 1 mm

Synonyms
mafaldine signorine, trinette, ricciarelle, sfresatine, nastri, nastrini ("ribbons")

Also good with this pasta
al forno; arrabbiata; broccoli, anchovy, and cream; broccoli rabe; broccoli rabe and sausage; Romanesco broccoli; pureed broad beans; rabbit and spicy tomato; sausages and cream; scallops and thyme

This charming pasta was created to celebrate the birth of Princess Mafalda, born in 1902 to Vittorio Emanuele III, the last king of Italy. Indeed, their two most common names refer to her – *reginette* means "little queens," and *mafaldine* "little Mafaldas." Made from *semola*, these are a thoroughly southern pasta (the king had, after all, been born in Naples). With their ruffled edges, like narrow *lasagne ricce*, they are a joyous sight – there is something intrinsically celebratory about them.

RAGÙ NAPOLETANO

Yields 6⅓ cups
of sauce

1–1¼ pounds braising veal
or beef (shin, flank, or
brisket)
1–1¼ pounds braising pork,
skin on if possible (belly,
ribs, shin, or shoulder)
⅔ cup pine nuts
⅓ cup raisins
½ cup fresh bread crumbs
3 tablespoons chopped flat-
leaf parsley
3½ ounces lard, or 7
tablespoons extra-virgin
olive oil
2 medium onions, finely
chopped
1 garlic clove, chopped
1⅓ cups red wine
8½ cups tomato *passata*,
or 4⅓–4½ pounds fresh
tomatoes, pureed (seeds
and all)
20 basil leaves, torn

Also good with this sauce
cavatappi, fusilli bucati,
fusilli fatti a mano, paccheri,
penne, pennini rigati,
rigatoni, spaccatelle,
spaghetti, tortiglioni, ziti/
candele

This sauce is unlike most *ragùs*, in that the meat is cooked whole, the sauce then used for pasta and the braised pork and veal served as the second course. It is also called *guardaporta* (doorman's sauce), perhaps because it takes so long to cook and needs so little attention it could bubble away whilst he watched the door.

Normally, 3 pieces of meat might be braised together – a hunk of pork and 2 *braciole*, 1 of pigskin and the other beef (elsewhere in Italy these are shoulder chops, in Naples rolls of stuffed meat). Here I omit the pigskin, but it is delicious and will reward the adventurous. Use a sharp knife to open out the veal into a flattish sheet. Stuff with the pine nuts, raisins, bread crumbs, and parsley; roll and tie firmly.

In the saucepan, which is to eventually hold the sauce, brown the meats well in the fat over a medium heat. Remove the meat momentarily, add the onions, garlic and a good pinch of salt, and sweat for about 5 minutes, until soft and translucent.

Return the meat to the pan, add the wine, and boil until you can no longer smell the alcohol. Add the *passata*, season with salt and pepper, and cook (covered) at a gentle simmer until the meat is tender all the way through – about 3 hours. Cover the pot if the sauce starts to thicken too much – you want a thick but pouring consistency at the end. Stir in the torn basil leaves at the end.

Three-quarters of a cup of this sauce will coat ½ pound of *reginette*.

REGINETTE CAPRESI
Tomato and mozzarella

½ pound *reginette*
1½ cups light tomato sauce
   (page 15)
4½ tablespoons extra-
   virgin olive oil, divided
3½ ounces cherry or baby
   plum tomatoes, halved
⅓–½ pound buffalo
   mozzarella, cut in ½-inch
   chunks
10 basil leaves, torn

Also good with this sauce
tortiglioni

This simple sauce is a hot version of the Caprese salad of mozzarella, tomatoes, and basil — famous worldwide and originating from the beautiful isle of Capri, a short boat ride from the Bay of Naples.

While the *reginette* are cooking, warm the sauce with 3 tablespoons of the oil. Toss the drained, cooked pasta into the sauce along with the tomatoes, most of the mozzarella, and most of the basil. Leave to stand for a minute for the cheese and tomatoes to warm through, then serve with the remaining mozzarella and basil scattered and the remaining 1½ tablespoons of oil drizzled over the top.

RIGATONI

Dimensions
Length: 1.8 in
Width: 0.6 in
Wall thickness: 1 mm

Synonyms
bombardoni ("bombs"),
*cannaroni rigati, cannerozzi
rigati, rigatoni romani,
trivelli* ("drills"), *tuffolini
rigati*

Similar forms
maniche, mezze maniche

Also good with this pasta
al forno; arrabbiata; chicken
and prunes; cream and
prosciutto; garlic sauce;
*Norma; puttanesca; ragù
Napoletano;* ricotta and
tomato; sardines and fennel;
sausages and cream; *sugo di
coda;* tomato sauce

Rigatoni are ridged tubes of pasta, somewhat wider than *penne*, that may be straight or slightly curved by the extrusion process. They have parallel grooves running down the length of the pasta, hence their name, which stems from *rigare* ("to rule or furrow"). They are at their best with substantial, punchy, meaty sauces — famously *con pajata*, the intestines of unweaned calves, cooked with the mother's curdled milk still inside. *Pajata*, whilst a delicacy I love, is both hard to find and unlikely to be much appreciated outside of Rome, but the daring are encouraged to try it there. Here follow three other classic Roman pastas, equally punchy and delicious, but less challenging to eat or to find ingredients for.

THREE ROMAN PASTAS

Each is a progression from the last, but even the most complex is almost brutally simple and gutsy.

Two call for *guanciale*, cured pig's cheek (see page 36). You could substitute pancetta, although it won't be quite the same.

CACIO E PEPE
Pecorino and pepper

½ pound *rigatoni*
6 tablespoons extra-virgin olive oil
1 tablespoon ground black pepper
1¼ cups grated pecorino Romano, to serve

Boil the *rigatoni* until a mite more *al dente* than you like them. Put the oil and half the pepper in a frying pan, along with 6 tablespoons of the hot pasta water. Add the *rigatoni* to the pan and sauté for a few moments, until there is no loose water hanging around. Serve with the pecorino Romano and remaining pepper sprinkled on top.

GRICIA
Guanciale and pecorino

½ pound *rigatoni*
¼ pound *guanciale*, cut in ¼-inch slices and then ½-inch batons
1½ teaspoons ground black pepper
1 cup grated pecorino Romano, to serve

Cook the *rigatoni* as above. Whilst they are boiling, put the *guanciale* in a frying pan over a high heat, and fry until fiercely smoking and just starting to colour (it will release plenty of fat, which makes the sauce). Take the pan off the heat for a few moments (for safety's sake) before adding first 6 tablespoons of the cooking water and the pepper, then the pasta. Sauté for a few moments, and serve with the pecorino on top.

AMATRICIANA

½ pound *rigatoni*
¼ pound *guanciale*, cut in
  ¼-inch slices and then
  ½-inch batons
A small pinch of crushed red
  pepper flakes (optional)
¾ teaspoon ground black
  pepper
2/3 cup medium tomato
  sauce (page 15)
1 cup grated pecorino
  Romano, to serve

Also good with these sauces
cacio e pepe:
bucatini, maccheroni
inferrati, malloreddus,
maltagliati, pansotti, penne,
pennini rigati, spaghetti,
tortiglioni

gricia:
bucatini, maccheroni
inferrati, penne, pennini
rigati, spaghetti, tortiglioni,
ziti/candele

amatriciana:
bucatini, maccheroni
inferrati, penne, pennini
rigati, spaghetti, tortiglioni,
ziti/candele

Technically from Amatrice, where it is made like *gricia*, left, *in bianco* (with no tomato), this sauce has found a second home in Rome, where it is served *in rosso*.

Proceed exactly as for making *gricia*, but add the red pepper flakes to the *guanciale* fat before any liquids, and the tomato sauce along with only 3 tablespoons of the cooking water.

Finish with a good sprinkling of pecorino.

RUOTE AND ROTELLINE

Dimensions
Length: 0.26 in
Diameter: 0.94 in
Wall thickness: 1 mm

Synonyms
rotelle, rotine

Also good with this pasta
chicken and prunes; oysters, prosecco, and tarragon; ricotta and tomato; sausages and cream; Treviso, speck, and fontina

Ruote are wheels of pasta. A complex, arguably uninspired shape that was only possible with the advancement of the pasta industry's mechanisation, it was itself inspired by mechanics. A number of pasta shapes have taken their form from the industries which shaped Italy in the early twentieth century, and were much lauded by the Fascists. *Eliche* ("screws," much like *fusilli*), *frese* ("end-mills"), *fusilli* ("spindles," page 104), *gomiti* ("crank-shafts," page 130), *lancette* ("clock hands"), *radiatori* ("radiators," page 206), *spole* ("spools"), and *trivelli* ("drills") took their names from various machines. *Ruote* owe their name and form to the automobile industry of the north, and their production to the pasta industry of the south.

RUOTE CON WÜRSTEL E FONTINA
Frankfurters and fontina

½ pound *ruote/rotelline*
4 frankfurters (or about 5 ounces)
1 medium red onion
3½ tablespoons butter
1½ teaspoons finely chopped fresh rosemary
3½ ounces fontina, diced about ¼ inch
¼ cup heavy cream (optional)

Also good with this sauce
fusilli, gomiti

Wheel-shaped pasta must seem somewhat trailer-trash to the Italian eye. With this in mind, here is an indisputably trashy recipe. It might not do for your soirées, but the kids will love it.

Put your pasta in the boiling water.

Slice your frankfurters on a bias, 2 inches thick. Peel, halve, and slice your onion with the grain. Fry it in the butter over a high heat for 3–4 minutes, until starting to brown and smell like a hot-dog stand. Turn the heat down to medium-low, add the frankfurters and rosemary, and cook for a few minutes more. Add the drained pasta to the pan with about 4–5 tablespoons of its cooking water. Bubble together until the pasta is nicely coated, then stir in the fontina and take the pan off the heat. A little cream, added to the sauce, helps to bring it together, but isn't necessary. Leave to rest, covered, so the cheese can melt, for a minute or so before serving.

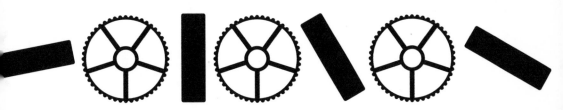

SEDANINI

Dimensions
Length: 1.6 in
Width: 0.26 in
Wall thickness: 0.8 mm

Synonyms
sedani, cornetti ("horns")
diavoletti, diavolini ("little
devils") and *folletti* ("elves"
or "goblins")

Also good with this pasta
macaroni and cheese;
macaroni salad; *Norma;*
puttanesca; salad of
zucchini, lemon zest, and
pine nuts; sardines and
fennel; sausages and cream;
Treviso, speck, and fontina

Once known as *zanne d'elefante* ("elephant tusks") for their
slightly curved shape, these elongated, narrow ridged tubes
of pasta were renamed when ivory became taboo. They are
now called *sedanini*, or "little celery stalks," which is just as
descriptive, if less exotic.

SEDANINI CON CARCIOFI, FAVE E PISELLI
Artichokes, peas, and broad beans

1/3 pound *sedanini*
1 pound broad beans in their
   pods
1/2 pound peas in their pods
3 baby artichokes
1 bunch green onions, cut
   into 3/4-inch lengths
2 garlic cloves, thinly sliced
6 tablespoons extra-virgin
   olive oil
1 cup chicken stock (or
   water)
3 tablespoons chopped flat-
   leaf parsley
10 basil or mint leaves (or
   both), shredded
Grated pecorino Romano, to
   serve (optional)

Also good with this sauce
*campanelle/gigli, canestri,
dischi volanti, farfalle,
farfalle tonde, fazzoletti,
garganelli, gramigne,
maltagliati, pappardelle,
spaccatelle, strozzapreti,
tagliatelle, torchio*

Pod the broad beans – if they are larger than your fingernail, blanch them for 1–2 minutes in boiling water, refresh in cold water, and shell them, too. Pod the peas. Cut away the tough (darker) parts from the artichokes, leaving only the tender leaves and heart (keep them in water acidulated with lemon juice right up until you cook them).

In a smallish saucepan, fry the green onions and garlic in the oil for a couple of minutes. Cut the artichokes into 1-centimeter wedges, and add to the pan with a pinch of salt. Cook for 2 minutes more, then add the peas, broad beans, and stock. Allow to boil, uncovered, until the vegetables are meltingly tender and the sauce reduces to a thick liquid.

The sauce will take 12–15 minutes to cook once the stock has been added. Put your pasta on so that it can be drained, only a touch undercooked, to be combined with the sauce for the last few seconds of cooking. Stir in the herbs, and serve with grated pecorino (or if you prefer, just a drizzle of oil).

SEDANINI CON POLLO E PRUGNE
Chicken and prunes

½ pound *sedanini*
½ pound skinless, boneless
   chicken thighs
5¼ tablespoons butter,
   divided
1⅓ cups pitted prunes (6⅓
   ounces) – soft ones are
   best
⅓ cup red wine
¾ cup chicken stock
1½ tablespoons chopped
   fresh oregano or
   marjoram
Grated Parmesan, to serve

Also good with this sauce
*casarecce, cavatappi,
chifferi rigati, ditali, ditalini,
garganelli, gemelli, gomiti,
maccheroncini, penne,
pennini rigati, rigatoni,
strozzapreti, ruote, ruotellini,
tortiglioni*

There is something almost medieval about this recipe, a sauce that is neither sweet nor savoury (or rather is both at once). If it tastes a little confused before you serve the dish, try it again with a touch of Parmesan, and the flavours should begin to make sense.

Start the sauce a bit before you put the pasta on. Dice the chicken thighs (½-inch pieces), and fry in half the butter over quite a high heat until browned. Add the prunes, chopped the same size as the chicken, and fry for a minute more. Season with salt and pepper, add the red wine, and reduce by half. Now add the stock (this is probably the time to put the pasta on), and allow to bubble reasonably rapidly until the sauce has some body; taste for seasoning. Drain the pasta a mite undercooked, and add to the sauce along with the remaining butter. Cook together until the sauce coats and the pasta is nicely *al dente*. Stir the oregano or marjoram through, and serve with grated Parmesan.

SPACCATELLE

Dimensions
Length: 1.44 in
Width: 0.96 in
Diameter: 4.2 mm

Also good with this pasta
artichokes, peas, and broad
beans; arugula, tomato,
and onion; broccoli rabe
and sausage; cabbage and
sausage; duck sauce; green
olives and tomato; *Norma*;
puttanesca; rabbit and
asparagus; *ragù Napoletano*;
Romanesco broccoli;
sausages and cream;
sausage, tomato, and saffron

Arced in cross-section, and curved in the shape of a crescent,
spaccatelle are like *gramigne* (page 134), but over double the size.
The name possibly has something to do with there being a
speccatura ("cleft") along the middle. These are one of the few
originally Sicilian pasta forms – bent like the local politics.

SPACCATELLE CON TONNO E MELANZANE
Tuna and eggplant

⅓ pound *spaccatelle*
⅓ pound drained top-quality canned tuna in oil (or ½ pound fresh tuna, plus 3 tablespoons extra-virgin olive oil)
1 smaller-than-average eggplant (⅔ pound)
Vegetable oil for deep-frying
1 red onion, finely chopped
1 garlic clove, finely chopped
¾ teaspoon crushed red pepper flakes
3 tablespoons extra-virgin olive oil
½ pound cherry or plum tomatoes, cut into chunks
4½ tablespoons white wine
3 tablespoons chopped fresh mint
3 tablespoons chopped flat-leaf parsley

Also good with this sauce
maccheroncini

This recipe would traditionally be made with swordfish. Given our huge appetite and lack of regard for this majestic creature, which has been hunted to the brink of extinction, I use tuna from sustainable sources instead. Best to direct our consumption temporarily elsewhere until the swordfish have recovered from our excesses.

If using canned tuna, break it up into chunks. If using fresh, dice ¾ inch, season with salt, and sauté briefly in the oil, just to seal the outside.

Dice the eggplant ¾ inch, season lightly with salt, and deep-fry in very hot vegetable oil (corn or sunflower are best) until golden brown. Drain and set aside.

About 20 minutes before you're ready to eat, fry the onion, garlic, and red pepper flakes with a pinch of salt in the olive oil over a medium heat until soft and lightly coloured (10 minutes). Add the tomatoes and fry for a few minutes (about 5, until starting to break down), then add the wine, tuna, and eggplant, and let the mixture boil for a few minutes, until the sauce is thickened. Season with salt and pepper. Add the drained pasta (which you have of course timed perfectly and drained when just a touch firmer than you might like to serve it), a dribble of pasta water, and most of the mint and parsley. Allow to cook for a minute until the sauce coats and the pasta is done, then serve with the remaining herbs on top.

SPAGHETTI

Dimensions
Length: 10.4 in
Diameter: 2 mm

Synonyms
vermicelli, fidi (from
the Arabic *al-fidawsh,*
"devotional"), *fidelini,
spaghettini, spaghettoni*

Also good with this pasta
aglio e olio; amatriciana;
anchovy sauce; *arrabbiata;*
cacio e pepe; carbonara;
clams; garlic sauce; fried in
nests; *fritta alla Siracusana;*
gricia; lentils; lobster,
mussels, and ginger; *Norma;*
pesto Genovese; pesto
Trapanese; rabbit and spicy
tomato; *ragù Napoletano;*
raw tomato; ricotta and
tomato; Romanesco broccoli;
sardines and fennel; sausage
sauce; *sugo di coda; tartufo*
dei poveri; tocco; tuna belly
and tomato

For me Italians have only got two things on the brain . . . and the other one is spaghetti.
—Catherine Deneuve

What is pasta, if not *spaghetti*? Simpler is always better, and it doesn't get any simpler than a cylindrical strand of *semola-*and-water dough. The name is also as obvious as can be – the diminutive form (for a shorter length) of string or twine (*spago*). The most popular form of pasta in the world, *spaghetti* account for two-thirds of global pasta consumption. Given the pasta's history, this may be a surprise. The word appeared relatively late, in 1836, the invention delayed because *spaghetti* are an intrinsically industrial form of pasta which can be extruded only by mechanical press.

Spaghetti being known worldwide came even later. Canned *spaghetti* were invented in the last moments of the nineteenth century in America, and this product (that would make an Italian turn in his grave) became widely available in Britain at the end of the Second World War. The Italian journalist Giuseppe Prezzolini once noted *spaghetti* had done more to spread Italian genius across the globe than the work of Dante. He wasn't wrong – we watch spaghetti westerns, laugh as our children greet pasta with the phrase "Uh-oh, Spaghetti-Os," and take our defining image of romantic dinner from *Lady and the Tramp*'s famous spaghetti-kiss scene.

SPAGHETTI AL POMODORO
Tomato sauce

½ pound *spaghetti*
1 cup plus 2 tablespoons light tomato sauce or ½ cup plus 1 tablespoon rich tomato sauce (page 15)

Also good with this sauce
campanelle/gigli, conchiglie, gemelli, gnocchi shells, *malloreddus, penne, pennini rigati, rigatoni, tortiglioni, trenette*

The original and the best — the first recipe for a tomato sauce for pasta occurs in a book by the Duke of Buonvicino, Ippolito Cavalcanti's *Cucina teorico pratica* in 1839, just a few years after *spaghetti* itself first appeared.

Drain the *spaghetti* just before they are cooked to your taste. Cook in the sauce in a frying pan with a splash of the pasta water. Light tomato sauce is best served with a little extra-virgin olive oil and maybe some torn basil leaves on top, rich sauce with some cheese – pecorino or Parmesan.

FRITTATA DI SPAGHETTI
Spaghetti and *bottarga* or Parmesan omelette

¼ pound *spaghetti*
3½ tablespoons butter
4 eggs
½ cup coarsely grated mullet *bottarga* (2 ounces) or 1⅓–1½ cups grated Parmesan
3 tablespoons chopped flat-leaf parsley (only if using *bottarga*)
2¼ tablespoons extra-virgin olive oil, divided

This recipe, when made with Parmesan, is a Neapolitan classic. There slices may be bought on the street where they compete with pizzas and fried foods as substantial and delicious snacks. Hot and fresh from the pan, a *frittata* is even more delicious - either simply with Parmesan, or with the added complexity of *bottarga*.

Put your pasta on to boil; balance a bowl over the pot and allow the butter to just melt in it. Remove from the heat, and beat in the eggs and either *bottarga* and parsley or just Parmesan. Season with a little salt and lots of pepper. Drain the pasta when still rather *al dente* and stir well, still hot, into the egg mixture. Have an 8-inch frying pan, one which your *frittata* will pretty much fill, already heated (very hot). Reduce the heat to low, add 1½ tablespoons of the oil, swirl it around, and pour in the pasta. Shake for a few moments and fry for

2–3 minutes or until golden brown. Turn out onto a plate which just fits the pan, return the pan to the heat, add the remaining ¾ tablespoon oil, and slide the *frittata* in. Cook gently for another 2–3 minutes before turning the *frittata* twice more, cooking for 1 minute each time. It should be cooked, but slightly runny in the middle. Serve with a little salad and a wedge of lemon if you like.

Also good with this sauce
capelli d'angelo, spaghettini, tagliolini, tajarin, vermicelli

SECCHIO DELLA MUNNEZZA
Mixed nuts with raisins, capers, and olives

½ pound *spaghetti*
1½ tablespoons each of shelled walnuts and hazelnuts
4½ tablespoons extra-virgin olive oil
1½ tablespoons pine nuts
3 tablespoons raisins
2 ounces cherry tomatoes, halved
1½ tablespoons salted capers, soaked in water until tolerably salty, then drained
¾ teaspoon dried oregano
1½ teaspoons finely chopped flat-leaf parsley
5–6 black olives (Gaeta are best), pitted and roughly chopped

Also good with this sauce
fusilli fatti a mano

This recipe for "garbage pail" pasta, so called because it uses the dregs of almost everything in the store cupboard, came to me via the inimitable Faith Willinger. She, in turn, discovered the recipe at e' Curti in Sorbo Serpico in Campania. *Curti* means "the shorties" — so named because the restaurant was founded by a couple of diminutive members of a travelling circus.

First chop the walnuts and hazelnuts. Put the pasta in the water straightaway, and everything should come together at the same time. Brown the chopped nuts gently in oil, and when they are a pleasing colour add the pine nuts, raisins, tomatoes, capers, and oregano, and cook over low heat until the tomatoes start to melt. Add the parsley and olives, and salt to taste.

Drain the pasta when a little more *al dente* than you like, and add to the sauce along with a small ladle (3 tablespoons or so) of pasta water. Sauté together for a minute or so, adding more water if the sauce dries out.

SPAGHETTI ALLA PUTTANESCA
Whore's sauce

½ pound *spaghetti*

3 tablespoons extra-virgin olive oil

6 ounces cherry tomatoes, halved

¾ teaspoon crushed red pepper flakes

1 garlic clove, thinly sliced

¼ cup salted capers, soaked until tolerably salty, then drained

¾ cup black olives (Gaeta, if possible), pitted and roughly chopped (4 ounces)

4 anchovy fillets, roughly chopped

⅓ cup light tomato sauce (page 15) or tomato *passata*

¼ cup chopped flat-leaf parsley

1½ tablespoons chopped fresh basil, or ¾ tablespoon chopped fresh oregano

Also good with this sauce
bavette, bigoli, bucatini, campanelle/ gigli, conchiglie, farfalle, fusilli fatti a mano, gomiti, linguine, lumache, rigatoni, sedanini, spaccatelle, spaghettini, torchio, tortiglioni

What more colourful name could there be than "whore's pasta"? This Neapolitan recipe may have originally been cooked by the proprietor of a brothel for his customers, a quick and cheap substantial dish to give them energy; or it may have been inspired by the lurid colours of the ladies' *biancheria* (undergarments). In any case, it is delicious, widespread, and enjoyed by people at every grade of respectability.

Cook the spaghetti in boiling, well-salted water. A few minutes before the pasta is cooked, heat a wide frying pan until smoking hot. Add the oil, followed immediately by the tomatoes, red pepper flakes, and garlic. Fry for a minute until the garlic just starts to colour and the tomatoes soften. Add the capers, olives, and anchovy, reduce the heat to medium, and fry for a minute more before adding the tomato sauce.

Simmer for a minute or so until the pasta is cooked a touch more *al dente* than you want it on the plate; drain it and add to the sauce along with the herbs. Stir together for 30 seconds over the heat, adding plenty of black pepper but probably no extra salt. Serve straightaway.

SPAGHETTI CON BOTTARGA E PANGRATTATO
Bottarga and bread crumbs

½ pound *spaghetti*
3 tablespoons fresh
    bread crumbs
1½ tablespoons extra-
    virgin olive oil
Grated zest of ¼ lemon
1½ tablespoons chopped
    flat-leaf parsley
6 tablespoons grated
    mullet *bottarga* (1⅓–1½
    ounces)
2 tablespoons butter

Also good with this sauce
*bavette, linguine,
malloreddus, spaghettini,
trenette*

Spaghetti with *bottarga* is another classic, especially in Sardinia. The addition of bread crumbs is my own — they can easily be omitted, but add a pleasing crunch.

Rub the bread crumbs with the oil, and toast in a moderate oven until golden brown. Leave to cool, then mix with the lemon zest, parsley, and half the *bottarga*. Put the pasta on to boil. When nearly done, warm the remaining *bottarga* in a frying pan with the butter and a few tablespoons of the pasta water over a very low heat, just to make a sauce – don't let it boil. Drain the pasta *al dente*, and toss in the sauce. When well coated, serve with the bread crumbs on top.

BREAD CRUMBS AND SUGAR

½ pound *spaghetti*
1½ teaspoons extra-virgin
    olive oil
½ cup fresh bread crumbs
¼ cup superfine sugar
5¼ tablespoons butter (or
    another 3 tablespoons
    extra-virgin olive oil)

Also good with this sauce
fusilli

My grandmother Agnes used to tell me how much she loved this dish as a kid in Hungary. I can't quite make up my mind whether it is too weird to love or just weird enough. It would make a good breakfast . . .

Rub the oil into the bread crumbs, then bake in a moderate oven until a rich golden brown. Mix with half the sugar. While your pasta cooks, take 6 tablespoons of its water and boil separately with the remaining sugar and the butter until emulsified and the texture of cream. Toss the drained pasta in this sauce, and serve with the sweet bread crumbs on top. Olive oil, instead of butter, adds a more savoury complexity to the dish, but takes it even further into the grey area between sweet and savoury. If you want to try it, just toss the pasta together with the oil, sugar, and 3 tablespoons of water — no need to boil the sauce in a pan, as it won't emulsify anyway.

SPAGHETTINI

Dimensions
Length: 10.4 in
Diameter: 1.5 mm

Also good with this pasta
arrabbiata; bottarga and
bread crumbs; clams; fried
in nests; garlic sauce; lentils;
lobster; *pesto Genovese;
puttanesca;* Romanesco
broccoli; scallops and thyme;
tuna belly and tomato;
zucchini and prawns

As *spaghetti* is the diminutive of *spago* ("string"), so *spaghettini* are "little *spaghetti*." Their finer texture means they cook faster, take up a little more sauce, and have less resistance to the tooth – you feel them less in the mouth. It seems many, especially non-Italians, prefer this experience to the original *spaghetti*. Largely, this is a matter of taste, and the two may be used more or less interchangeably. In general, *spaghetti* will be better with a heavier sauce and *spaghettini* with a lighter one.

SPAGHETTINI AGLIO E OLIO
Garlic and oil

½ pound *spaghettini*
4 garlic cloves, finely
    chopped
½ cup plus 1 tablespoon
    extra-virgin olive oil
¾ teaspoon crushed red
    pepper flakes
3 tablespoons chopped flat-
    leaf parsley

Also good with this sauce
gemelli, spaghetti

This pasta dish is pungent and well-loved. Lots of garlic, red pepper flakes, and oil make for powerful flavours, but delicious ones . . .

Put the garlic and oil in a cold pan, and cook over a medium heat until the garlic has sizzled for a minute, but not coloured. It is best to start this just a minute or 2 before your pasta is cooked. Add the red pepper flakes to the pan, then the drained pasta along with about 6 tablespoons of the cooking water. Sauté together for a few seconds, toss in the parsley, and serve.

You can halve the red pepper flakes for the faint-hearted.

SPAGHETTINI AL POMODORO CRUDO
Raw tomato

½ pound *spaghettini*
3–4 ripe tomatoes
    (14 ounces)
6 tablespoons extra-virgin
    olive oil
1 large garlic clove, crushed
15 basil leaves, torn

Also good with this sauce
fusilli bucati, spaghetti

A classic from Lazio all the way down to Naples, raw tomatoes make one of the simplest and tastiest sauces. My grandmother, who makes this pasta almost every other day when in Italy, calls it *primavera* (meaning "springtime") — but it is a far cry from the Italian–American sauce of the same name. The American sauce is poorly named — it relies heavily on summer produce, but my grandmother's is just as inaccurate. The tomatoes must be at their peak (mid- to late-summer produce) and are not so flavoursome earlier in the year.

At least 10 minutes but no more than an hour before you eat, chop the tomatoes (1–2 centimeters) and mix with the oil, garlic, salt, and pepper. Leave to macerate at room temperature. Put the pasta on to boil. Given that you can't cook the sauce, it is a good idea to warm it gently in a bowl over the boiling water. Drain the pasta when *al dente,* and toss with the sauce and basil leaves. Some add Gaeta olives, pitted and chopped, but I think it is just fine without. I hold pecorino (on top) and chopped red onion (stirred through) in the same regard. Serve immediately.

SPAGHETTINI "AL MERLUZZO FELICE"
Seafood and ginger

½ pound *spaghettini*
6 large prawns,
   6 langoustines,
   or 1 small lobster
12 clams
12 mussels
2¼ tablespoons very finely
   chopped fresh ginger
1 garlic clove, finely
   chopped
Scant ¾ teaspoon crushed
   red pepper flakes
½ cup extra-virgin olive oil
¼ cup white wine
3 tablespoons chopped flat-
   leaf parsley

Also good with this sauce
*bavette, linguine, spaghetti,
trenette*

I first had this dish at Al Merluzzo Felice in Milan (one of the finest Sicilian restaurants in Italy), then repeated the experience in Sicily itself. A version can also be found, from time to time, on our menu at Bocca di Lupo, but there we have corrupted it by adding tomato.

It is normally served with a mixture of lobster and prawns or langoustines — difficult to achieve when cooking for two as below, but if you scale the recipe up, consider a little more variety.

Halve the prawns/langoustines/lobster lengthways (if using lobster, cut into chunks and split the claws). As the pasta boils, heat a wide frying pan over a high heat. All at once, add the seafood, ginger, garlic, red pepper flakes, and oil, and fry for a couple of minutes (until the crustacean shells have turned red). Add the wine, and let it bubble until all the clams and mussels have opened. Drain the pasta, *al dente* as ever, and add to the pan with the parsley. Stir together over the heat until most of the sauce has been absorbed. Serve straightaway.

STELLINE AND STELLETTE

Dimensions
Length: 4 mm
Width: 4 mm
Thickness: 0.5 mm

Synonyms
alfabeto, anellini, astri,
avemarie, fiori di sambuco,
lentine, puntine, semini

Also good with this pasta
acquacotta; alphabet soup;
stracciatella

The defining characteristic of these stars, other than their points, is the pin-prick of a hole in their center. *Stelline* ("little stars"), *stellette* (bigger stars), or *fiori di sambuco* (elderflowers) are also sometimes called *avemarie* – they are so tiny they cook in the time it takes to say one Hail Mary. Miraculously they have been around for much longer than industrial pasta production – since at least the sixteenth century. It is hard to conceive how such delicate forms could be made by hand.

Like most *pastina*, *stelline* are normally served in broths and soup, and normally to the elderly and children. They appeal to both because of the ease with which they may be eaten and digested, and the romantic inspiration of their form, evocative of the night sky, constellations, and angels, and the ancient world from which they came.

BRODO
Clarified chicken or capon broth

Serves 4–5

1 medium chicken or capon without giblets (about 4 pounds)
2 celery stalks
1 carrot, halved
1 onion, halved
3 bay leaves
3 egg whites

Also good with
agnolotti; agnolotti dal plin; canestri/canestrini; capelli d'angelo; cappelletti; orzo; pappardelle; passatelli; quadretti/quadrettini; tagliatelle; vermicelli; vermicellini

This yields 6–8 cups clear broth, enough for 4–5 people.

Cut 1 breast from the chicken and set aside. The rest of the meat will be boiled in the broth, but can be used again:

- sliced and served with boiled potatoes, *salsa verde*, and *mostarda*.
- cooked with rice.
- made into a pasta filling (such as *cappelletti*, page 58).
- chopped up and used in a salad.

Put the chicken, vegetables, and bay into a large pot and cover with cold water. Simmer for 3 hours, topping up the water to keep the level just over the carcass. Strain, skim, season with salt, and leave to cool to room temperature.

Finely mince the raw breast, and mix with the egg whites. Stir this mixture well into the stock, and return to a low heat until it comes to a bare simmer – keep it with just the occasional bubble for about 10 minutes, then turn off the heat and leave to stand at room temperature until partly cooked and looking clear. Strain gently through muslin or cheesecloth.

STELLINE IN BRODO

¼ pound *stelline*
3 cups clarified chicken
broth (see opposite)
Grated Parmesan, to serve

Season the chicken broth with salt, and cook the *stelline* in it until as *al dente* as you like. Serve with grated Parmesan.

If you are especially particular about the clarity of your broths, you might want to cook the *stelline* in another pot of unclarified, seasoned chicken stock, then strain them and serve in a limpid pool of clarified broth that has been warmed separately. This hardly seems worth the bother.

STELLETTE BRAISED IN CHICKEN STOCK

½ pound *stellette*
1¾ cups good chicken
stock
3½ tablespoons butter
6 tablespoons grated
Parmesan

This delicate, comforting dish almost qualifies as baby food. Use a little more salt and fat than would do a baby good, and you have a dish fit for a king.

Simmer the little stars of pasta with the stock and butter (and salt and pepper to taste) over a medium heat until the liquid is absorbed and the pasta just cooked. This should be done without a lid on, with a regular stir to prevent sticking.

The cheese can be stirred through just before serving (for a softer taste) or sprinkled on top for something marginally more piquant.

Serve the pasta spread out flat on the plate – this dish has such density that it cools slowly, and so entails a risk of burning palates and tongues if you don't take such a precaution.

STROZZAPRETI

Dimensions
Length: 1.4 in
Width: 5 mm

Synonyms
strangolarpreti, gnocchi di prete in Friuli; *frigulelli, piccicasanti, strozzafrati* in Le Marche; *cecamariti* in Lazio; *maccheroni alla molinara* in Abruzzo; *strangulaprievete* in Naples; *strangugliaprieviti* in Calabria; *affogaparini* in Sicily

Also good with this pasta
arrabbiata; artichokes, peas, and broad beans; braised bacon and peas; broccoli rabe and sausage; cannellini beans; chicken and prunes; ham, peas, and cream; lentils; morels; pureed broad beans; rabbit and asparagus; scallops and thyme; squid and tomato; *sugo di coda;* white truffle

Cooks seem to have it in for priests. Turkish *imam bayildi* ("the priest fainted") is so called because it is rich enough to floor a priest, whilst Italian *strozzapreti* ("priest stranglers"), are clearly even more lethal. There are a few stories behind the name . . .

One theory is that the *azdore* (Romagna housewives) would make pasta for men of the cloth as partial payment for land rents. Their husbands would be so angered by the sight of fat churchmen feasting on their wives' food they might wish them to choke as they stuffed their faces. It is also said that the pastas resemble rolled towels, with which one might strangle a priest if one felt so inclined. Perhaps the most commonly told story is the simplest, and probably closest to the truth – that gluttonous priests were so enamoured with the savoury pasta that they would eat it too quickly, often choking, sometimes to death. The common thread in these stories is the gentle anticlericism of the people of Tuscany and Romagna.

At any rate, *strozzapreti* are a common pasta, easily made by rolling small strips of dough (¾ inch by 2½ inches) between the hands to produce an almost tubular shape, similar in section to *cavatelli* (page 70) and *maccheroni inferrati* (page 160) that may be fairly straight or distinctly twisted.

STROZZAPRETI CON STRIDOLI E VONGOLE
Cowbells and clams

1/2 pound dried
  strozzapreti
3½ ounces *stridoli*,
  monksbeard, or samphire,
  or ½ ounce chives in
  1-inch lengths plus 1¾
  ounces wild arugula
2 shallots, very finely
  chopped
1 garlic clove, finely
  chopped
2¾ tablespoons butter
3 tablespoons extra-virgin
  olive oil
¾–1 pound Manila clams
  (*vongole veraci*) or *tellines*

Stridoli or *strigoli* are the young shoots of bladder campion (cowbells), a wildflower common in central Italy and the UK. These leaves are a delicious wild herb, bitter with saponin. You can forage for them yourself or buy them in the markets of the Veneto and Emilia-Romagna. Substitutes, equally delicious in this recipe but different in flavour, could be *barba dei frati* (monksbeard, occasionally available in shops) or common samphire. A mixture of arugula and chives is tasty, too.

Cut any roots from the *stridoli* and discard; wash the leaves and set aside. Put the pasta on, and start the sauce at the same time. Gently fry the shallots and garlic with a little salt in the butter and oil over a medium heat until nice and soft – about 6–7 minutes. When these are ready, a few minutes before the *strozzapreti*, add the clams, and cover with a blanket of the leaves. Increase the heat to high – you'll see some rummaging action in the foliage as the clams start to pop open. When you think they have all done their thing, stir in the leaves to make sure they are fully wilted. Drain and add the pasta, taste for seasoning, and serve immediately.

STROZZAPRETI, CALAMARI E BROCCOLI
Squid and broccoli

½ pound dried *strozzapreti*
1 pound fresh whole squid
  (or ⅔ pound cleaned)
⅔ pound broccoli (1 small
  head "normal" or ¾ head
  Romanesco)
½ cup plus 1 tablespoon
  extra-virgin olive oil,
  divided
1 garlic clove, thinly sliced
4 small (or 3 large) anchovy
  fillets, roughly chopped
¾ teaspoon crushed red
  pepper flakes
6 tablespoons white wine

Slice the bodies of the squid into fine, 2–3-millimeter rings, and cut the tentacles into equivalent-sized bunches. Cut the broccoli into fairly small florets. Put the pasta and the broccoli on to cook, at the same time and in the same water – the *strozzapreti* should be *al dente* at the same time as the broccoli are soft and almost mushy, which is how both should be for this dish.

A few minutes before the pasta is done, heat a wide pan over a high heat. Add 6 tablespoons of the oil and the garlic, which should fry until it barely begins to colour. Add the squid, anchovy, and red pepper flakes, and sauté for a minute or 2 until the squid is opaque and the rings hold a circular shape. Add the wine, let it bubble for a few seconds until the smell of alcohol is gone, then add the *strozzapreti* and broccoli, which you have just drained well, shaking to get rid of all the water.

Toss together in the pan, then serve drizzled with the remaining 3 tablespoons of oil.

TAGLIATELLE

Dimensions
Length: 10 in
Width: 0.4 in
Thickness: 0.75 mm

Synonyms
tagliolini; tagliatelle smalzade in Trentino-Alto Adige; *lesagnetes* in the Veneto; *bardele* in Lombardy; *fettuccine* in Lazio; *pincinelle* in Colonna; in Sicily *tagghiarini*; in Sardinia *taddarini; nastri* ("ribbons"), *fettucce romane, fettuccelle, fresine, tagliarelli*

Also good with this pasta
artichokes, peas, and broad beans; *carbonara;* ham, peas, and cream; *in brodo;* langoustines and saffron; lemon and butter; oysters, prosecco, and tarragon; porcini; pureed broad beans; rabbit and asparagus; smoked salmon, asparagus,

Short bills and long tagliatelle, say the people of Bologna, knowing whereof they speak, for long bills frighten husbands, while short tagliatelle are proof of the inexperience of she who made them, and, when served, look like leftovers.
—Pellegrino Artusi

Tagliatelle comes from *tagliare*, "to cut." As with almost all ribbon pastas, these are made by rolling up a sheet of thinly rolled egg pasta dough like a roll of cloth, then cutting it across to make ribbons, curled like party streamers which can be fluffed up and laid out to dry a little. As ribbon pastas are so simple to make, and *tagliatelle* are of a medium size, they can be found across Italy. Their heartland, however, is Emilia-Romagna and especially Bologna, where they are de rigueur with *ragù Bolognese*. They were reputedly invented there by the Bolognese maestro Zefirano – personal chef to Giovanni II de Bentivoglio, to mark the marriage of Lucrezia Borgia to Alfonso I d'Este, Duke of Ferrara. Where the other signature pasta of Bologna (*tortellini*, page 262) was modelled on the bride's navel, these were inspired by her blonde, silky hair. The pasta was supposedly so thin the Basilica di San Luca could be seen through it, via the cook's window. Both stories are likely to hold as much water as a colander, but are romantic nonetheless.

Tagliatelle production is still an art form in a few shops and restaurants in Bologna, the fresh dough being hand-rolled

and cream; *tocco*; walnut sauce; white truffle; wild boar sauce; zucchini and prawns

on pins 1.5 meters long (see a note on technique, page 11). As said, they are available throughout the rest of Italy. Regional variations crop up in the north, such as in Lombardy where *bardele coi morai* are *tagliatelle* made with borage. And in Alto Adige and Friuli–Venezia Giulia, on the day of slaughter some of the fresh pig's blood is mixed into the pasta dough itself, and the resultant pasta served with kale. Further south, in Abruzzo and Molise, *tagliatelle* are cooked in milk – a reminder of times when lean days (when meat was abstained from) were not limited to Lent, but comprised 150 of the days in each year.

Although normally eaten *asciutte* ("dry," i.e., with sauce), they can also be served *in brodo* (with broth, page 242).

TAGLIATELLE AL RAGÙ BOLOGNESE
Bolognese sauce

Serves 8

1¾ pounds dried, or about 2¼ pounds fresh, *tagliatelle* (made with the simple or enriched egg pasta dough, page 13)
½ cup grated Parmesan, to serve

RAGÙ BOLOGNESE
1 pound minced pork
1 pound minced veal (or beef)
3½ ounces chicken livers, finely chopped (optional)
1 carrot

This sauce is a million miles from the "Bol" that we Brits like to serve with pasta, which is about as close to the real McCoy as our *chile con carne* is to a true version. It is orange, not red; it is more oil- than water-based; it is delicate, aromatic, creamy, and subtle. This is one of many recipes where the cooking technique is as important to the finished dish as the ingredients — buy best-quality pancetta and Parmesan, spend as much money as you can afford on the eggs and flour for your pasta (or the packaged *tagliatelle*), and the few pennies remaining on the other ingredients. There are words to describe how good this is, but they shouldn't appear in print . . .

It is worth having a butcher mince the meats coarsely (⅓ inch thick), for the improved texture. Peel and dice the carrot, dice the celery, chop the onion, and slice the garlic.

2 celery stalks
1 medium onion
4 garlic cloves
7 tablespoons butter
4 tablespoons extra-virgin
  olive oil
3½ ounces pancetta (not
  smoked), cut in strips
1⅓ cups white wine
2¼ cups milk
14 ounces canned
  tomatoes, chopped
1 cup beef or chicken stock
  (optional; otherwise an
  additional 1 cup milk)

Also good with this sauce
campanelle/gigli, farfalle
tonde, pici, torchio, tortellini

Take a very wide frying pan (12 inches), and melt the butter in the oil over a medium heat. Add the vegetables and pancetta along with a good pinch of salt, and sauté for 10–15 minutes until softened. Increase the heat to high and add the meat in 4–5 additions, allowing time for any water to evaporate, stirring and breaking up any lumps with a spoon. After the last addition, wait until the pan starts to splutter slightly, then decrease the heat to medium and fry, stirring occasionally, until the meat has browned with a fair proportion of crispy bits – about 15–20 minutes. Deglaze with the wine, then transfer to a saucepan along with the milk, tomatoes, and stock as well as a good grinding of pepper and more salt to taste. Cook at a very gentle simmer, uncovered, for about 4 hours until the sauce is thick, more oil- than water-based (add a little stock or water if it dries too much or too quickly). When ready, the liquid will be as thick as heavy cream and, stirred up, the whole should be somewhat porridgy. Adjust the seasoning one last time.

The addition of bay and/or dried red pepper flakes along with the meat is heretical, but not displeasing.

Heat the *ragù* in a frying pan with a little pasta water. Drain the boiled pasta when marginally undercooked, then add to the sauce to finish cooking for about 20 seconds, with some butter. Serve with grated Parmesan on top.

TAGLIATELLE CON TREVISO, SPECK E FONTINA
Treviso, speck, and fontina

About ½ pound (less for
    dried, more for fresh)
    tagliatelle
2 tablespoons butter
½ a head of Treviso
    (elongated radicchio),
    shredded
⅓ cup heavy cream
4 slices speck (1¾ ounces),
    cut into ½-inch strips
3½ ounces fontina

Also good with this sauce
*campanelle/gigli, conchiglie,
farfalle tonde, fettuccine,
garganelli, gnocchi* shells,
*gomiti, lumache, pici,
radiatori, ruote, sedanini,
tagiolini, tajarin, torchio,
tortiglioni*

Rich sauces, bitter lettuces, smoked hams. All speak of the far north of Italy, where they find their way into pastas, risottos, pizzas, and sandwiches in any combination. Here as part of a creamy sauce, the bitter lettuce helps to cut through the fat.

The sauce and the pasta will likely take the same time to cook. Melt the butter over a medium heat and sweat the Treviso, seasoned with plenty of salt and pepper, for a minute or until it begins to wilt. Add the cream and allow to bubble gently for a minute – it should thicken a little. Drain the pasta when *al dente*, and toss into the sauce along with the speck (broken up with your fingers to avoid clumps) and the fontina, diced about ½ inch. Stir over the heat until the sauce is velvety and stringy, and serve straightaway.

TAGLIATELLE CON CAPPESANTE E TIMO
Scallops and thyme

About ½ pound (less for
    dried, more for fresh)
    tagliatelle
10 dry-cut scallops of a
    decent size (⅔ pound)
3 tablespoons olive oil
7 tablespoons butter
8 cherry tomatoes, cut into
    quarters
3 tablespoons fresh thyme
    leaves
6 tablespoons white wine

The sauce will take 4–5 minutes to make – time the pasta accordingly.

Clean the tough muscle from the scallops, and cut each in half to make 2 thinner discs – it is up to you whether to leave the coral on. Season with salt and pepper, and rub with the oil to coat. Heat a wide frying pan over a very high heat until smoking, then place the oiled scallops evenly in the pan. Leave them to fry for a minute, until they start to brown, then dot the butter between them. Be sure not to move the scallops – if they sit still they will sear better, and the aim is to achieve a dark sear on one side. When the scallops are well browned, and you are fearful that a second more will burn the butter beyond palatability, scatter the tomatoes and thyme into the pan. Shake, to settle the new addition between the scallops, and fry for half a minute more. Deglaze the pan with the wine, shaking vigorously this time to emulsify the sauce, and allow the wine to reduce until the sauce is as thick as light cream. Drain the *tagliatelle*, just a little more *al dente* than you like them, and toss into the sauce. Serve promptly.

TAGLIATELLE AL SUGO D'ARROSTO
Stew juice

We often turn to the potato or to rice when we have a sauce from a stew or pot-roast to mop up. But noodles (especially rich, eggy *tagliatelle*) provide not only one of the most traditional, but one of the best ways to do so.

In some of the recipes (*ragù Napoletana*, page 216; *sugo di coda*, page 197; *coniglio all'Ischitana*, page 37; *cuscussù* with fish and almonds, page 85) we are already doing this, although these tomato-based sauces seem designed for their pasta. Almost any stew's juices will go well – indeed, the drippings in a pot-roast and the deglazings from a conventional roast will be excellent. Your only quandary will be whether to follow the Italian fashion and serve the pasta dressed in the sauce before the meat, or the Austrian and serve it as an accompaniment.

In any case, allow 3 ounces of egg noodles per person as a side. Deglaze your roasting pan with water if the good bits are sticking, or reduce your stew's juices until they coat a spoon. Add butter (1–1¾ tablespoons per portion) to give a bit of body, toss the pasta well in the sauce, and serve with Parmesan.

Of course, if you don't feel like serving pasta and meat in 1 meal, save the pan juices and use them to dress a plateful of pasta for yourself another day. This is a great delight: to sit alone in the kitchen, and know you have the very best part of the roast or stew – the juices with a few measly pickings scraped from the carcass – all to your very self.

TAGLIOLINI AND TAJARIN

Dimensions
Length: 10 in
Width: 2 mm
Thickness: 0.8 mm

Synonyms
taglierini

Also good with this pasta
fried in nests; *frittata;* lemon
and butter; lokshen pudding;
oysters, prosecco, and
tarragon; soufflé; Treviso,
speck, and fontina

Tagliolini are nothing more than very thinly cut *tagliatelle*.
The art of cutting sheets of *lasagne* into finer noodles was
discovered in the fifteenth century. Maestro Martino (author,
and the world's first celebrity chef) wrote in his *Libro de Arte
Coquinaria* in 1456 that "*macharoni alla Romana*" (*fettuccine*)
should be cut to the width of your finger, but "*macharoni alla
Genovese*" (*tagliolini*) should be cut as finely as the width of a
needle. Their delicacy is both a boon and a burden – these
pastas are so fine they have an ethereal delicacy, but they are
easily overcooked by a miscalculation of a few seconds and
can be swamped by clumsy saucing.

Tajarin, from Piedmont, are a variation made with a supremely
rich pasta dough, rolled a little thicker than the *tagliolini* made
elsewhere. These have slightly more body and bite, and are
the classic pasta to serve with the king of the soil, the white
truffle.

TAGLIOLINI GRATINATI CON GAMBERI E TREVISO
Prawns and Treviso au gratin

¼ pound dried *tagliolini*, or ⅓ pound fresh
Scant ½ pound peeled raw prawn tails, or ½ pound potted shrimp (see text)
3½ tablespoons butter (omit if using potted shrimp)
½ a smallish red onion, thinly sliced across the grain
1 medium head Treviso (or radicchio), thinly shredded
3½ tablespoons white wine
¼ cup heavy cream
6 tablespoons grated Parmesan

This recipe is an approximation of a dish served at Da Fiore in Venice. The combination of prawns, bitter radicchio, cream, and cheese is rather unusual but utterly delicious.

It is a struggle to get great prawns outside of southern Europe. The best prawns for this dish would be Venetian ones, raw Mediterranean red prawns, or live langoustines. The latter 2 are occasionally available in the UK (to peel langoustines, split the head to kill them, plunge for 3 seconds in boiling water, refresh in ice water, and then peel like a prawn). For British readers, the best bet is to buy whole cooked Atlantic prawns (1–1¼ pounds) and peel them yourself, or to buy cleaned brown shrimp. If you can't get either, buy some potted shrimp — the cayenne and mace are actually pleasing additions to the dish. In the US, rock shrimp are the way to go.

Melt the butter (or potted shrimp) over a medium heat. Add the onion and a pinch of salt, and fry for a few moments, then the radicchio and gently sauté for 4 or 5 minutes until wilted. Add the prawns, then the white wine, and let bubble for a couple of minutes until most of the liquid has evaporated. At about the same time, put the *tagliolini* in a pot of boiling, salted water and the cream into your radicchio and prawns. Let both pots boil until the *tagliolini* are marginally under-cooked, then drain and add to the sauce. Toss together, season with salt and pepper, and transfer to a suitable (4½-by-9½-inch) baking dish. Sprinkle with Parmesan. Brown the top, either in a fiercely hot oven or under the broiler. Serve immediately.

TAGLIOLINI CON GRANCHIO
Crab

1/3 pound dried *tagliolini*, or
  1/2 pound fresh
2 mildish fresh red chilis,
  seeded and finely diced
1 garlic clove, chopped
6 tablespoons extra-virgin
  olive oil
3 1/2 ounces brown crab
  meat, carefully picked
1/2 pound white crab meat,
  carefully picked
Grated zest of 1 small lemon

Also good with this sauce
bavette

The sauce is quick to make, so you can start at the same time as the pasta hits the water. Put the chilies, garlic, and oil into a cold pan, and heat over a medium flame until it sizzles. Add the brown crab meat along with about 6 tablespoons of the pasta water, and break up with a wooden spoon to make a sauce. Add the white crab meat and lemon zest to warm through now, stirring gently so as to keep intact any lumps of meat from the claws. Drain the pasta when *al dente*, add to the sauce, and stir together to mix, then remove from the heat and serve.

Three tablespoons of chopped parsley don't go amiss, but aren't necessary. A tablespoon of shredded mint leaves tastes nice, in an unauthentic way.

TAJARIN AL TARTUFO D'ALBA
White truffle

About 1/2 pound (less for
  dried, more for fresh)
  tagliolini or *tajarin*
2/3 cup butter
4 duck eggs
A little grated Parmesan
1 ounce fresh white truffle

Also good with this sauce
*agnolotti dal plin, fettuccine,
maltagliati, tagliatelle,
tortelli, cappellaci*

You will need three pans for this dish – one filled with boiling salted water for the pasta, one with simmering salted water for the eggs, and one to melt the butter.

Everything needs to start in quick succession: Put the pasta on to boil, melt the butter over a low heat with 3 tablespoons of the pasta water, drain the pasta, and toss into the butter. Set a slotted spoon in the simmering water. Crack open the duck eggs, discard the whites, and gently drop the yolks onto the spoon. Cook for just 20 seconds, until the thin film of egg white turns into a cloudy veil around the still-raw yolks.

Portion the buttered pasta into bowls, and carefully lay a yolk on top of each, in the center. Dust with a little Parmesan, then cover with thinly shaved truffles. A truffle shaver (obviously) works well, but then so does a potato peeler.

TORCHIO

Dimensions
Length: 1.4 in
Width: 0.8 in
Diameter: 0.42 in

Similar forms
campanelle, gigli

Also good with this pasta
artichokes, peas, and broad
beans; braised bacon and
peas; chickpeas and clams;
green beans; Hungarian fish
soup; lamb sauce; lentils;
mackerel, tomatoes, and
rosemary; pureed broad
beans; *puttanesca; ragù
Bolognese*; ricotta and
tomato; sausages and cream;
Treviso, speck, and fontina;
tuna belly and tomato

An abbreviation of *maccheroni al torchio* ("macaroni in the shape
of a torch"), *torchio* is another shape, near-identical in structure
and use to *campanelle* (page 42), but without the frilly edges;
this pasta instead is ridged and curved in profile to catch and
cup the sauce.

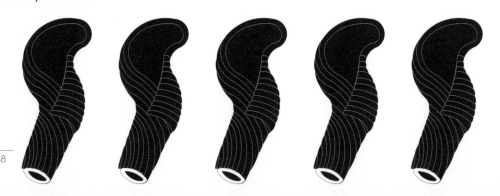

TORCHIO CON MIDOLLO E POMODORO
Bone marrow and tomato

½ pound *torchio*
⅓ pound bone marrow, diced*
⅔ pound tomatoes, chunked, or halved cherry tomatoes
2 garlic cloves, thinly sliced
3 sprigs rosemary
A pinch of crushed red pepper flakes
4 anchovy fillets, chopped
⅓ cup red wine
Grated Parmesan, to serve

*Buy one whole marrow bone from your butcher, and have him split it lengthways down the middle – the marrow can then be removed like the seeds of a cucumber. Otherwise, buy 1¾ pounds center-cut marrow bones in 2-inch lengths and push the marrow out with your thumb.

Also good with this sauce
campanelle/gigli

This dish is very, very meaty and very, very rich — not for the faint-hearted or those at risk of a heart attack. If you're the sort who likes to gnaw on a marrow bone, give it a go; otherwise be smart and try something else.

Heat a frying pan over a high flame. When smoking, add the bone marrow followed immediately by the tomatoes, garlic, rosemary, and red pepper flakes. Fry for 10 minutes, until some of the tomatoes have browned and others have softened. Reduce the heat to low, and add the anchovy and three-quarters of the wine. Simmer the sauce for 20 minutes until quite thick and oily-looking, breaking up the tomatoes a little with the back of a spoon; put the pasta on to cook towards the end of this process.

When the pasta is cooked but firm, drain it well and add to the sauce. Toss a few times in the pan to coat, then remove from the heat and add the remaining wine. This helps to emulsify the sauce, while the raw alcohol cuts through the fattiness a little. Stir together well and serve with a generous quantity of Parmesan grated on top.

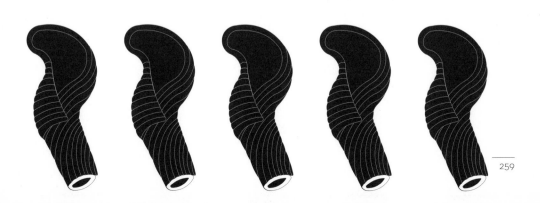

TORTELLI/CAPPELLACCI

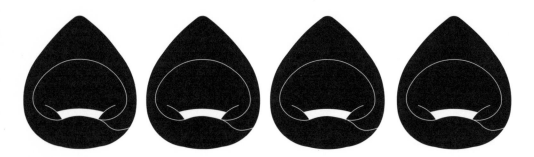

Dimensions
Length: 1.4 in
Width: 1.2 in

Synonyms
turtello in Emilia-Romagna;
turtej cu la cua in Piacenza;
tordelli in Toscana

Also good with this pasta
butter and sage; cream;
porcini and cream; white
truffle

Tortelli ("little cakes") resemble fortune cookies and are also called *cappellacci* ("little hats"). A square of pasta is stuffed and folded diagonally to make a triangle (or a circle to make a semicircle), the two longer arms are twisted to meet together, and the broader point is folded up to make a pleat around the bulge of filling, which acts as a trap for sauce. The form is particularly popular in Emilia-Romagna, along with *tortelloni* (larger ones, page 266) and *tortellini* (tiny ones, page 260), but the two most distinctive fillings come from Lombardy. *Tortelli Cremaschi* (*tortelli* in the Cremona manner) are filled with amaretti, raisins, candied citron, nutmeg, Parmesan, and sometimes a little mint or cocoa. The second classic (see opposite) is *cappellacci di zucca*, equally famous in Modena (Lombardy) and Ferrara (Emilia-Romagna), with the version from Mantua being made in a different shape more similar to *caramelle* (page 62). As with the *Cremonese* recipe, it blurs the boundary between sweet and savoury – in a delightful manner when well-executed, sickly when not.

Similar and worth noting are *casonsei* from Brescia and Bergamo (from the same stem as *calzone*, the folded pizzas), also stuffed with squash and *mostarda* or sometimes sausage, but curved only to a horseshoe shape with the ends not pinched together.

CAPPELLACCI DI ZUCCA
Sweet and savoury pumpkin filling

Serves 4

2/3 pound simple or enriched egg pasta dough (page 13)

FILLING (yields 13/4 pounds)
1 good quality squash (Marina di Chioggia, onion, kabocha, or butternut)
1/3 cup butter
20–25 amaretti cookies (31/2 ounces)
31/2 ounces *mostarda di frutta* (optional; apple is best if you can get it)
1/4 pound *grana* cheese, such as Parmesan
A good grating of nutmeg

Also good with these fillings
ricotta (page 267); spinach and ricotta (page 210)

This filling can be frozen or made instantly into pasta. I say this because there is enough filling to feed ten (you can scale it down, but the best squashes to use tend to weigh about 21/4 pounds each). You need 2/3 pound of filling for this recipe.

Preheat the oven to 390°F (or 355°F for convection ovens).

Clean the squash (peel and seed it) and cut into wedges – you should have 11/2 pounds prepared weight. Roast with the butter, covered tightly with foil, until completely soft and starting to brown. Uncover for the final minutes if it looks wet. Remove from the oven, leave to cool, then combine with the other ingredients, salt, and pepper in a food processor. Work until smooth. Cool before using to fill the *cappellacci*.

Roll the pasta to the desired thickness of just under 1 millimeter (0.7 millimeter if you're particular, the second-thinnest setting on most machines), cut into 21/2-inch shapes (round or square, with straight or frilly edges), and put a dollop of filling in the center of each (a heaped teaspoon, 1/4 ounce, or as much as you can fit and still be able to close the sides with a little room to spare). Mist lightly with water if the pasta is too dry to attach to itself. Fold in half (diagonally if you've cut squares), press to seal, and twist around a finger (with the triangular or rounded flap pointing up, as with the finger), pressing the 2 long arms together to close. You don't need to fold a flap over beforehand (as you would for *tortellini* or *tortelloni*, pages 260 and 264), but angling the flap slightly away from your finger will make a pleasing crease between the flap and the filling.

Best served with butter and sage (see page 23).

TORTELLINI

Dimensions
Length: 1 in
Width: 0.84 in

Synonyms
agnoli, presuner, or
prigionieri in Capri

Also good with this pasta
butter and sage; porcini
and cream; *ragù Bolognese;*
walnut sauce

Tortellini ("small *tortelli*") are the pride of Emilia-Romagna, Bologna in particular, alongside *tagliatelle* (page 248) and *lasagne* (page 136). Miniaturised *tortelli* formed around the tip of a finger, they require skill and patience to get right. Whilst there must be few Bolognese housewives who don't know how to make them, most are purchased even in their home town. There is still a healthy cottage industry making *tortellini* by hand for sale in the shops – anyone who knows anything prefers them handmade.

There are various enchanting and similar tales of their origin. In one, Lucrezia Borgia stopped off at an inn in Castelfranco Emilia. Smitten by his guest's beauty, the innkeeper crept up to her door in the night to sneak a peek through the keyhole. All he could see was Lucrezia's navel, but what a navel it was! He rushed to his kitchen and created a pasta in the exquisite belly button's image. In an alternative version, the tavern is in Bologna and the guests are the battle-weary Venus and Jupiter. As the two slept, the publican did what all seem to do in Italy – crept up to peer through the keyhole – and was taken by a beauteous navel.

The belly button is a good comparison – it does indeed look similar to *tortellini* and is as good at catching lint as the pasta is at catching sauce. And if there is a single defining characteristic of the Italians, it is an incomparable attachment to the mother. The choice of the umbilicus as the "elite" of pastas, which

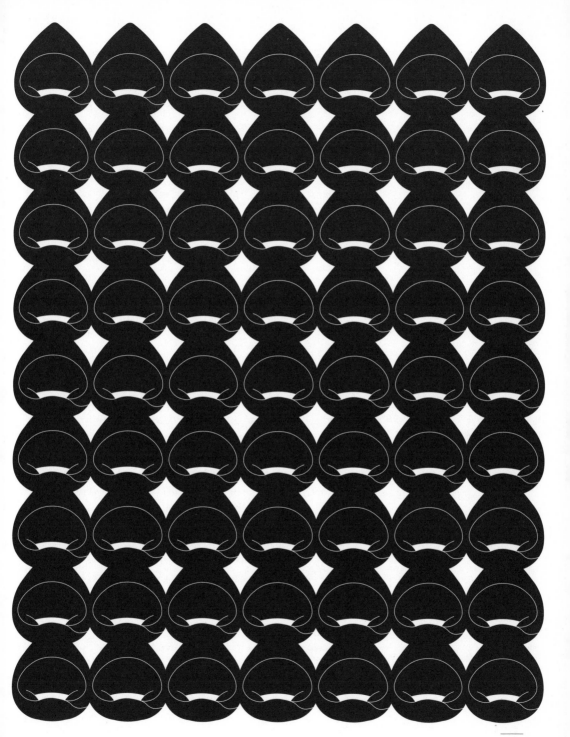

every Italian (or at least every Emilian) dreams of eating, is surely no coincidence.

So enshrined in myth are *tortellini* that there is only really one recipe – the filling is made of mortadella, pork, prosciutto, Parmesan, egg, and nutmeg; only a dab is used in each pasta, and the square of wrapping is as small as possible to enclose it. The ancient way of serving *tortellini* is *in brodo* – preferably in a capon broth, the surface covered with shavings of white truffle on special occasions. Today, they are more likely to be seen in cream, butter and sage, or *ragù*. I recommend either cream or broth to savour the flavour at its purest.

TORTELLINI

Serves 6

1¾ pounds simple or enriched egg pasta dough (page 13; quantity allows some spare for wastage)

FILLING
3½ ounces pork loin, diced
1¾ tablespoons butter
3½ ounces mortadella
3½ ounces prosciutto
3½ ounces Parmesan
1 egg
A grating of nutmeg, to taste

For the filling, gently fry the pork loin in the butter until just cooked and lightly browned. Turn off the heat and leave to cool in the pan. Combine the pork and its juices with the other ingredients in a food processor and mince until a smooth paste. Refrigerate if not using immediately.

For the *tortellini*, roll the pasta just under 1 millimeter thick. Just do 1 sheet at a time, make sure there is no flour on it, and lay out flat on a clean table. Cut into 2¾-inch squares, and dot a tiny (hazelnut-sized) piece of filling in the center of each. Check that the pasta is wet enough to stick to itself when you seal the *tortellini*. If it isn't, spray with a light mist of water. Cover loosely with plastic wrap, to keep the pasta from drying as you work.

Take 1 square of pasta from under the plastic wrap. Close it diagonally, to make a triangle, and gently squeeze the sides to seal and exclude any air. Fold the top of the triangle down, to make a trapezoid (like a Stanley blade), with the top of the triangle just sticking out. Put a finger gently against the lump where the filling is (keep the folded triangle on the outside), and wrap the 2 longer corners around your finger so they meet. Press together to join, then remove your finger. Do this again, and again, and again until it's time to roll out another sheet. Not for the impatient.

TORTELLINI IN BRODO
In broth

½ pound *tortellini*
4¼ cups clarified chicken or capon broth (page 242)
Grated Parmesan to serve
½ ounce fresh white truffle, to serve on extra special occasions

Also good in this soup
cappelletti, pansotti

Cook the *tortellini* at a gentle simmer in the broth; serve in wide bowls with the Parmesan sprinkled over, and a generous shaving of white truffle if the wallet permits.

TORTELLINI CON PANNA
Cream

½ pound *tortellini*
⅓ cup butter
⅓ cup heavy cream
A few gratings of nutmeg
Grated Parmesan, to serve

Also good with this sauce
agnolotti dal plin, cappelletti, tortelli/cappellacci

As your *tortellini* boil, warm the butter in the cream until it melts, stirring often. Add nutmeg, salt, and pepper to taste. Toss the pasta in the sauce over the heat for a few moments, then serve with plenty of Parmesan.

This sauce is a favourite of my grandmother. It is very, very rich and she very, very thin. Her portions are small for herself, generous to others. She sometimes adds 6 torn basil leaves, a few gratings of lemon zest, or both. All are delicious variations, as is the addition of thinly sliced strips of speck or prosciutto, but simplest is always best, and using the recipe above, unadorned, is recommended.

TORTELLONI

Dimensions
Length: 1.8 in
Width: 1.52 in

Also good with this pasta
butter and sage; morels;
porcini and cream; tomato
sauce; walnut pesto; walnut
sauce

The same shape as *tortelli*, again being formed from either a circular or square piece of dough, only a little larger. As such, they are not normally made with meaty fillings, which would dominate the pasta. More delicate farces – ricotta, pumpkin, or spinach and ricotta – work excellently, and so correspondingly delicate sauces (cream, butter and sage, or a light tomato) are used.

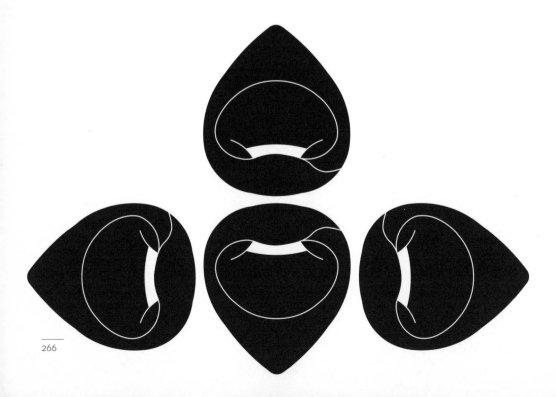

TORTELLONI DI RICOTTA

Serves 4

½ pound simple or
  enriched egg pasta dough
  (page 13)
1 cup sheep's milk (or mixed
  sheep's and cow's milk)
  ricotta
2 egg yolks
½ cup grated Parmesan
A hint of nutmeg

Also good with these fillings
spinach and ricotta (page
210)

Beat together the ricotta, egg yolks, and Parmesan by hand, and season with salt, pepper, and nutmeg to taste.

Roll the pasta relatively thinly (just under 1 millimeter, or the second-thinnest setting on most machines), making sure neither the pasta nor the work surface is floury, and cut into 3-inch squares. Spray lightly with water if too dry to stick to itself. Put a piled-high teaspoon (⅓ ounce) filling in the center of each square and fold the pasta diagonally to make triangles. Pick one up and fold the broader corner (the right-angle one) over to make a trapezoid, wrap around a finger (with the little flap you just folded over on the outside), and press the long ends together.

Keep on a tray dusted with *semola* until ready to cook – be sure the *tortelloni* don't touch each other, as the moist filling will make the pasta liable to stick.

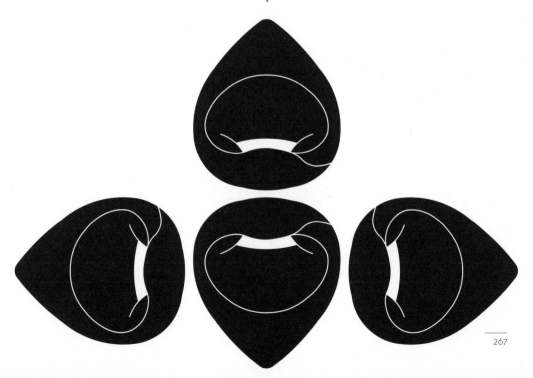

TORTELLONI DI RICOTTA CON ASPARAGI E PANNA
Asparagus and cream

½ recipe ricotta *tortelloni*, or ½ pound other fresh filled pasta
A good bunch of asparagus (¾ pound)
½ cup plus 1 tablespoon heavy cream
3½ tablespoons butter
Grated nutmeg
Grated Parmesan, to serve

Also good with this sauce
cappelletti

There are restaurants that specialise in this dish, but it is never so fresh and uplifting as when made at home.

Cut the woody ends of the asparagus away and slice the rest into ¾-inch lengths, leaving the tips intact. Put the pasta on to boil, and at the same time heat up the cream with the butter, a good grating of nutmeg, and salt and pepper to taste. Allow it to boil, and reduce until it regains the consistency of refrigerated heavy cream.

The pasta will probably take only a couple of minutes to cook. A minute in, or a minute before the end, add the asparagus to the pasta water. When both are done, drain and add to the cream sauce. This will be thinned a little by the water clinging to the pasta. Cook together until the sauce coats tenaciously, then serve swiftly with a good grating of Parmesan.

TORTELLONI DI RICOTTA AL PESTO DI NOCI TOSTATE
Burnt walnut pesto

1 recipe ricotta *tortelloni*, or
   1 pound other fresh filled
   pasta
1/2 garlic clove, very thinly
   and evenly sliced
Sunflower or corn oil for
   frying
3/4 cup shelled walnuts
3/4 teaspoon fresh thyme
   leaves
1/2 cup extra-virgin olive oil
Crunchy sea salt (such as
   Maldon)
Grated Parmesan, to serve

Ricotta and walnuts are a marriage made in heaven: a simple plate of fresh ricotta, wet walnuts, and arugula, or the recipe below for darker flavours. Any shape of pasta will do . . .

Starting from cold, fry the garlic in the oil (enough to eventually cover the walnuts) in a small pan over a medium-low heat. The garlic will sizzle for a while, then stop and turn an even golden brown. Remove with a slotted spoon and drain on paper. Add the walnuts to the oil, and fry until they are as dark as you can get them without burning. The colour of a very tan Mediterranean skin is good (break a nut in half to see inside), as they will continue to brown more as they cool.

Crush the crispy garlic with the thyme leaves in a mortar and pestle until fine, then add the walnuts and pound, but leave a little texture. Add the olive oil and stir in crunchy salt to taste, also seasoning with pepper. Allow plenty of salt to give this sauce a lift. It will keep for ages in the fridge, but should be brought to room temperature before using.

Boil the *tortelloni* until *al dente*, drain, and serve with the sauce sparsely drizzled over. A few shavings of Parmesan, best done with a potato peeler, are delicious scattered on top.

TORTIGLIONI

Dimensions
Length: 1.8 in
Width: 0.42 in
Wall thickness: 1.25 mm

Also good with this pasta
al forno; amatriciana; arrabbiata; cacio e pepe; chicken and prunes; chickpeas; *gricia;* mussels and beans; *Norma;* prosciutto and cream; *puttanesca; ragù Napoletano;* ricotta and tomato; Romanesco broccoli; sausage sauce; *sugo di coda;* tomato and mozzarella; tomato sauce; Treviso, speck, and fontina; tuna belly and tomato

My favourite tubular pasta, *tortiglioni* are similar to *rigatoni* (page 218), but with more pronounced grooves that are slanted, wrapping around the tubular pasta in a multiple helix, like the red-and-white rotating signs you used to see outside the barber's shop. The word *tortiglione* is also linked to heraldry, referring to the headband worn on the *testa di moro* ("Moor's head") on the Sardinian flag – it stems from the Latin *torquere*, "to turn." As with most industrial pastas, *tortiglioni* are popular in the south, in this case particularly Campania and Lazio.

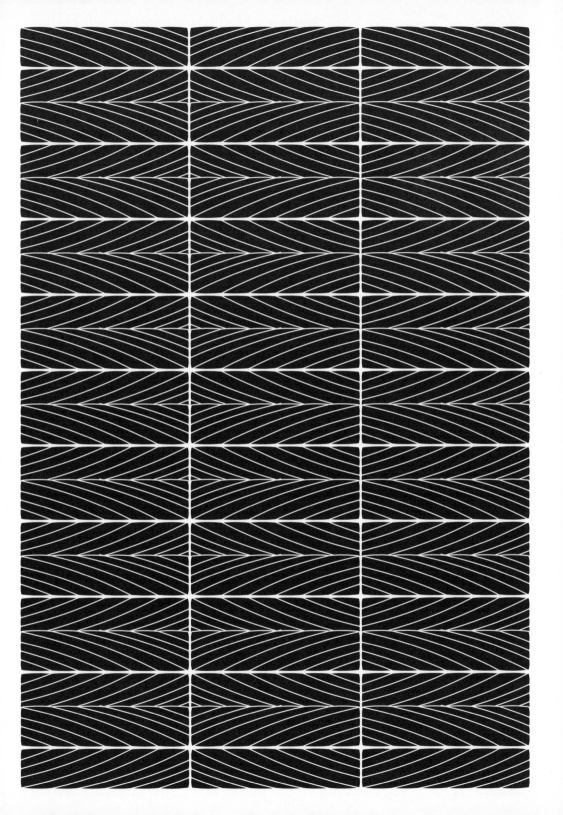

TORTIGLIONI ALLA NORCINA
Sausages and cream

½ pound *tortiglioni*
½ pound Italian sausage, skin removed
½ medium onion, thinly sliced across the grain
1½ tablespoons olive oil or lard
⅜ teaspoon crushed red pepper flakes
⅓ cup white wine
½ cup heavy cream
Grated pecorino Romano, to serve

Also good with this sauce
campanelle/gigli, casarecce, cavatappi, gramigne, maccheroni inferrati, mafaldine, paccheri, penne, pennini rigati, pici, radiatori, reginette, rigatoni, sedanini, spaccatelle, ruote, ruotellini, torchio

This recipe, found across Umbria, should in theory be made with the famous sausage from Norcia — so famous that the word *Norcina* has become synonymous with sausage.

Put the pasta on to boil. In another pan, fry the sausage and onion in the fat over a medium–high heat until partially browned (5–8 minutes), stirring occasionally and using your spoon to break up the sausage. Add the red pepper flakes, closely followed by the wine; reduce by half and then add the cream. Let the sauce bubble and thicken. When still a little too *al dente*, drain the pasta and add to the sauce. Cook together until the cream is thick enough to coat the pasta well. Serve with plenty of black pepper and grated pecorino Romano.

TORTIGLIONI CON LENTICCHIE
Lentils

½ pound *tortiglioni*
1 small or ½ medium onion, finely chopped
2 garlic cloves, sliced
6 tablespoons extra-virgin olive oil
2 bay leaves
½ cup small brown lentils (3½ ounces)
3 tablespoons chopped flat-leaf parsley

Also good with this sauce
bavette, campanelle/gigli, canestri, conchiglie, dischi volanti, ditali, ditalini, fettuccine, fusilli, linguine, orecchiette, penne, pennini rigati, spaghetti, spaghettini, strozzapreti, torchio, ziti/candele

This dish is my mother's favourite — wonderful and peasanty (the dish, not my mother). She normally uses long pasta (*spaghetti* or *spaghettini*); I prefer shorter tubes which make it easier to pick up the lentils.

Fry the onion and garlic gently in the oil for 5 minutes, until they lose any hint of rawness. Add the bay and lentils, then enough water to cook them in (for this quantity, cooking uncovered, 2 cups or slightly less). Boil gently until a few of the lentils have gone to mush and the rest are whole but completely tender. There should still be a little bit of liquid, but not a swimming amount. Season only now with salt and pepper. The lentils can be cooked just before you eat (allow 30–40 minutes) or a few days ahead if they are then refrigerated.

Boil the pasta, drain, and add to the hot lentils. Cook together for a few moments, stir in the parsley, and serve. This dish really doesn't need anything else, but if you are in possession of a particularly fine *cru* of olive oil, now may be the time to use a small drizzle.

TROFIE

Trofie are tightly spiralled, torpedo-shaped short pasta, which can be made in a number of ways to pretty much the same effect. Like *orecchiette* (page 170), they are infinitely superior when made fresh, unlike the majority of semolina pastas. I would go so far as to say that if you can't get fresh *trofie* (and you are unlikely to outside of Italy) or make them (and I imagine most readers may be reluctant to), it is better to substitute a simple dried pasta — *linguine* (page 146) or *spaghetti* (page 230) — in their place. The shape of *trofie* is a combination of ergonomic and functional design — they are easily handmade, and are efficient sauce traps.

Trofie originate from Liguria, where they are *the* pasta to eat with *pesto Genovese* (the basil one that follows). Their name may stem from the Greek *trophe* ("nutriment"), or be a bastardisation of *gnocchi* (pages 116 and 122): Their origins were as a bread-crumb-and-potato dough, rolled into the shape of modern *gnocchi*. Today, *trofie* are made from a simple semolina and water dough. *Trofie bastarde* are of the same form, but made with chestnut flour — a staple of the poor in olden days, giving a sweeter taste but less nutrition. These can occasionally be found today.

TROFIE AL PESTO GENOVESE
Pesto, potato, and green beans

Serves 2

1/3 pound *semola* (or 1/3 pound dried *trofie* or *linguine*)
5 new potatoes (1/3 pound)
31/2 ounces fine green beans

PESTO GENOVESE
31/2 ounces bunched basil
1 garlic clove
1 cup plus 3 tablespoons Parmesan
1 cup plus 3 tablespoons pecorino Romano (or a mature Sardo)
1 cup pine nuts, Italian if possible
2/3–3/4 cup extra-virgin olive oil
13/4 tablespoons butter, softened

Also good with this sauce
bavette, bucatini, busiati, casarecce, corzetti, fusilli bucati, fusilli fatti a mano, gnocchi, linguine, maccheroni alla chitarra, maccheroni inferrati, spaghetti, spaghettini, trenette

This basil pesto recipe is enough for about 10 people; there's no point making a small quantity as it freezes very well. Use 4¼ ounces of pesto for the pasta for 2.

To make the pesto, pick the basil leaves and wash them gently only if you have to (let them dry naturally, spread out on a cloth). Crush the garlic to a paste with a little salt. Put the cheeses, basil, and garlic into a food processor and work to a fine paste, then add the pine nuts and continue until quite fine, but with some texture from the kernels. Add the olive oil, butter, and some salt and pepper. It is best to let it stand for a few minutes before you finally taste for seasoning.

To make the *trofie*, put the *semola* out on a wooden board, make a well, and add 4½ tablespoons water at room temperature. Bring together to make a firm dough, knead, and leave to rest, covered, for at least 15 minutes. Make sure your board is completely free of any flour. Break off a walnut-sized lump of dough and roll to make a long, 3-millimeter-wide strand. Cut into 1½-inch lengths. There are 2 ways to proceed from here.

1) Take 1 section of pasta. Using the flat of a knife (or a metal palette knife) at a 45° angle to both the board and the pasta, draw it across and along the pasta to produce a deep, spiralling groove along its length. Close inspection will show that the groove extends within the pasta, whose inner surface will be rough (like *orecchiette*, page 170) and outside smooth. The dough has effectively been rolled and stretched into a rectangle in the process, the angle of the knife causing the pasta to roll up diagonally, hence the torpedo shape.
2) Roll these sections between your hands to start the torpedo shape. One by one, roll the lengths between the ball of your palm and the board with considerable pressure, sliding your hand along the length as you go.

The friction should cause the strip to flatten and twist into a sort of irregular helix. A little more pressure at the start and finish will taper the ends into a torpedo shape even more. You need some friction between the pasta and the board – if you're skidding, dampen the board slightly.

Without too much practice, it should take about 15 minutes for this quantity. They don't all need to look the same – they are homemade! Leave the *trofie* spread out to dry slightly for about 20 minutes, until just a little leathery outside.

To make the dish, peel the potatoes and slice very evenly, 1–2 millimeters thick. Trim the tops of the green beans (I like to leave the tails on), and cut in 1¼-inch lengths. In a pan of well-salted water, boil the pasta, beans, and potatoes together for 5 minutes or until cooked. Drain, and serve with a dollop of the pesto on top to stir in at the table.

As I made clear on page 274, I have no time for dried *trofie*. If you don't want the hassle of making your own fresh ones, I suggest using *linguine* and adding the vegetables 5 minutes before the end of cooking.

VERMICELLINI

Dimensions
Length: varies 0.8–4 in
Diameter: 1 mm

Also good with this pasta
in brodo; soufflé

These are nothing more than short-cut lengths of *capelli d'angelo* (page 54). Primarily used in soups in Italy, *vermicellini* have broken out and gone global. In India, they are roasted in oil and then cooked in condensed milk as a sweet; in Armenia and Iran, again roasted in oil, then cooked with rice to make a pilaf; in China, cooked with mung beans; in Mexico, in chicken soup; in Spain, in *fideuà* (page 281); and as an ancient tradition in Jewish cookery as *vermishelsh*. Strangely, they do not seem so popular in Italy.

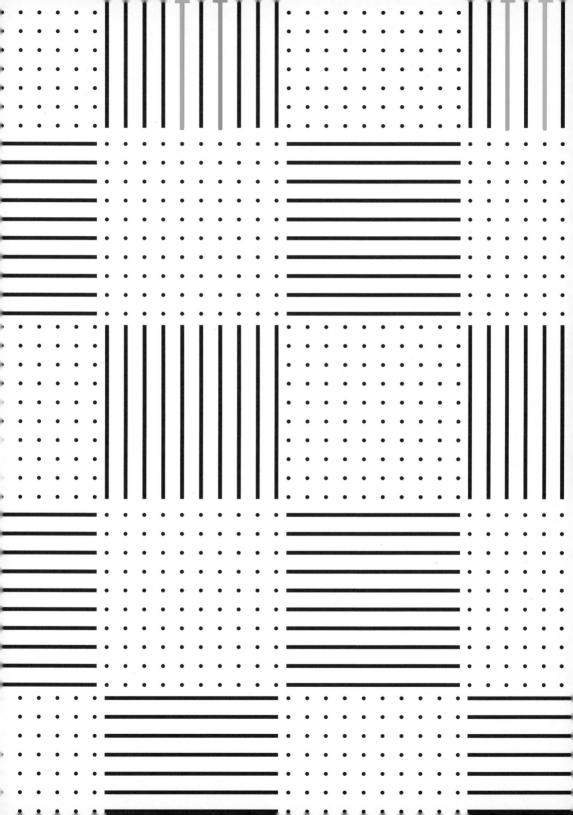

STRACCIATELLA
Egg-drop soup

2 ounces *vermicellini*
3 cups clarified chicken
   broth (page 242)
A few drops of lemon juice
   (optional)
2 eggs
½ cup grated Parmesan
A few gratings of nutmeg

Also good with this soup
*canestrini, capelli d'angelo
orzo, quadretti, quadrettini,
stelline, tagliolini*

This Roman egg-drop soup is normally made without any pasta. Agnes, my grandmother on my father's side, makes it with noodles for more substance.

Bring the broth to a boil, seasoned with salt and, if you like, a few drops of lemon juice. Beat together the eggs, cheese, and nutmeg. Crush the pasta into the broth; when it returns to the boil, stir vigorously, and add the egg mixture (either all at once or as a slow stream). Continue stirring for a few moments, then allow the soup to simmer until the pasta is just cooked.

LOKSHEN PUDDING

Serves 6–8

1 pound *vermicellini*
¾ cup plus 2 tablespoons
   butter
8 eggs
2 cups sugar
1½ teaspoons vanilla
   extract
4⅓ cups cottage cheese

Also good in this dish
*capelli d'angelo, tagliatelle,
tagliolini, tajarin, vermicelli*

An Ashkenazi noodle pudding. To our embarrassment neither Caz (the inventor and designer of this book) nor I, despite our Jewish ancestry, knew how to make this dish. Nigella Lawson came to our rescue. It was generous of her to give us this recipe — it not only filled a gap in our knowledge, but also gave us the opportunity to taste something our mothers really should have made for us.

Preheat the oven to 355°F (or 320°F for convection ovens).

Cook the *vermicellini* until *al dente* in less salty water than usual, breaking up the nests of pasta before they drop into the boiling pot. Drain well. Melt the butter and let it cool until no more than warm. Beat the eggs and combine with the butter, sugar, vanilla, and cottage cheese, then add the noodles and mix well. Put into a 9-by-12-inch or 10-by-11-inch baking dish, then bake for 1–1¼ hours, until the top is just golden. Leave to cool for a while before serving — this dish is best served warm rather than cold or hot.

FIDEUÀ

Serves 4

½ pound *vermicellini*
1 medium onion, chopped
    relatively finely
1 red bell pepper, seeded
    and chopped like the
    onion
1 *ñora* pepper, seeded and
    soaked in hot water then
    chopped (or 1½ more
    teaspoons smoked paprika)
4 garlic cloves, thinly sliced
⅓ cup extra-virgin olive oil
2 ripe tomatoes, cut in ¾-
    inch chunks
1 medium red mullet or
    gurnard (⅔ pound),
    scaled and gutted
1 bay leaf
1½ teaspoons smoked
    paprika
A small pinch saffron
    (20–30 strands)
2–2¼ cups fish stock
12 clams
12 mussels
12 smallish shell-on prawns
Homemade aïoli and lemon
    wedges (optional), to
    serve

Also good in this dish
capelli d'angelo, vermicelli

Punctuating this book, like well-hidden Easter eggs, are a few non-Italian recipes. This Valencian recipe made the cut because it is perhaps the best thing to do with *vermicellini*. It is basically a paella, with noodles in place of rice.

Fry the onion, both kinds of pepper, and the garlic in the oil with a pinch of salt over a medium-low heat. Cook for a good 15 minutes, until jammy. Add the tomatoes and cook for a few minutes more. Cut the head from the fish (do this in advance and use in the fish stock, if making your own), and cut the flesh across into 6–8 bone-in chunks.

Season the fish well and add to the pan along with the bay, paprika, and saffron. Cook for 2 minutes, until the outside of the fish turns white, then add the uncooked *vermicellini*. Mix as best you can (a tall order), then add the stock. Increase the heat to medium, and press down with the back of a spoon to submerge the noodles. Taste for seasoning.

When boiling, reduce the heat to low and tuck in the shellfish. Cook uncovered until the pasta is *al dente*, the clams opened, and the juices scarce – shake the pan from time to time to prevent sticking. Cover with parchment paper or foil, lay a cloth on top to keep some heat in, and leave to stand for 10–15 minutes before serving with aïoli, and lemon wedges if you like.

ZITI/CANDELE

Dimensions
Length: 2 in
Width: 0.4 in
Wall thickness: 1.25 mm

Similar forms
ziti candelati

Also good with this pasta
al forno; amatriciana;
arrabbiata; gricia; lentils;
Norma; ragù Napoletano;
ricotta and tomato

Intrinsically Neapolitan, *ziti* cannot be separated from marriages. The word in fact means "the betrothed" or "the bridegroom," and *ziti* are invariably served as the first course of a wedding lunch. One by one, the long tubes are broken into four pieces before cooking. Their stout tubular shape works well with robust, meaty sauces as well as simpler ones. *Candele* ("candles"), or *ziti candelati*, are an outsize version – twice the width, three times the length, and with thinner walls, they must also be broken – not only for tradition, but to fit in any pot. *Ziti* are eaten almost exclusively in the south and could be considered symbolic of the great divide – northerners can be just as sneery about *ziti* as about the people who eat them.

There is a charming tale (how true, who knows?) that Pope Leo turned Attila the Hun away from invading Rome not by convincing him it mightn't be the best idea, but by feeding him a dish of baked *ziti* that led the Hun to develop a bout of wind, considered a bad omen, that made him decide not to go ahead with the invasion. The year was 452, and here I smell a rat – this far pre-dates pasta's arrival in Italy, according to my understanding.

TIMBALLO DI CANDELE E MELANZANE
Baked in a pastry case with eggplant

Serves 4–6

PASTRY
2²/₃ cups all-purpose flour
3 tablespoons superfine or
    confectioner's sugar
¹/₃ pound lard
1 egg
2 egg yolks

FILLING
²/₃ pound *candele*
1¹/₂ cups *ragù Napoletano*
    (page 216)
³/₄–1 pound Italian sausage,
    or 1 recipe meatballs from
    lasagne ricce Napoletane
    (page 144)
1 eggplant (optional), plus
    corn oil for deep-frying
12 quail eggs, hard-boiled
    and peeled
1 cup plus 3 tablespoons
    grated Parmesan
12 basil leaves, torn

This baked pasta dish is rather retro but still found in full force, especially in the south of Italy. It may not be trendy, but is impressive nonetheless.

Preheat the oven to 425°F (or 390°F for convection ovens).

For the pastry, with cold hands (go for a walk if it's wintery), rub together the flour, sugar, and lard with a pinch of salt until it looks like bread crumbs. Add the egg and extra yolks, and just bring together. Flatten out a bit, wrap in plastic wrap, and refrigerate for at least an hour before use.

For the filling, boil the *candele*, leaving them *al dente*. This is easier said than done, as they are ridiculously long – a fish poacher seems the only practical way (or else break the pasta to fit into your largest pot).

Dress the pasta with the *ragù*. Cook the sausages in the oven until firm and browned, about 10–15 minutes, then slice them into ¹/₂-inch discs. (Leave the oven on; the assembled dish will bake at the same temperature.) If using the eggplant, cut into ³/₄-inch dice, salt lightly, and fry in very hot oil until golden brown.

Roll out the pastry quite thinly (3 millimeters). It is very short, and so liable to crack, but can always be patched. Grease a 2¹/₂- to 2³/₄-quart metal or ceramic ovenproof dish (a Bundt pan or any deep dish or bowl would suit), and line with the pastry – you should have some left over, which you'll need to cover the top. Coil a *candela* or 2 to fill the bottom, making sure it is coated in plenty of sauce (your hands will get messy, but not to worry). Dot with sausage and eggs (and eggplant, if using), sprinkle with Parmesan and basil, and cover with another layer of *candele*.

This pasta is rather hard to handle (it looks great in the finished dish, but there is a lot to be said for using shorter shapes). Your life will be slightly easier if you coil from the outside in, rather than the other way around. Repeat until you have used everything up, finishing with a layer of pasta, topped with any last drops of sauce. Cover with the remaining pastry, seal and tuck in the edges and bake for an hour until golden and fragrant.

Leave to stand at room temperature for 10 minutes before trying to unmold.

ZITI LARDATI
Lardo and cherry tomatoes

½ pound *ziti*, broken into 4 even lengths
2¾–3 ounces *lardo* (cured pork back fat), diced ½ inch or slightly smaller
7 ounces cherry tomatoes, halved
1 garlic clove, thinly sliced
A good pinch of crushed red pepper flakes
Grated pecorino Romano, to serve

First boil the pasta. When the *ziti* seem about 4 minutes from being done, heat a wide frying pan over a high heat until smoking. Add the *lardo* and fry for 20 seconds, until just beginning to colour on all sides (this will produce a lot of smoke, so open the windows). All at once, add the tomatoes, garlic, and red pepper flakes, and sauté for a couple of minutes, until hot through. Season with salt and pepper, add a ladleful of the pasta water (about 3 tablespoons), and allow to bubble for a few seconds. Drain the pasta (now just seconds away from being as *al dente* as you like) and add to the sauce. Cook together for 30 seconds or so and serve, piping hot, with grated pecorino atop.

ACKNOWLEDGEMENTS

I offer my thanks to:

Victor, without whose support I'd never be able to write a book, nor have anyone to buy it, and all the members of my family who invested their time, money and love into Bocca di Lupo. Your faith has always been our biggest asset.

My parents, and theirs in turn, for giving me the will to eat, the love of food. Also for showing me how to cook, and how to live.

Nancy Oakes and Sam and Sam Clark also, for having faith and for teaching me everything I know. I have had the best teachers.

The staff at Bocca di Lupo, especially David Cook and Alberto Comai, who have contributed directly and indirectly to many of the recipes herein. Along with Angelo Guida and Simone Remoli (thank you, too), they often covered for my absence from the restaurant when I went off writing. Also thank you Cristina Bagnara, who helped even though she has long been back home in Italy, and to Faith Willinger, who provided one recipe and inspiration for many more.

Caz Hildebrand for dreaming this book up and for offering me the writer's part, and for making it so damn beautiful. Jon Butler, for taking a leap of faith and publishing it. Antony Rettie, for guiding it into the public eye. Kitty Travers, for her sterling research on the shape and history of every pasta we could think of.

And lastly, to every Italian hand that ever made pasta, for turning it into such a delicious thing, which I have the pleasure to enjoy almost every day of my life.

Jacob Kenedy

I am indebted to so many people for their contributions to this book.

To Jon Butler, for your editorial wisdom and consistent enthusiasm, thank you. To the team at Boxtree/Macmillan: Tania Adams, Antonia Byrne, Jacqui Graham, Amy Lines, Sophie Portas, and Mark Richmond, thank you all for being fantastic to work with.

To Susan Fleming, and to Sarah Barlow, thank you both for bringing calm, rigour, and order to the book.

I am grateful to numerous people who have contributed advice, suggestions, and material as the book has evolved, especially Ann Bramson, Anna Del Conte, Louise Haines, Nigella Lawson, Lily Richards, Amanda Ross, and Kitty Travers, thank you.

To Kate Marlow and Mark Paton, my wonderful partners in Here Design, who have lived with this project as long as I have and deserve much gratitude, for keeping the faith all these years and for believing we could make it happen. And, Mark, for your brilliant animation skills that brought the book to life, thank you. And to everyone else in the studio, thank you for being Here.

Jacob, they say that good things come to those who wait – and you are that good thing – your recipes and your writing are more than I could ever have wished for – I can't imagine a better collaborator, or a more passionate pastaphile.

Last, and most of all, to Lisa Vandy, for drawing almost a hundred pasta shapes perfectly, making it so easy to design this book, and for everything else that you do so perfectly, I can never thank you enough.

Caz Hildebrand

INDEX OF SAUCES